CREDIT DERIVATIVES

Law, Regulation and Accounting Issues

AUSTRALIA
LBC Information Services—Sydney

CANADA AND USA
Carswell—Toronto

NEW ZEALAND
Brooker's—Auckland

SINGAPORE AND MALAYSIA
Sweet & Maxwell Asia
Singapore and Kuala Lumpur

CREDIT DERIVATIVES

Law, Regulation and Accounting Issues

Edited by

Dr Alastair Hudson

LONDON
SWEET & MAXWELL
1999

Published in 2000 by
Sweet & Maxwell Limited of
100 Avenue Road
Swiss Cottage
London NW3 3PF
http://www.smlawpub.co.uk

Typeset by Dataword Services Limited, Chilcompton
Printed and bound in Great Britain
by MPG Books Ltd, Bodmin, Cornwall
Indexed by Indexing Specialists, East Sussex

No natural forests were destroyed
to make this product, only farmed
timber was used and replanted.

ISBN 0 421 627900

A CIP catalogue record for this book
is available from the British Library

Acknowledgment

Grateful acknowledgment is made to the *International Swaps and Derivatives Association Inc.* for permission to reproduce the following in the appendix:

The confirmation form listed as an exhibit in the 1999 ISDA Credit Derivatives Definitions.

Introduction

This book began life as a conference in London in December 1997 when credit derivatives were creatures of myth emerging from the primeval ooze of the financial derivatives markets. By the time the contributors were approached and handed over their parcels of expertise on various manifestations of credit derivatives, those products had emerged onto dry land and had begun to take recognisable shape.

This book seeks to be the first to address the legal, accounting and risk context of credit derivatives in one place; the first to assess in detail not only structuring issues, questions raised by the documentation of transactions, and complex risk assessment, but also to point to potential future problems as diverse as the termination of contracts, liability for mis-selling these products and accounting for depreciation of credit derivatives. All-in-all, the aim is a lofty one: to collect in one place all that can be said about these aspects of credit derivatives and to inform either the practitioner or the academic about their structure and practice.

The smorgasbord of contents begins with Schuyler Henderson's encyclopaedic dissection of the various types of credit derivatives. He looks at the wide range of swaps and options which make up this type of product. Importantly, he considers many of the terms which have grown up around the documentation and structuring of credit derivatives, such as "materiality", and places them in the context of the new standard form documentation.

At a fundamental level, Schuyler examines the importance of placing the credit derivatives, whether in the form of a total return swap or a credit option, within the definition of a derivative as an "unbundling of financial obligations" rather than simply as a kind of funded participation in a loan issue. The role of the reference entity, the particular problems of conceiving of documentation to establish credit-worth, and these products' legal proximity to insurance contracts were among the specific issues teased out.

John Jakeways considers some very specific legal issues which are raised by credit derivatives. In particular, the question of the voidability of these instruments on grounds of being gaming contracts, of being classified as insurance contracts, or otherwise. These are issues whch arise in relation to each type of new financial product which operates by taking a position on underlying market movements. The general legal nature of credit derivatives is analysed in this Chapter.

Martin Hughes's Chapter on sovereign credit derivatives and related issues considers a number of particularly intricate issues relating to the documentation of credit derivatives in that context. Sovereigns raise a number of questions aside from the usual corporate questions considered hitherto. Many of the initial difficulties in the marketplace have arisen from the use of these instruments by sovereigns and therefore this detailed analysis is particularly welcome.

The Chapter on termination of derivatives contracts deals with the vast range of caselaw in England and Wales concerning the ability of parties to achieve restitution of moneys paid under contracts where those contracts are held to have been void on grounds of incapacity, mistake, fraud, or (potentially) supervening illegally or regulatory intervention. In the context of a new financial market trading in particularly complex products like credit derivatives, these issues of termination will form an essential part both of calculating credit risk and assessing documentation risk in putting transactions together. The consequences for English law generally have been wide-reaching, in that they involve derivatives or have application directly to derivatives transactions, and makes their consideration particularly important.

Peter Cossey, Jonathan Davies and Ben Galbraith then consider the particularly complex issues surrounding accounting for credit derivatives. The complexity of the products offers a number of opportunities for accounting for them in a number of ways — each of which have advantages in different contexts. The importance of these issues (for liquidity and other purposes) as part of the structuring process is considered in that Chapter.

Similarly, Collier and MacDonald consider the taxation treatment of credit derivatives. Of particular concern is the issue of deciding in which category a new product like the credit derivative should fall when the tax rules set out a number of existing categories. The taxation of variable cash flows is always a complex question, never more so than in relation to credit derivatives. As part of the structuring issue, then, taxation forms an essential part of this business.

The final two Chapters consider the risks raised by credit derivatives. Alan Morrison considers in detail the way in which the appraisal and measurement of risk in relation to credit derivatives has developed over time from the Black-Scholes model. The final Chapter then examines the legal risks arising from the complex credit derivatives for the seller in relation to undue influence, fraud, misrepresentation, and fiduciary liability.

In short, the book seeks to inform the professional in the full range of issues which surround the structuring of credit derivatives beyond the mathematics of the transactions. We are all conscious of the fact that as word processor is put to paper on a project of this sort, a development on some trading floor somewhere in the world will have made a part of that discussion obsolete. However, we do believe that the main part of this book considers questions which will remain of such fundamental importance that they will never go out of date nor out of fashion.

For my part, I would like to thank the contributors for their efforts and, at times, their great patience. Thanks to Victoria Wright and Andy Hill at Sweet & Maxwell who have steered this project forwards to the form which you currently hold in your hand. Also to Ruth Clougherty and Sarah Kemm at IBC who organised the conferences which gave birth to this project. Finally, to those who supported me, to my mother, to Andy and to Helena, for all they mean to me, much thanks.

Any errors, omissions or infelicities of expression remain, in true banking fashion, the fault of prevailing market rates.

Dr Alastair Hudson
Mile End

August 1999

Contents

Table of Cases

Table of Statutes

Table of Statutory Instruments

Chapter 1

Credit Derivatives

by Schuyler K. Henderson*

1.001 The application of derivatives technology to credit is one of the more recent innovations in the financial markets. The credit derivative is a transaction the value of which is based on the credit of a third party. In addition to the market having grown to noticeable proportions, the product has received "official" recognition through publication by the International Swaps and Derivatives Association, Inc ("ISDA") of a form of credit swap confirmation principally for use with its 1992 Master Agreement.[1] While presenting many of the enforcement, regulatory and tax issues which arise with respect to all derivatives, credit products present some additional complexities and require familiarity with the lending, securities and derivatives markets. Part I of this Chapter endeavours to place credit derivatives in the context of the broader financial markets, describe the basic structures, analyse why credit derivatives constitute true derivatives and are different than traditional financing arrangements which in some cases are replicated through credit derivatives, and identify some of the risks involved in treating credit as a derivative product. The second part discusses selected documentation issues, with a focus on the ISDA credit swap confirmation. The third part discusses selected legal issues.

Part I: The Context

Market background

1.002 The practice of financial law, on the debt side, can be characterised as advising financial institutions or their customers with respect to products involving cashflow and credit. Traditionally, there were two broad categories of finance lawyers: advisers to bank lenders in extensions of credit which traditionally involved a long term, direct credit relationship between the lenders and their customers; and advisers to underwriters, which traditionally were exposed to short term underwriting risk. There are clearly common elements between bank lending and debt securities underwriting, but the tendency to specialise in one or the other resulted in part from procedural differences (syndicated lending mechanics distinguished from underwriting mechanics) and also from substantive factors. The securities markets, reflecting the tradable (*i.e.* readily marketable) nature of

* Partner, Baker & McKenzie, London. This Chap. was originally presented at the W.G. Hart Legal Workshop, Institute of Advanced Legal Studies, July 1998, and was first published in the form of three articles in Butterworths *Journal of International Banking and Financial Law* ((1998) 8 J.I.B.F.L. 332, (1998) 9 J.I.B.F.L. 399 and (1999) 5 J.I.B.F.L. 193). The author wishes to thank his partners, David Geen and James MacLachlan, for their review of and comments on this Chapter.
[1] Defined terms in this Chapter refer to those used in the ISDA form, many of which terms are described in the annex or more fully explained in Part II of this Chapter.

securities and the potentially large number of public holders, emphasise regulatory and statutory requirements dealing principally with disclosure, with less emphasis on ongoing monitoring of credit performance. The bank lending markets, reflecting the need of a creditor to monitor a long term lending relationship which cannot be unilaterally terminated by sale of the instrument, tend to require more stringent credit documentation. Each therefore presents its own particular complexities in understanding mechanics of cashflows, regulatory and tax risks, levels of tolerance of, and protection against, credit risk and, of course, jargon.

In the mid 1980s, the distinction between bank lending and the debt securities markets became less distinct with the disintermediation of financial institutions, the increasingly direct access of borrowers to the capital markets and the desire of financial institutions to increase fee income while reducing asset exposure. Two important elements of this development were: from a broader economic perspective, the quest for liquidity, or the existence of a market in which there would be a readily ascertainable price and opportunity for buying or selling risks or rights; and, as a corollary in documentation, development of structures which permitted tradability, or the right freely to transfer those risks and rights. The Euronote facility, the transferable lending facility, refinement of the traditional sale of sub-participations between lending institutions on a silent basis, direct trading in loan agreement debt (particularly of emerging market borrowers) and securitisation techniques all represented different aspects of this trend. The transferable or public element in securities and the long-term relationship implicit in bank lending declined in significance as a bright line dividing finance lawyers.

1.003 At about this time, and contributing in a substantial way to blurring further the distinction between lending lawyers and securities lawyers, a third practice area emerged: derivatives. While based on cashflow and credit, and therefore in the same family as bank lending and securities, and in many ways a link between the two markets, derivatives developed their own procedural and mechanical conventions. Roughly speaking, the term "derivatives" includes three very different groups of financial products: exchange traded futures and options[2]; debt securities with an "unusual" rate of return, where the return is based on something other than a fixed rate of interest or a commonly recognised floating rate such as LIBOR and the instrument is often characterisable as having an embedded option or swap ("embedded" securities); and over-the-counter ("OTC"), individually negotiated, bilateral notional amount agreements including swaps, providing for cash flows based on movements in interest, currency, equity, commodity or other indices (or a combination thereof), and swap-related products which are, or have certain characteristics similar to, options (including caps and floors and OTC options on those indices or on securities or commodities themselves).

OTC derivatives of the third category, originally referred to simply as swaps, developed out of back-to-back loans, usually intermediated by a bank, in the mid 1970s. A critical mass of swaps developed in the period 1983 to 1985, when interest rate swaps were linked to the international capital markets. Building on the greatly increased end-user base, financial intermediaries became dealers in swaps, pricing the transactions over the phone and using sophisticated portfolio hedging techniques. For purposes of this Chapter, this involved three noteworthy developments. First, while swaps remained non-transferable credit-based instruments, liquidity

---

[2] Being traded on an exchange, these instruments lack a long-term credit element, and thus form a distinct, regulatory-oriented practice area. The term "derivatives" herein will refer only to over-the-counter derivatives.

was simulated through rapid entry (*e.g.* telephone trade call followed by a short form confirmation usually under a master agreement) and willingness of dealers to agree to termination at a negotiable but immediately quoted price or the ability to close out the market risk by a reverse swap with the same or another dealer. Second, in order properly to manage the pricing and hedging of the transactions, it was necessary to mark each swap to market on a current basis. This fundamental shift in thinking, the pricing of a product based on the current valuation of cashflows in a long-term non-transferable credit relationship, was revolutionary. Third, the financial risk of these instruments was viewed and managed on a portfolio basis. By 1986, swaps could be fairly characterised as trading instruments creating long-term non-transferrable credit risk, a unique financial product.

Derivatives technology then proceeded, slowly at first but with accelerating rapidity later, to span the spectrum of financial indices and assets, including interest rate, currency, commodity and equity. Derivatives were increasingly used in conjunction with, or as integral parts of, virtually every other type of financial transaction, ranging from leveraged buy-outs to project finance to securitisation to share transactions to provision of leveraged investment management services. The range of indices used in derivatives has since expanded out of the financial (*i.e.* lending and price) markets, to include indices based on almost anything, including shipping freight utilisation, insurance losses, utilisation of electricity, telecommunication usage and weather. As the line between the bank lending and securities markets had blurred in the mid 1980s, the line between derivatives financing on the one hand and bank loans or debt securities on the other also became blurred in the early 1990s.

The credit derivative is the latest, perhaps conceptually the crucial, bridge between the lending markets and securities markets, requires skills generic to those markets and the derivatives markets and, finally, merges credit with cash flow.

Description of credit derivatives

1.004 A credit derivative is:

- an individually negotiated OTC transaction or a note structure,

- between two parties, one of which can be referred to as the buyer of protection/seller of risk and one of which can be referred to as the seller of protection/buyer of risk

- in which the value of at least one of the obligations is based on performance by a third party (Reference Entity) or parties under specified debt obligations (Reference Obligations) or on the change in creditworthiness of the Reference Entity

- which obligations are often but not necessarily triggered by the occurrence of a specified credit event (Credit Event) or events.

In general, a credit derivative may be structured as a swap, an option or an embedded security (often termed a credit-linked note). If the credit obligations are triggered by the occurrence of a Credit Event, it is called a default product. The credit payment may track payments on the Reference Obligations (total return), be a flat amount (digital) if a Credit Event occurs or be based on the quantified amount of the change in creditworthiness of the Reference Entity (credit decline). As with all derivatives, it should be borne in mind that each of the structures and payment methods, although categorised as a credit product, may present different issues to analyse.

Basic structure: credit default swap

1.005 In the most common form of credit derivative, the default swap, one party, in return for a fee, agrees that, on the occurrence of a Credit Event, it will acquire credit-impaired securities at a pre-agreed price or pay the difference between that price and their current value. In the typical structure provided for in the ISDA credit swap confirmation, the buyer of protection/seller of risk pays a Fixed Amount periodically to the seller of protection/buyer of risk. On the occurrence of a Credit Event, as reflected in a Credit Event Notice delivered by one of the parties and, if the parties have so agreed in the confirmation, confirmed by a Notice of Publicly Available Information, a Materiality test or both, the seller of protection/buyer of risk:

(a) if Physical Settlement applies, pays a purchase price determined by applying the Reference Price (an agreed percentage specified in the confirmation) to the Floating Rate Payer Calculation Amount (generally the face amount of the Reference Obligation in respect of which protection is sold) against receipt of Deliverable Obligations (the Reference Obligations, other specified securities or securities of the Reference Entity selected by the buyer of protection/seller of risk subject to certain limitations), or

(b) if Cash Settlement applies, pays either (i) the positive amount determined by applying the remainder of the Reference Price minus the Final Price (a percentage based on the Market Value of the Reference Obligations at settlement) to the Floating Rate Payer Calculation Amount, or (ii) an agreed amount set forth in the confirmation.

FIGURE 1
Cash-Settled Default Swap

Fixed Amount: 0.5% p.a. on Floating Rate
Payer Calculation Amount ($10MM)

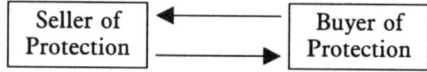

On Credit Event,
(Reference Price—Final Price) X
Floating Rate Payer Calculation Amount
($10MM)

Total return products

1.006 In a total return swap, the buyer of protection/seller of risk pays periodic amounts equal to interest paid on the Reference Obligations. On final settlement after the Scheduled Termination Date of the swap, or earlier if Credit Events are specified and one occurs: if physically settled, the buyer of protection would be obligated to deliver Deliverable Obligations; or if cash settled, the buyer of protection would be obligated to pay an amount equal to principal paid on the

Reference Obligation, if the settlement date is the maturity date of the Reference Obligation, or the value of the Reference Obligation based on its Final Price, if the Reference Obligation has not matured or been accelerated at that date. The seller of protection/buyer of risk periodically pays the notional funding cost (*e.g.* LIBOR) of the buyer of protection/seller of risk and at maturity pays the purchase price, which is usually the Reference Price applied to the notional amount, against either delivery of Deliverable Obligations or the Final Price-based payment. The periodic payments, if in the same currency and falling due on the same date, would be netted, as would the payment of the Reference Price against the Final Price in a cash-settled transaction.

FIGURE 2
Physically-Settled Total Return Swap

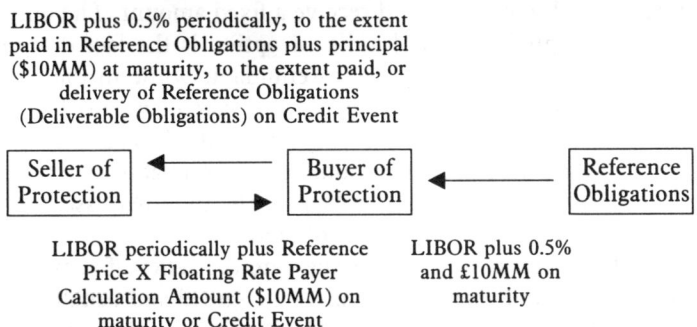

LIBOR plus 0.5% periodically, to the extent
paid in Reference Obligations plus principal
($10MM) at maturity, to the extent paid, or
delivery of Reference Obligations
(Deliverable Obligations) on Credit Event

| Seller of Protection | Buyer of Protection | Reference Obligations |

LIBOR periodically plus Reference
Price X Floating Rate Payer
Calculation Amount ($10MM) on
maturity or Credit Event

LIBOR plus 0.5%
and £10MM on
maturity

In a total return credit-linked note, on the issue date the seller of protection/buyer of risk buys the note for its face amount. Thereafter the buyer of protection/seller of risk makes payments under the note equivalent to those made on the Reference Obligations. On maturity of the note, whether as scheduled or occurring by reason of a Credit Event, the buyer of protection/seller of risk either delivers Deliverable Obligations or pays an amount equal to principal paid on the Reference Obligation, if it matures on the maturity date of the note, or the value of the Reference Obligation, if it matures thereafter, in either case in full redemption of the note.

1.007 The total return swap bears more than passing resemblance to a traditional "risk participation": if the seller of protection (risk participant) performs, the buyer has no credit exposure on the Reference Obligation which it may hold. The total return credit-linked note is similar to a traditional "funded participation": on receipt of the sale proceeds of the note from the seller of protection (participation purchaser), the buyer of protection, regardless of the future solvency of the seller of protection, has no credit exposure on the Reference Obligation which it may hold since it is only obligated to pay the seller of protection amounts equal to those which it actually receives on the Reference Obligations. It is therefore commercially indifferent as to whether or not the Reference Entity performs. There are those who say that a total return transaction without Credit Events is, for that reason, not a credit product. While it is not in its fundamental nature a default product in the sense that a Credit Event is not necessary for it to work, the principal value of the transaction lies in the ability of the Reference Entity to perform. The total return transaction is more aptly described as a credit product which also transfers market and other risk.

Under some circumstances, the basic credit default swap described above could be appropriately characterised as a total return swap. For instance, in a cash-settled total return swap with Credit Events relating to a Reference Obligation which pays interest based on LIBOR and which matures on the Scheduled Termination Date of the swap, payments may be netted. In this case, a fixed amount, representing all or part of the spread over LIBOR on the Reference Obligations, is paid by the buyer of protection on an ongoing basis and the seller of protection pays only the difference, if any, at maturity or on the occurrence of a Credit Event.

Digital products

1.008 In a digital swap, the seller of protection receives a fixed amount periodically and on the occurrence of a Credit Event pays the agreed amount. In a digital option, the buyer of protection pays a premium and, on the occurrence of a Credit Event, is entitled to exercise and receive a fixed amount. The only significant difference between a digital swap and a digital option is the fact that in an option the premium is paid in advance and is non-refundable while in the swap the fixed amount is paid over time until the occurrence of the Credit Event. The premium on the option should therefore equal the present value at the Effective Date of the fixed amount under the swap, adjusted to account for the probability of a Credit Event occurring and the fixed amount ceasing to be payable. In either case, the transaction bears some resemblance to a standby letter of credit.

In a digital credit-linked note, on the issue date the seller of protection pays the face amount of the note and thereafter receives an agreed and usually above market rate of return until the occurrence of a Credit Event, whereupon the note is redeemed at an agreed price which is less than the issue price of the note. The discount is the agreed amount of protection. If no Credit Event occurs, on maturity the note is paid in full.

FIGURE 3
Digital Credit-Linked Noted

Payments of $10MM, as note purchase price
on Effective Date

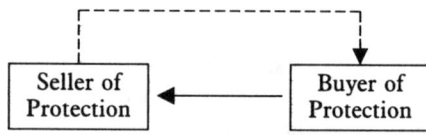

Periodic payments under Note on agreed basis
(*e.g.* LIBOR plus 2.0%) and payment of $5MM
on occurrence of Credit Event, if one occurs, or
$10MM at maturity if not Credit Event occurs

Credit decline products

1.009 The third type of transaction provides for a payment expressly based on the quantified change in creditworthiness of the Reference Entity, and may or may not include Credit Events. This change in credit is usually (though, of course, need not be) a negative change, and these products can be referred to as credit decline products. In a swap or option, the seller of protection/buyer of risk has a single obligation: either to buy Deliverable Obligations at the Reference Price or, if cash settled, to pay an amount based on the excess of the Reference Price over the Final

Price of the Reference Obligation. The buyer of protection/seller of risk pays a periodic fixed amount if a swap, or a premium if an option. In a cash settled credit decline note, the buyer of protection/seller of risk receives full payment from the seller of protection/buyer of risk on its issue date, pays an agreed and usually above-market rate of return on the issue amount and, on the occurrence of a Credit Event, pays the value of the Reference Obligation. If no Credit Event occurs, the note would be paid in full on its maturity.

This type of transaction differs from a total return transaction in two fundamental ways. First, it does not provide for periodic payments equivalent to those on the Reference Obligations. Secondly, in a credit decline product relating to a fixed rate Reference Obligation, adjustments to either the Reference Price or Final Price are often made in order to back out changes in value resulting from changes in market required interest rates in order to arrive at a payment based purely on quantification of the credit change.[3].

There are several ways the removal of the effects of external interest rates can be achieved for a fixed rate Reference Obligation. The first method, which would not require changes to the ISDA credit swap confirmation, would be through structural choices. The Reference Price would be agreed on a basis that it was interest-rate neutral. It would not necessarily reflect the Market Value at the Effective Date but would represent an agreed valuation which backed out the portion of the value at the Effective Date which was based on the relationship between the coupon on the Reference Obligation and then current market fixed rates for its term. On settlement, Reference Obligations or Deliverable Obligations would be specified as instruments which were then due and owing (Due and Payable) in an amount equal to the Floating Rate Payer Calculation Amount.

1.010 The second method[4] is to use a Reference Price based on the Market Value at the Effective Date but couple it with a contingent or notional asset swap written at the Effective Date, with the fixed leg equalling the coupon on the Reference Obligation and the floating leg having a spread above or below LIBOR sufficient to bring the value of the swap to par as of the Effective Date. If physically settled, the swap would become effective on the date of delivery of the Deliverable Obligations. If cash settled, the termination value of the swap, expressed as a percentage of the notional amount, would be aggregated with the Market Value of the Reference Obligations at the time and would in effect back out the interest rate portion of any change in value between the Effective Date and the Settlement Date resulting from changes in interest rates (and currency rates, if a currency swap).

A third way is to define the Reference Price, not as an agreed percentage set forth in the confirmation, but as the value (expressed as a percentage of face amount) of an instrument with a yield equal to an agreed spread over the yield on a benchmark

---

[3] If the Reference Obligation and, if different, Deliverable Obligation are floating rate obligations, there is, at least in theory, no interest rate factor reflected in its value. The cash-settled difference, based on the remainder of the Reference Price minus the Final Price, or the difference between the Reference Price and the value of Deliverable Obligations, if physically-settled, would thus reflect the change in the market's view of the ability of the Reference Entity to pay the face amount: the market quantification of the decline in creditworthiness.

[4] The second and third methods are essentially similar to the tests for Price Materiality and Spread Materiality in the ISDA credit swap confirmation, discussed in Part II. These are worth analysing and understanding as they represent the basic way of pricing credit as an independent product. As with total return transactions, there are those who claim that, absent a Credit Event, credit decline transactions are not "credit" products. The principal reason, however, for a widening of the spread or a decline in value after backing out the effect of interest rates is a credit decline and thus it is appropriately classed as a credit product, even if not a default product.

obligation as of the settlement date. The value of this product lies in the widening of the spreads between the yield on the Reference Obligation and the yield on a benchmark such as a "riskless" security (*e.g.* U.S. Treasuries) or the current fixed rate prevalent in the swap market. If physically-settled, the seller of protection would pay this against delivery of Deliverable Obligations. If cash-settled, it would pay the difference between the Reference Price and the Final Price based on the Market Value of the Reference Obligation at maturity or on the occurrence of a Credit Event. These transactions are also called "yield products".

FIGURE 4
Physically Settled Yield Option

On Effective Date
Premium

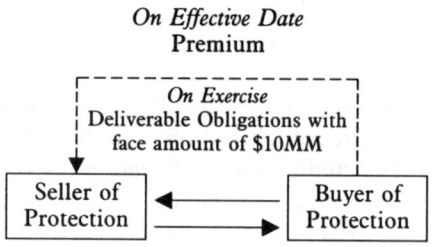

Reference Price (based on
benchmark yield) = $10MM

1.011   The second and third methods would generally be applied through an option structure without Credit Events, since profitability of exercise depends on the credit change. Accordingly, all of the variations in option structure for exercise could be used, including American, European or Bermudan, single or multiple, and full or partial exercise.

If, however, one of the above methods or a different method is not used to back-out interest rate effects on a fixed rate Reference Obligation, a Credit Event is necessary and the difference between the Reference Price and Final Price or value of the Deliverable Obligations, as the case may be, would also reflect a change in the market view on interest rates. In this situation, the transaction would not be a pure credit decline product. It would, however, represent more accurately the actual loss incurred on a default on the Reference Obligations, and thus may protect the buyer of protection more accurately against its actual loss resulting from a Credit Event.

Variations

1.012   The structures and payment flows described above, of course, represent generalisations to which there are variations limited only by the imagination of the parties and applicable law. Credit derivatives can be combined with currency swaps, either explicitly or implicitly, so that the credit is transferred in a currency different than that of the Reference Obligation. There are ways of "leveraging" credit risk which result in higher fees to the seller of protection and higher risk undertaken by it. Reference Obligations could include a basket of obligations of different Reference Entities. Credit Events could apply to any of them and, on the occurrence of a Credit Event, there could be partial settlement with respect to the affected Reference Obligation or final and full settlement either with respect to one of the Reference Obligations or the entire basket. If the separate Reference Obligations in a final and full settlement transaction have little risk correlation, the fee or premium receivable (and the risk undertaken) would be even greater. Leverage can also be obtained by buying protection from one party for the amount of non-payment on a Reference Obligation up to a stated amount (in effect the first portion defaulted) and buying protection from another party for the excess, if any, of the actual amount not recovered and the first portion. The first seller of protection takes the greater risk, and receives the greater fee, and the second seller of protection the lesser risk.

Uses of credit derivatives

1.013 There are a number of uses for credit derivatives. One party, the buyer of protection/seller of risk, may obtain credit protection with respect to its exposure to the Reference Entity or an entity with credit characteristics similar to the Reference Entity. It may hold outstanding debt (a loan or security) of the Reference Entity, be a derivatives counterparty of the Reference Entity or in any number of other ways be exposed to the Reference Entity's inability to perform its obligations. It may wish to reduce this risk in exchange for giving up part of its return. For instance, the holder of Forint bonds issued by a Hungarian corporate entity could buy protection against all or a portion of these bonds for a limited period, at a price which left it with some profit in the position and the opportunity for longer term gain. Alternatively, it could buy protection against a particular type of event occurring, *e.g.* political risk as distinguished from commercial inability of the issuer to perform, by buying protection with respect to the Government of Hungary.[5] Of course, it need not necessarily be a traditional type of credit exposure which is being hedged: a financial institution underwriting a bond offering or a loan syndication in a period of high volatility may wish to protect itself during the syndication period through a credit decline option; or the holder of shares may buy a digital option with a Downgrade Credit Event applicable to the issuer to hedge its equity position.[6] Further, the buyer of protection/seller of risk, if a dealer, may have acquired the debt in order to sell the risk, and may be using this structure to sell the risk to its customers through a total return transaction rather than the more complicated form of repackaging or securitisation using a special purpose vehicle. Alternatively, if the buyer of protection does not have actual exposure to the Reference Entity or on the Reference Obligation, buying protection is equivalent to selling debt of the Reference Entity short. The credit derivative is particularly useful in this respect if there is not a developed repo or securities lending market in the relevant Reference Obligation.

The other party, seller of protection/ buyer of risk, is notionally extending credit to the Reference Entity. It may be seeking yield enhancement through investment in a high yielding instrument but is unable to acquire debt of the Reference Entity.

---

[5] The holder of Forint corporate bonds wishing protection against sovereign risk could buy protection under a credit decline default swap designating the Hungarian government as the Reference Entity, appropriate Credit Events relating to its default on debt (its debt being the Obligation), declaration of a moratorium, imposition of exchange controls and other similar sovereign type events, and the Reference Obligations (used only for valuation) being the underlying Forint corporate bonds. The ISDA credit swap confirmation would require some adjustment for use with a sovereign Reference Entity.

[6] From a "technology" perspective, there are of course similarities between certain equity products and credit products, such as a total return equity swap and a total return debt swap, or a share option and a spread option on a bond. The major differences lie in the more complicated and varied possibilities included in equity products for the requirement to adjust the number of shares or price if there are capitalisation changes. More interesting will be to see the development of cross-hedging techniques between the debt and equity markets.

A party may wish to buy certain types of obligations, say, Russian GKOs, but may be unable to do so because of either regulatory constraints applicable to it or to the Reference Entity or lack of liquidity in the instrument. This party could simulate the purchase through a total return swap or a default swap. Indeed, even though the zero coupon GKOs are expressed in roubles, the total return swap could be structured to simulate a dollar investment in the Russian obligations without exposure to currency fluctuations, with the dealer in effect (and perhaps invisibly) combining a credit derivative with a dollar/rouble forward transaction to create a purely synthetic investment.[7] Alternatively, a total return, physically-settled swap, coupled with a sale of the Reference Obligations on the Effective Date by the seller of protection to the buyer of protection, can achieve certain benefits otherwise obtained through a secured loan.

Finally, the application of derivatives methodology facilitates the management of credit exposure on a portfolio basis through development of methods of measuring and managing credit risk and pricing illiquid bank loans to borrowers which may or may not have public (*i.e.* readily priceable) debt outstanding.[8] A commercial bank in particular now has the ability rapidly to transfer the credit risk of an asset from its books to another party wishing to acquire that exposure and to adjust its loan portfolio in the same way that it adjusts its trading portfolio. Rather than wait until the loans mature, until it can find a purchaser for a funded participation or until it can structure a securitisation vehicle, it can apply derivatives technology to its loan portfolio, decrease exposure to that industry while retaining the customer relationship with its borrowers, reduce its capital maintenance requirements and, perhaps, simultaneously acquire exposure to a different industry. It may become a structurer, originator and seller of debt while maintaining its customer relationships with only limited credit exposure to its customers.

Why are they derivatives?

1.014 As noted above, each of these credit products bears some resemblance to a traditional financial arrangement of one form or another, such as a risk participation, funded participation, standby letter of credit or repackaging program. But there are characteristics of these credit products which firmly place them in the derivatives category.

The most common, if not terribly helpful, definition of a derivative is that it is an instrument the value of which is derived from another instrument or product. A credit derivative, in which the value is based on the credit of a third party, clearly falls within this broad definition. Another technical definition of derivatives is that they are "notional" contracts, or contracts involving contingent payments based on changes in an index applied to a notional amount. The typical credit transaction is purely "notional" in that there is no requirement that the Reference Obligations be held and payments, even in a total return product, are expressed as being equivalent

---

[7] If the Reference Obligation paid interest periodically rather than on a zero coupon basis, the credit derivative would be combined, expressly or implicitly, with an asset currency swap.

[8] Complementing this capability and methodology are new approaches to analysing credit risk. For instance, J. P. Morgan has developed CreditMetrics, and Credit Suisse Financial Products has developed CreditRisk, each of which is a programme which values a bank's lending book, or selected parts of it, on a portfolio basis, *i.e.* based on probability of performance and correlation of risks rather than (or more properly in addition to) individual credit analyses and establishment of reserves.

to those made on the Reference Obligation, even if not actually received.[9] Market Value, used for determining the Final Price for cash settled transactions, is also, at least in the ISDA credit swap confirmation, a notional value based on averaging of quotes, perhaps over a period, rather than the actual sale price of a Reference Obligation by the buyer of protection.

Once credit is treated as a notional product, it can be separated from a relationship or from a particular instrument. All the credit products discussed above are thus derivatives in the classic sense that they unbundle rights and obligations in financial transactions, and transfer the different pieces to the parties who, in the case of an obligation, are best able to bear it and who, in the case of a right to receive, regard it as most valuable. The unbundling permits creation of an instrument which replicates another instrument (a total return transaction), or of a purely synthetic risk/right relationship which exactly meets the expectations of the parties even where the desired risk asset does not exist and never has existed. Even a total return swap can be synthesised, *e.g.* where the credit risk of a four year Reference Obligation is effectively transferred for a period of three years[10] or where the Reference Obligation is a rouble security but payments are expressed in dollars at an agreed exchange rate. Country risk can be sold while retaining the ongoing credit risk of the commercial operations of the Reference Entity. The Reference Entity might not be the borrower to whom the buyer of protection has credit exposure and the Reference Obligations might not be the actual debt held by the buyer of protection, but protection, not otherwise available, may be approximated. Parties can negotiate between themselves on precisely what they want. As with all derivatives, credit derivatives, properly used, increase market efficiency and choice and can be used to reduce risk.

1.015 Finally, credit derivatives are properly classed as derivatives because they are in fact treated as derivatives. They are documented under derivatives documentation. More significantly, they are treated commercially, in terms of pricing and liquidity, as derivatives. Even the total return swap transaction, which is the least "derivative-like" of the credit products, represents the transfer of credit and market risk through a derivatives structure which is valued as a derivative on early termination, and for this reason is properly classed as a derivative. In the credit decline product (or the Materiality tests described in Part II of this Chapter), where pure credit is priced by backing out interest and currency risk, credit is truly treated as an independent product like any other priceable rate or index. In fact, the treatment of "credit" as a priceable product, the development of various pricing methodologies to value credit as a "thing" artificially created or separate from an instrument in which it is first embedded, is the single most compelling element leading to the conclusion that a credit derivative is a derivative. In this regard, it may be tempting to differentiate credit derivatives from more traditional derivatives because of fewer "objective" criteria in pricing credit as a product. In this view, credit expectations are highly subjective, uncertainties abound (particularly in the emerging markets) and perceptions as to values differ substantially. On the other hand, one would argue that the "science" underlying, *e.g.* foreign exchange, is not

---

[9] It is important to note in a participation or total return transaction that no right to or interest in the Reference Obligation is transferred until, if applicable, delivery in a physically settled transaction. Payments under the transaction are expressed to be equivalent to those paid under the Reference Obligation rather than an obligation to pass those payments on. Described in Parts II and III of this Chapter are additional legal and tax reasons for structuring the arrangements in this manner.

[10] Its effectiveness depends on either a reliably liquid market for the Reference Obligation or a reliably liquid credit derivatives market.

as refined as outsiders believe and, in the early days of the interest rate swap market, there were also substantially wider spreads. The fact that subjectivity, uncertainty and varying perceptions result in wide spreads do not differentiate credit derivatives from other derivatives; they simply provide tremendous opportunities to derivatives dealers for profit (and, of course, loss).[11]

Central to the pricing of these products, and to the actual risk in them, is a market in which pricing and transfer can readily occur. While relatively new and relatively small, the market is growing rapidly. It was estimated that in 1997 there were "only" $40 billion of notional value credit derivatives outstanding.[12] A soon to be published report by the British Bankers Association reportedly estimates 1998 outstandings to be in the range of $170 billion, expected to grow to $380 billion by 2000. There are now a number of dealers which regularly offer to enter into credit derivatives and maintain bid/offered prices in respect of a variety of Reference Entities. The fact that even total return transactions as well as digital or credit decline transactions can now be quoted, terminated or "sold" means there is a growth in liquidity which facilitates pricing at current valuation, which pricing facilitates further liquidity. Another element of liquidity, speed of execution, is facilitated by the emergence of market acceptable documentation, such as the ISDA credit swap confirmation. With European Monetary Union, the disappearance of eleven currencies and the risk incident thereto and the creation of a pan-European market, it can also be expected that derivatives dealers will divert their attention and their skills to credit in an increasingly innovative way to meet investor demands for yield enhancement and risk opportunity. While the prospects of growth seem good, it should be borne in mind that the market is still relatively thin and liquidity can quickly disappear, and documentation in the credit markets, as discussed in Part II of this Chapter, is unlikely to achieve the degree of standardisation found in the interest rate and currency swap market. .

Risks in treating credit as a derivative product

1.016 While the credit derivative offers the advantages and opportunities common to derivatives in general, it also presents certain additional risks and uncertainties common to derivatives. As noted above, OTC derivatives are illiquid, credit-based transactions but are treated as if they are tradable instruments. There is inherent tension in the derivatives market between competitive dealing requirements and an institution's customary credit standards. This tension crosses over into credit derivatives. Transferring complex credit risk on a notional basis, or rapidly incurring credit risk which once involved, during the period of the time needed to document the transaction, a close review of the underlying asset documentation, creates new challenges.

Structural basis risk

1.017 Since the credit derivative is a notional product, there may be basis risk in the structure where the buyer of protection actually holds a specific exposure in

---

[11] At first glance, one would describe a credit derivative as pure credit risk equivalent to its notional amount, and not comparable to, say, the notional amounts of an interest rate swap or, a more apt analogy, a currency swap of which credit exposure is a small percentage. Even with a total return or digital product, however, if the credit exposures can be freely transferred or closed out by a reverse transaction, the exposure can be quantified as the likelihood at any given time that the exposure will arise in the near future or the value at which the exposure can be terminated (*e.g.* sale, close-out or hedge). This is classic derivatives valuation.

[12] See *International Financing Review* 1187, June 14, 1997.

respect of which protection is sought. The debt held by the buyer of protection might be illiquid (*e.g.* a bank loan) and the buyer may acquire protection based on the trading price of public securities of its borrower. Using the price of the security to value the loan presupposes that the market would price the assets in the same manner. In fact, publicly traded debt and privately held loans may be treated differently in a default context and liquidity itself may be a factor affecting the value. Further, the borrower might not have publicly traded (*i.e.* priceable) debt outstanding and the buyer may acquire protection based on the trading price of securities of similar entities. The basis risk widens further.

The credit-linked payment, being notional, may differ from actual exposure. Market Value, averaged over time, may only approximate the actual loss on an actual disposition of the Reference Obligations. In a digital product, the buyer of protection may be entitled to receive $5,000,000 on the occurrence of a Credit Event relating to a Reference Obligation in which it has a $10,000,000 exposure. Its protection is based on the historical fact that defaulted debt of this type of Reference Entity trades at 50 per cent of face, a fact which may or may not be true at a future date. In a yield product, the use of a swap rate rather than a "riskless" security as the benchmark introduces basis risk to the extent that the swap spread (*e.g.* difference between the U.S. dollar fixed rate for a given term in the swap market differs from the U.S. treasury rate for a similar term) may itself vary over time for financial and liquidity rather than credit reasons.

Anything other than a matched payment total return transaction, which exactly mirrors the payment flows and impediments to those flows (*e.g.* withholding tax) in respect of which protection is sought, leaves some structural basis risk. In short, the advantages of the product, the ability to synthesise protection, may in many cases not be absolute. This is not in itself a disadvantage of the product, as long as the buyer of protection is aware of and has properly allowed for the basis risk it is retaining.

Due diligence

1.018 More worrisome are the risks flowing from ease of entry and speed of execution. If the buyer of risk/seller of protection were in fact buying a security or making a loan it might typically make a detailed analysis of the risks inherent in the extension of credit. Purchase of a funded participation by a bank usually involved a detailed review of all underlying documentation, including legal opinions. The speed and flexibility of credit derivatives are unavailable if such a review is to be made. There is a risk that notionally buying the debt through a credit derivative with a respected financial institution will lull the buyer of risk/ seller of protection into a false sense of security. The buyer of risk/seller of protection may not fully investigate the jurisdictional peculiarities of the Reference Entity and Reference Obligations, some of which are described in Part II, or the tightness and enforceability of the underlying documentation. While this poses obvious problems for the buyer of risk/seller of protection who may "trust" the seller of risk/ buyer of protection, the latter may have some concerns over the legal effect, if any, of this fiduciary-like reliance even if there are self-serving representations alleging that there is no such reliance..

Part II: Selected Documentation Issues

1.019 Part I considered exposure in credit derivatives which arises from using notional products to replicate or hedge actual exposures and the need for due diligence with respect to the Reference Entity, the Reference Obligations and the documentation related to them. An analysis of credit derivatives also requires close attention to the particular derivatives agreement in order to determine what risks have been or have not been transferred and whether the settlement procedures reflect the parties' expectations. Since the credit derivative bridges the bank lending, securities and derivatives markets, the lawyer analysing a credit derivative agreement must apply a broad range of financial expertise in this process.

Forms of documentation

1.020 There are three generally used documentation structures for credit derivatives: note form, specialised agreement and confirmation under a standard derivatives master agreement.

A seller of protection/buyer of risk may have a preference for holding notes. An institution may in fact be prohibited or restricted in its legal ability from entering into swaps or writing options, but it may be permitted to acquire notes where the rate of return is based on factors other than interest rates. Viewed from a different perspective, the credit-linked note permits a dealer to buy protection/sell risk without incurring credit exposure to the seller of protection/buyer of risk, thereby broadening the customer base to which the dealer can market the product. Credit-linked notes may be structured as standard notes (with, of course, some non-standard payment provisions), either individually issued and documented or issued under an existing medium term note programme or similar programme. The extent to which a dealer's MTN programme requires revision to provide for credit pricing may well depend on when it was first put in place, as many earlier dealer MTN programmes may not provide for appropriate pricing supplements for credit-linked notes. If a suitable MTN programme is in place, the credit-linked note structure is cheaper and simpler than other structures such as repackaging or securitisation vehicles which are used to market illiquid assets or securities coupled with an asset swap to a potentially large number of investors. Both investor and dealer will, however, wish to consider the fact that the buyer of risk/seller of protection in a credit-linked note incurs full credit risk to two parties: the Reference Entity and the seller of risk/buyer of protection. This double risk will affect pricing, as well as utilise, at least on the margin, the dealer's capacity to issue debt in the market.

Credit swaps or options are drafted as either separate agreements or as confirmations under existing derivatives agreements. A separate agreement may be preferable for use with a counterparty which wishes only to deal in credit products or where the nature of the underlying assets or the structure is particularly complex. In the first case, the parties may not wish an agreement of a standard nature which is overly complicated as a result of the need to cover a broad range of other products which are not relevant. In the second case, the standard agreement may require too many alterations for the particular transaction.

1.021 Most credit swaps and options, however, are documented under derivatives master agreements. Potential advantages to executing a credit derivative under an existing derivatives master include: faster execution, as a result of many general protective provisions such as representations, covenants, events of default, tax procedures and enforcement provisions already having been agreed between the parties; and potential reduction of the credit risk between the parties and recognition thereof for capital purposes based on termination netting of exposures across a variety of transactions. Additional advantages of using the ISDA Master Agreement are its market acceptance and familiarity, its general even-handedness between the parties and the general confidence in its enforceability. The last advantage is based on legal opinions obtained with respect to the ISDA Master Agreement in many jurisdictions by ISDA collectively and derivatives dealers individually and in some cases on express regulatory recognition of the effectiveness of the ISDA Master Agreement for termination netting and capital purposes.[13]

If a derivatives agreement other than an ISDA Master Agreement is used, the parties will wish to assure themselves that it is suitable for use with credit derivatives. If an ISDA Master Agreement or another standard form is used, the parties will further wish to consider whether all terms of the standard master agreement should apply to credit derivatives in the same way as they apply to other derivative transactions. For instance, the parties may be more comfortable with Loss as the measure of damages in respect of a credit derivative under the ISDA Master Agreement rather than the more customary Market Quotation, given the relative lack of liquidity in the credit derivatives market compared to, say, the dollar interest rate swap market.

1.022 The typical derivatives master, such as the ISDA Master Agreement, provides for the entry into transactions either in writing or orally over the phone confirmed by writing.[14] Either method typically requires a confirmation. The confirmation is thus the document which contains the essence of the transaction, subject to the general terms of the master agreement. Prior to ISDA's efforts in creating its credit swap confirmation, documentation for credit derivatives varied widely over a range from reasonably good to embarrassingly bad. ISDA's publication of its credit swap confirmation was somewhat unusual, since normally ISDA waits for market practice in a product area to develop prior to "codifying" that practice in one of its forms. The ISDA credit swap confirmation was, uniquely, intended to focus the market. Even during the lengthy drafting period, some terms from then current ISDA drafts in fact began to be used regularly in the market and are now becoming common market standard. In part because the ISDA form only provides for a limited type of transaction, many dealers continue to use their own form of confirmation, even if under the ISDA Master Agreement. While these proprietary forms often incorporate some or all of the ISDA credit swap definitions, there are sometimes minor changes which are barely noticeable but may have substantive effect.

Regardless of which forms are used, care must be exercised. Even the best documents may not cover all the risks inherent in the Reference Obligations or may allocate some risks in a way which one or both of the parties, on full consideration, would not wish. Drafting choices made for the purpose of standardisation and general acceptance may not be appropriate for all situations. There is no rule that says "standard" documentation must be used. The balance of this Part II will discuss specific issues with respect to the ISDA credit swap confirmation which are in general relevant also to proprietary documentation or credit-linked note structures: Credit Events and other events which create risk but may not be accounted

---

[13] For instance, the French netting statute focuses primarily on the nature of the parties (or at least one of them) and on the market standard terms of the relevant master agreement rather than the particular form of transaction. The ISDA Master Agreement or the AFB Master Agreement (which, however, is not presently geared towards credit derivatives) would, in general, be highly recommended for use with a French counterparty for the maximum possible range of derivative products. That having been said, Part III will discuss issues which may arise in other jurisdictions relating to the degree of protection offered some types of credit derivatives in the insolvency of a local counterparty.

[14] Given the complexities and potential variations in credit derivatives, an oral agreement leaves the draftsman of the confirmation exposed to the risk that the other party will not accept its final terms and the basic agreement will fall apart and it leaves the other party exposed to the risk that it may be deemed to have unwittingly agreed to terms unfavourable to it.

for; the Credit Event Notice; Notice of Publicly Available Information and Materiality tests; issues on valuation and settlement; and the degree of discretion of one or both of the parties.

ISDA credit swap confirmation

1.023 The ISDA credit swap confirmation, the financial elements of which were described in Part I, provides for a credit default swap with respect to a single non-sovereign Reference Entity. It is drafted as a confirmation under the 1992 ISDA Master Agreement. It can in theory be used as a free-standing contract for the transaction in question, but would not then contain protective provisions found in the Master Agreement relating to representations, taxes, covenants, events of default, termination events, termination netting and enforcement. In addition, the confirmation incorporates the 1991 ISDA Definitions. By incorporating those Definitions, many technical matters such as determining business days, methods of calculating accrued amounts and the like need not be expressly set forth but certain awkward expressions result such as "Floating Rate Payer" (seller of protection), "Fixed Rate Payer" (buyer of protection) and "Floating Rate Payer Calculation Amount" (generally, the face Amount of Reference Obligations to which the Transaction relates). Of course, each party must assure itself that the Definitions work in harmony with anticipated payment flows under the swap as well as with the payment conventions applicable to the Reference Obligations and the delivery conventions applicable to the Deliverable Obligations. This is particularly important in arrangements designed to approximate total return products, for which the ISDA confirmation is not designed, or for use in structured financings.

Credit Events

1.024 As noted in Part I, a total return transaction and some types of credit decline option may not include any Credit Events, although in a total return transaction a Credit Event can be used to provide for early settlement where the Reference Obligation itself, for example, is accelerated. In a default transaction, however, whether a digital or credit decline product, the Credit Event is absolutely central to operation of the transaction, since valuation and settlement only occur on satisfaction of the conditions: occurrence of a Credit Event, delivery of a Credit Event Notice and, if agreed by the parties in the confirmation, delivery of a Notice of Publicly Available Information, satisfaction of a Materiality test, or both.

The menu of Credit Events set forth in the ISDA credit support confirmation are:

- *Bankruptcy:* a standard clause relating to insolvency and bankruptcy situations applicable to the Reference Entity, including objective occurrences such as the institution of proceedings by or against it and, if against it, failure to discharge within 30 days, the appointment of an insolvency representative, and a secured party taking possession of substantially all its assets, and some more subjective occurrences, such as the Reference Entity becoming insolvent or unable to pay its debts, entering into general arrangements with its creditors and taking any action leading to those and other enumerated events.

- *Failure to Pay:* the Reference Entity fails to make payments (presumably including interest) under defined Obligations when due, after allowing for any applicable grace period, in an amount in excess of an agreed Payment Requirement. In this regard, payment not required to be made on the Reference Obligations by reason of a subsequent illegality or lack of capacity will not excuse a default.

- *Cross-acceleration:* a default by the Reference Entity which results in defined Obligations in an aggregate amount in excess of an agreed Default Requirement being accelerated.

- *Cross-default:* a default by the Reference Entity which permits holders of defined Obligations in excess of an agreed Default Requirement to accelerate, whether or not they have done so.

- *Repudiation:* the Reference Entity repudiates a defined Obligation.

- *Restructuring:* conclusion of a waiver, rescheduling, standstill or other similar arrangement with respect to a defined Obligation such that the terms of such Obligation become materially less favourable to the holder of the Obligation, the latter condition of course having a subjective element.

- *Downgrade:* the credit rating of the Reference Entity or a specified Downgrade Obligation dropping below a Specified Rating set forth in the Confirmation.

- *Credit Event upon merger:* a merger or sale of substantially all of its assets by the Reference Entity in which the surviving entity is materially weaker than prior to the action, again introducing a subjective element.

It is important to note that the Credit Event must occur on or after the Effective Date and on or before the Scheduled Termination Date. This time limitation is a reasonable provision, but it highlights the need for due diligence: any event prior to the Effective Date but not known until later, even if its subsequent publication has an adverse effect on the Reference Obligation, cannot be used to trigger protection. Any event for which all conditions are not met until after the Scheduled Termination Date (*e.g.* lapse of a grace period in Failure to Pay where the Scheduled Termination Date is the maturity date of the Obligations) cannot be used to trigger protection.

1.025 If the seller of protection/buyer of risk views the product as a synthetic extension of credit, the Credit Events should in theory be structured to replicate normal events of default for the Reference Entity, the creation of a synthetic bond. There is, however, a difference in function between an event of default in a bond and a Credit Event in a credit derivative. While the actual holder of a debt obligation would wish stringent credit controls and easily triggered defaults in order to have an early warning and, perhaps, exert leverage on the borrower to enable the lender to obtain additional protection, the Credit Event in a credit derivative is a trigger to the obligation of the seller of protection to pay. The seller of protection/buyer of risk might therefore prefer to keep the Credit Events to a minimum. For instance, it might argue that Cross Default is intended to give negotiating leverage to a holder of the Obligation and is thus not appropriate as a triggering device in a notional product.

The buyer of protection/seller of risk would wish the maximum number of Credit Events drafted as widely as possible. It might argue that the circumstances specified in Cross Default would have significant effects on the perception of creditworthiness of the Reference Entity and accordingly on the value of the Reference Obligations. If a party is buying protection with respect to specific debt it is seeking to hedge, it would wish the Credit Events to be drafted to create the maximum possible symmetry between the derivative and the hedged debt, including at a minimum Bankruptcy, Cross Acceleration and Failure to Pay. If the Reference Obligation matures after the Scheduled Termination Date, it will wish the widest possible range of Credit Events, with more sensitive triggers.

Other events

1.026   To the extent events can occur which may result in non-payment at maturity of the hedged position (if that maturity falls on or before the Scheduled Termination Date of the derivative) or decline in value of credit (if the maturity of the hedged position is after the Scheduled Termination Date) but do not constitute Credit Events, protection may have been lost or weakened. The fact that ISDA has published eight Credit Events does not mean that the parties cannot alter them or devise additional triggering events based on the credit of the Reference Entity or other events which, while not relating directly to the Reference Entity, may reflect the broader credit considerations in any particular financial transaction.

First, the buyer of protection may wish to alter the Credit Events or to consider other events, not included in the ISDA menu, which could occur with respect to the Reference Entity and have a material effect on the value of the Reference Obligations, particularly if the debt matures after the Scheduled Termination Date of the credit product. For example, Credit Events such as Bankruptcy may be expanded where the Reference Entity, *e.g.* a Japanese bank, is subject to a regulatory scheme which provides for regulatory actions which are interim steps intended to avoid actual insolvency proceedings in serious credit crises, perhaps including a partial government bail-out prior to actual insolvency which keeps the Reference Entity limping along, at least for a while. Restructuring might be amended to include announcement of negotiation for a standstill agreement, in addition to just its conclusion. Cross Default might be altered to include a waiver of defaults prior to their acknowledgement as occurring.[15]

1.027   Other external events, part of the broader risk parameters an actual investor faces, could occur which result in payments being properly made by the Reference Entity but not actually received by a holder of debt. If the buyer of protection/seller of risk in a total return swap is actually holding the Reference Obligations and the Reference Entity is deemed to have made the payment, the buyer's obligation to pay the equivalent under the credit derivative might arise but it may not in fact have received the funds on which it was relying in order to make the payment. If the buyer of protection/seller of risk in a default product is holding the Reference Obligation and the external event is not a Credit Event, it cannot deliver a Credit Event Notice even though the Reference Obligation may have declined in value substantially as a result of the external event. If the documentation does not address these risks, the buyer of protection may therefore remain exposed to them. On the other hand, the seller of protection/buyer of risk in a

---

[15] Other occurrences which could result in unexpected risks are credit support ceasing to be binding, new money obligations imposed on the holder of a Reference Obligation, unscheduled prepayment or redemption of Reference Obligations or conversion of the form of Reference Obligations not constituting a Restructuring. The ISDA credit swap confirmation specifies that some of these events will permit or require the Calculation Agent to determine substitute Reference Obligations.

synthetic transaction or a total return swap may base its decision to enter into the transaction solely on an analysis of the credit of the Reference Entity and would resist inclusion of other such external events. If the documentation does pass these risks on, the seller of protection acquires an exposure it may not have planned on or may not have bothered to analyse.

One example of these external risks is custody risk. If the buyer of protection is holding the Reference Obligations through a custodian and the custodian becomes insolvent, defaults on its obligation to pass on moneys or is negligent, the buyer of protection may discover that it is obligated to make a payment in respect of funds which, though paid by the Reference Entity, were not passed on to the buyer of protection by the custodian. Other similar fiduciary risks include the refusal of a registrar to record a transfer or a clearance system failure. Such risks, often ignored in dealing with OECD debt, are increasingly being considered in the context of emerging market debt. If these risks have been passed on, it may take a careful reading of the confirmation for the buyer of risk/seller of protection to notice that it has taken them on. Even if it notices the risk, it is the rare transaction in which the buyer of risk/seller of protection seeks to review the laws of the jurisdiction where the Reference Obligations are held to determine legal recourse against the custodian or right to assets held by an insolvent custodian. Even rarer is a review of the custodian agreement under which the Reference Obligations are held to determine whether or not the custodian is obligated to segregate assets or to permit the owner of assets to inspect its records. Unheard of is the transaction in which the seller of risk/buyer of protection agrees to inspect the records of the custodian and monitor its performance.

1.028   Other examples include a range of political or sovereign events which could affect access to payments made on Reference Obligations, even where properly made by the Reference Entity.[16] For instance, the imposition of foreign exchange controls or other foreign exchange risks should be allocated, particularly if the credit product is expressed to be payable in a currency other than the currency of the Reference Obligation.[17] Payment by a Reference Entity which cannot be transferred out of the country or converted into the currency of the derivative payment may leave the buyer of protection exposed if it is required to pay out under a total return transaction or cannot deliver a Credit Event Notice in a default transaction. If the risks have been passed on, the buyer of risk/seller of protection needs to consider them. For both parties, ISDA's recently published 1998 FX and Currency Option Definitions contain an interesting menu of lessons learned over the last several years resulting from dislocation of the currency markets. These events include: it becoming impossible to convert a currency or to transfer it to an account outside the jurisdiction or between accounts within a jurisdiction or to a party non-resident in the jurisdiction; the development of a dual or split exchange rate; illiquidity rendering a party unable to get firm quotes on the exchange rate; and disruption of pricing sources.

Taxes may also affect net receipts. Imposition of a withholding tax on a payment under Reference Obligations could result in the buyer of protection receiving

---

[16] The ISDA credit swap confirmation specifies that lack of capacity, invalidity or a change in law, such as a moratorium imposed by the Reference Entity's sovereign on payment of an Obligation, does not excuse a Failure to Pay or other Credit Event.

[17] Note that a credit derivative in which payment is made in a currency other than that of the Reference Obligation contains an implied FX transaction or currency swap which must be taken into consideration on any early termination.

substantially less interest than anticipated and will affect their value in the market. Arguably, since a withholding tax is a tax on the payee, deduction by the payer at source is technically a payment to the payee forwarded to the government by the payer on the payee's behalf. The buyer of protection/seller of risk might, unless there were careful drafting to the contrary, be obligated to pay equivalent amounts to the seller of protection based on the full payment. If an unexpected direct tax is imposed on holders of a Reference Obligation (*e.g.* road user's tax on holders of GKOs) for which provision is not made in the confirmation, the buyer of protection will incur a loss and not be indemnified for it by the seller of protection. If these risks are passed on, the seller of protection/buyer of risk will wish to consider in advance the withholding or other tax implications regarding the Reference Obligations.

Credit Event Notice and Notice of Publicly Available Information

1.029 The occurrence of a Credit Event is not sufficient by itself to trigger an obligation under the ISDA credit swap confirmation. One of the parties must deliver a Credit Event Notice which contains a description in reasonable detail of the facts asserted as constituting a Credit Event. If a Credit Event occurs on or before the Scheduled Termination Date but does not become known or verifiable until after the Scheduled Termination Date, protection will be lost unless the agreement provides an extension for notice purposes. Some proprietary credit derivative forms require satisfaction of all conditions prior to the Scheduled Termination Date, thereby exposing the buyer of protection to timing risks with respect to satisfaction of procedural conditions such as delivery of the Credit Event Notice. The ISDA credit swap confirmation requires satisfaction of the procedural conditions prior to the date which is provisionally specified, in brackets, as 14 days after the Scheduled Termination Date. The parties would wish to review what the appropriate period is given the nature of the Credit Events, the Reference Entity and the Reference Obligations (and the Obligations if different).

The ISDA credit swap confirmation allows the parties to specify delivery of the Credit Event Notice by the buyer of protection, the seller of protection, or either of them. The party entitled to deliver the Credit Event Notice of course has a crucial role, particularly given the subjective nature of some of the Credit Events. Arguably, the party which is in the business of managing the credit risk with respect to the Reference Entity or Reference Obligations would be the party most likely to become aware of the relevant event. That having been said, one may question whether or not that party, if it is the seller of protection, would be as diligent and aggressive in determining the existence of a Credit Event as the buyer of protection would like, particularly if the Scheduled Termination Date of a credit default swap was approaching. One can also consider whether or not the buyer of protection is apt to be more diligent and aggressive in determining a Credit Event than the seller of protection would like. Either party could, of course, also be influenced in its diligence and aggressiveness by its view of where the market was going. If the seller of protection thought the credit of the Reference Entity was going to deteriorate, it might have an incentive to deliver a Credit Event Notice earlier rather than later and thereby minimise its loss. The buyer of protection under these circumstances might defer delivering since it is not at risk with respect to the anticipated further deterioration, particularly if there is a Materiality test which might not be met, as discussed below. Parties may therefore wish to consider different designations of the party entitled to deliver depending on the Credit Event (*e.g.* the seller of protection on Cross Default and the buyer of protection on Failure to Pay) or a third party could be requested to assume the responsibility (for a fee and subject to additional documentation, of course). Alternatively, the parties may simply conclude that these issues cannot be resolved to the complete satisfaction of both parties, that they are not of a type which can be adequately addressed contractually given the notional nature of the product or that the risks balance out.

1.030 Since the typical credit product is notional, a number of Credit Events contain subjective elements and neither party may be holding Obligations or have regular contact with the Reference Entity, it may be difficult to prove the existence of a Credit Event in a way satisfactory to both parties whose respective interests are opposed. The ISDA credit swap confirmation permits the parties to agree to a condition to settlement based on public information: the Notice of Publicly Available Information specifying publication of information reasonably confirming the event in a specified number of internationally recognised sources, including, but apparently not limited to, Public Sources designated by the parties.[18] While the seller of protection would generally wish this condition, it is not an unmitigated good from its perspective. If the Notice of Publicly Available Information is properly given, the condition is technically satisfied even if a Credit Event is subsequently shown not to have occurred. For example, in times of volatility rumours may abound and the Public Sources selected may not always distinguish between fact and rumour. Although to a limited extent the Materiality test described below serves as a control in this respect, parties may also wish to consider other procedures for looking behind the Publicly Available Information.[19]

The buyer of protection would, of course, generally prefer no such condition. A buyer of protection which actually holds Obligations would, in theory, receive notice at some point of the relevant events. If it is nevertheless required to deliver a Notice of Publicly Available Information, it may not be able to find reports in the specified Public Sources or other internationally recognised sources. For example, prior to restructurings, it is to the benefit of the borrower as well as the waiving banks not to state publicly that defaults have occurred, waivers have been given or that a borrower is insolvent. In a period of economic crisis, newspapers may not bother to list each bankruptcy, a concern which has been expressed with respect to the bankruptcies of various Indonesian counterparties. Alternatively, perhaps the Publicly Available Information is not usable since it cites the buyer of protection or its affiliate as a source (*e.g.* it is the agent in a defaulted syndicated loan). Parties may therefore wish to provide a mechanism for supplying other supplementary evidence of a commercially reasonable nature.

Materiality

1.031 As noted, certain of the Credit Events have elements which are subjective, difficult to ascertain or both, with the result that good faith views may differ as to their occurrence. Published rumours which satisfy the requirement for Publicly Available Information might not in fact be viewed as significant by the market. Certain Credit Events could in fact occur but not have the expected effect on the Reference Obligations. Some Credit Events, the purpose of which is primarily to

---

[18] It is important to note that the Publicly Available Information cannot have as its source either party or an affiliate and need not confirm any subjective criteria or threshold levels contained in the Credit Events.

[19] It is unlikely that the dispute resolution clause in the ISDA credit swap confirmation would apply to looking behind information in fact appearing in a Public Source.

give lenders leverage in advance of serious problems, may be too sensitive in a transaction designed to price only the most serious problems. These concerns, coupled with the fact that there is no time limit on giving a Credit Event Notice in relation to the occurrence of a Credit Event, create the risk that the notional credit product does not in fact transfer or price credit risk adequately and that it may create a simple option the value of which is based on other factors.[20]

The Materiality tests are designed to address these concerns and to assure that there is at least a measurable decline in credit from the Effective Date which is agreed by the parties to be sufficiently significant. Even though these tests do not require a causal connection to be shown between the credit decline and a given Credit Event, the parties may agree to provide for Materiality to apply with respect to all or none of the Credit Events. They may agree to apply the test to only some Credit Events, perhaps those with a more sensitive trigger or subjective elements, while not applying it to the obviously threatening events such as Bankruptcy.[21] .

The ISDA credit swap confirmation provides a choice of two approaches for determining Materiality: Price Materiality which can apply to a floating rate Reference Obligation or a fixed rate Reference Obligation; and Spread Materiality which can apply only to a fixed rate Reference Obligation.[22]

Price Materiality is satisfied if the excess, if any, of the Initial Price (expressed as a percentage and specified in the confirmation, presumably representing the agreed value on the Effective Date) exceeds the Final Price (a percentage determined on the basis of Market Value on the Valuation Date or, if more than one is specified, the Valuation Dates) by an amount greater than the Price Decline Requirement (a percentage set forth in the confirmation). There are a number of issues one might wish to consider with respect to this test.

1.032 First, the Price Materiality formula with respect to a floating rate Reference Obligation is based solely on the difference in the two Prices without backing out values reflecting changes in market requirements for the margin over the floating rate. While a floating rate obligation is, in theory, always tradable at par (absent credit issues), this is not quite right. Floating rate debt is usually expressed with a margin over a commonly used floating rate such as LIBOR, and the margin required by the market in general will vary from time to time. The ISDA credit swap confirmation thus creates a minor basis risk in the determination of Price Materiality with respect to a floating rate Reference Obligation.

Secondly, the determination of Price Materiality for a fixed rate return by reference to a change in the value of a notional interest rate swap entered into on the Effective Date with fixed rate calculation and payment provisions corresponding to the coupon on the Reference Obligation and a floating rate calculated at three

---

[20] Since default products are in some respects similar to options and a Credit Event is analogous to a condition to exercise, satisfaction of that condition (if it is the only one) can be viewed as resulting in an unrestricted right to put or call. Following a Credit Event, the relevant party can choose to exercise (*i.e.* deliver a Credit Event Notice) based on changes in market value resulting from factors other than credit. Therefore, after the occurrence of a Credit Event, a party entitled to deliver a Credit Event Notice in effect has an interest rate sensitive put, if it is the buyer of protection, or an interest rate sensitive call, if it is the seller of protection, particularly if the transaction is physically-settled (see below, para. 1.035).
[21] Even under Bankruptcy, however, some of the specified events may be highly subjective or difficult to determine, such as the Reference Entity's insolvency or inability to pay its debts, or technical, such as a frivolous petition for insolvency against the Reference Entity which, due to court delays, cannot be dismissed within 30 days and thus constitutes a Credit Event.
[22] If there is a basket of Reference Obligations, different tests could be applied to different Reference Obligations and the parties may choose to base satisfaction of the condition on the Materiality test being met with respect to any Reference Obligation (Individual) or to each Reference Obligation (Joint). Note that key terms (*e.g.* Initial Price or Initial Spread) would probably need to be defined separately for each Reference Obligation in the basket.

month LIBOR plus an agreed Initial Spread. Price Materiality is deemed to exist if the sum of the Market Value of the Reference Obligation at the Valuation Date and its Interest Rate Adjustment Amount is below its Initial Price by more than the Price Decline Requirement. The Interest Rate Adjustment Amount is the difference between the Mark to Market Value of the notional swap on the Valuation Date, from the perspective of the fixed rate payer, and the remainder of 100 per cent minus the Initial Price. While the purpose of this provision is to back out changes in value resulting from changes in interest rates, significant concerns have been expressed as to whether this formulation works as desired.[23]

The Spread Materiality test compares the yield on the Reference Obligation based on its Market Value to the Interpolated Swap Rate, being the fixed rate in the market on the Valuation Date for a fixed rate against LIBOR interest rate swap for the remaining maturity. The difference between these two is the Final Spread.[24] If the Final Spread exceeds the sum of the agreed Initial Spread and the Spread Widening Requirement, Spread Materiality exits. The general procedure is essentially that referred to with respect to the yield option described in Part I of this Chapter, using the rate in the swap market as the benchmark. Since the swap market yield is based on a spread over "riskless" securities such as U.S. treasuries, which spread changes from time to time, again a minor basis risk is present.[25]

1.033 The ISDA credit swap confirmation provides for the Calculation Agent to determine Materiality on the same agreed Valuation Dates which would apply in determining the Final Price in cash settlement, permitting, however, the parties to select the first, the last or any Valuation Date or an average over all Valuation Dates for purposes of the test. In determining the number of Valuation Dates appropriate for the test, the parties will wish to consider issues such as volatility and the length of time required for the market to "digest" news of the event.

There are several critical timing issues which arise in application of the Materiality test and weaken the already notional link between the occurrence of the Credit Event and the credit decline. First, the parties may wish to consider the fact that there is no time limitation on imposing the Materiality test. A Credit Event can be used as a triggering event, once it occurs, regardless of any subsequent cure and the passage of time. After occurrence of the Credit Event, an option (as described in footnote 20) exists subject to external market factors as to the profitability of exercise and to a decline in credit for *any* reason as a condition to

---

[23] It is not at all apparent from the confirmation itself how this provision works or how the Initial Spread should be determined. According to market sources, the only way in which the formula works is to determine an Initial Spread that would be required so that the aggregate of the value of the swap, from the perspective of the fixed rate payer, and the Reference Obligation (each expressed as a percentage) would be 100 per cent as of the Effective Date. A problem in the drafting arises through use of the "difference" concept. The difference between two numbers is always positive. The provision should read ". . . the remainder of (i) the Mark to Market Value minus (ii) . . .". A simpler way of backing out the effect of interest rate movements is to select the Initial Spread so that the swap alone is at par (or zero) value at the Effective Date, delete the definition of Interest Rate Adjustment Amount and revise sub-clause (ii) of Price Materiality to read "(ii) the Market Value of the fixed rate Reference Obligation is below the sum of its Initial Price and its Mark to Market Value by more than the Price Decline Requirement".

[24] Note again the technical problem resulting from the "difference" concept. The test is really meant to apply only where the Reference Obligation yield has widened against the benchmark. However, if the Reference Obligation yield is below this benchmark yield, there is still a difference and the difference between two numbers is always a positive number. The drafting problem here is not as serious as with Price Materiality, as it is presumably unlikely that the Reference Obligation yield would ever be below the Interpolated Swap Rate.

[25] Proponents of the Interpolated Swap Rate take the position, which is not necessarily logical, that it is the appropriate rate because it is the funding rate which they use in their derivatives business.

exercise. Even the limited nexus in the default product between a specified Credit Event and credit decline may therefore be lost.[26]

1.034 Secondly, it is not clear from the drafting if a party can give repeated Credit Event Notices, or if the other party can give a subsequent Credit Event Notice, if the Materiality test has not been met on delivery of the first Credit Event Notice. There is no provision which expressly bars more than one Credit Event Notice for a given Credit Event. Nonetheless, there is a possible interpretation, based on the definition of "Valuation Date"[27] and the context of the confirmation, that on giving the Credit Event Notice the Valuation Date or Dates automatically occur and, if Materiality is not found to exist, the Credit Event has been "lost" as a triggering event. If this interpretation is correct, there is an incentive for the seller of protection to deliver earlier, since it may be able to trigger the test prior to a significant decline.[28] From the perspective of the buyer of protection, there would be a "Russian roulette" element in delivering a Credit Event Notice if it is not clear as to the Materiality of the event. The buyer of protection, if it has the right to deliver a Credit Event Notice, would therefore wish to defer delivery until it is reasonably certain the test will be satisfied so as not to risk losing the "benefit" of the Credit Event.

Depending on their interpretation of the ISDA credit swap confirmation and their views on the above, the parties may wish to amend the form to clarify the position with respect to the ability to deliver repetitive Credit Event Notices. They may also wish to consider a mandatory application of the Materiality test within a specified period following occurrence of a Credit Event, particularly in default products where only a limited number of Credit Events have been selected.

Valuation and delivery issues

1.035 The ISDA credit swap confirmation provides for settlement after satisfaction of all conditions within the defined period either on a cash basis or by physical delivery. The method may be specified or one of the parties may be given the right to select the method prior to final valuation. Whether the transaction is cash or physically settled, non-credit related payments such as a Fixed Amount payable by the buyer of protection continue up to the settlement date even if after the Scheduled Termination Date.

---

[26] By way of example, assume that a Credit Event such as Cross Default occurs but, because the underlying event is quickly cured, it would not meet the Materiality test. The buyer of protection does not deliver a Credit Event Notice. Subsequently, the credit of the Reference Entity actually improves. Three years later, still prior to the Scheduled Termination Date, the credit deteriorates for other reasons but there is no new Credit Event. The three-year old Credit Event can still technically be used by the buyer of protection, and the Materiality test might be satisfied as a result of circumstances unrelated to the Credit Event.

[27] "[Valuation Date]: With respect to a particular Credit Event, the day that is [ ] calendar days after the delivery of a Credit Event Notice [and a Notice of Publicly Available Information] for such Credit Event [and each [ ] successive calendar day thereafter, ending on and including the [ ] such Valuation Date]." Other issues relating to this definition are discussed below.

[28] By way of example, assume a Credit Event occurs and, while it is reasonably clear to an objective observer that the Credit Event does not have a material effect, the seller of protection still has the right to deliver a Credit Event Notice. On delivery of the Credit Event Notice, the Valuation Date or Dates automatically occur. The Calculation Agent commences its determination of Price Materiality and determines that Materiality does not exist. Therefore, that Credit Event arguably ceases to be of relevance, even if the particular occurrence in question, *e.g.* the filing of an insolvency petition and it not being dismissed within 30 days, subsequently turns out to be not as frivolous as the market thought and the other (or the same) party subsequently attempts to deliver another Credit Event Notice.

If cash settlement applies, the Calculation Agent values the Reference Obligations by determining a Final Price based on market quotations from five leading dealers, after disregarding the highest and lowest quotations obtained.[29] All or some of the dealers may be specified, subject to the right of the Calculation Agent to appoint substitutes after consultation. The parties may choose from a menu of alternatives to base the Final Price on the bid, offered or mid-market quotations of the dealers, and on the highest quote or average of quotes on each Valuation Date. If there is a basket of Reference Obligations, the averaging is on an unweighted basis, with the effect that each Reference Obligation carries the same weight.

1.036 Valuation procedures are important not only in the sense that they quantify the actual liability, but they are important in structural terms when analysing the symmetry between protection obtained and any actual exposure with respect to the Reference Obligations. The parties may agree that the Final Price is determined on one Valuation Date or over a number of Valuation Dates. The first may be preferable for the buyer of protection which is actually selling or intends to sell the Reference Obligations on that date and can arrange to sell them at or about the specified Valuation Time. The basis risk to the buyer of protection in this case is limited to any difference between the notional calculation of Market Value and the actual sale price. The seller of protection/buyer of risk in a synthetic product, or the buyer of protection/seller of risk which is not hedging a saleable exposure or which is more comfortable with selling hedged debt over a period, would typically wish Valuation Dates spread over a period for the effect of the Credit Event to be naturally worked out in the market. This also avoids risks to both parties flowing from short-term volatility and allows the market to "settle" and arrive at a consensus value.[30].

A physically settled transaction requires delivery of a Portfolio of Deliverable Obligations by the buyer of protection against payment by the seller of protection of the Physical Settlement Amount, which is the product of the Reference Price and the Floating Rate Payer Calculation Amount. A party may, without reducing its own obligation, designate an affiliate to make or take delivery. To the extent the parties are concerned with future delivery risk, they can include an optional clause permitting either party to require delivery against payment in escrow at its expense.

1.037 The determination of what are Deliverable Obligations is, of course, important. To the extent that the Deliverable Obligations do not correspond to actual exposure thought to be transferred, basis risk in protection arises. The ISDA credit swap confirmation contains alternative provisions for determining Deliverable Obligations: specification of the Reference Obligations, the most common choice; or one of the parties designating obligations of the Reference Entity at the

---

[29] It is interesting to note the trend in the ISDA credit swap confirmation and proprietary confirmations providing for pricing of a transaction on, *e.g.* voluntary terminations towards using five reference dealers rather than the four used in Market Quotation.

[30] As noted above, the ISDA credit swap confirmation provides for Materiality and Final Price to be determined on the same Valuation Date or Dates, or at least one of them. Note the quandary posed to the buyer of protection which holds Reference Obligations and wishes to sell them on the Valuation Dates which are also used for the Materiality test: it may not know on those dates if the test will be satisfied. Parties may choose to alter this in a given transaction such that there are different dates used, as the purpose of the two calculations may not coincide in all transactions. Further, as noted above, Valuation Dates are defined by reference to calendar days rather than Business Days. If Market Value is being determined as an average over a period, it is not clear how Market Value for a non-Business Day Valuation Date is determined, how the Calculation Agent should give weight to quotations obtained in respect of such days or how deferred Valuation Dates relate to subsequent Valuation Dates which are Business Days on which quotes are obtained.

time of delivery subject to certain limitations.[31] The ISDA credit swap confirmation permits the parties to agree to limit a party's discretion in selecting Deliverable Obligations to those which are Due and Payable, and in any case provides two further sets of limiting conditions, one or both (or neither) of which may be selected to apply. The first relates to financial terms of the Deliverable Obligations in order to assure that they bear at least some similarity to the Reference Obligations: same currency, lack of contingency as to payment, maturity, simple periodic interest and the like. The second relates to legal and structural elements which could affect adversely the value of the Deliverable Obligations regardless of their financial terms: absence of set-off, no liabilities on the holder and no restrictions on trading. The parties will wish to consider these, and perhaps other, conditions in the context of each particular transaction.

Care should also be taken with respect to determining the quantity of Deliverable Obligations. Deliverable Obligations with a face amount equal to the Floating Rate Payer Calculation Amount, whether or not Due and Payable, could have accrued interest to the disadvantage of the buyer of protection. A Deliverable Obligation with a face amount equal to the Floating Rate Payer Calculation Amount could be worth less than its face amount if it is a zero coupon bond prior to its scheduled maturity or bears a fixed rate below the current market rate and is not Due and Payable, in either case to the disadvantage of the seller of protection.

1.038   It should also be noted that if the Reference Obligation is fixed rate, the Reference Price is based on its market value at the Effective Date, and market rates drop between the Effective Date and the settlement date, it is possible that a Materiality test, if one applies, could be satisfied and Deliverable Obligations could still be worth more than the amount payable by the seller of protection based on the Reference Price. This possible benefit to the seller of protection is not available in cash settlement, where payment is made only if the Final Price is lower than the Reference Price, and should particularly be considered if one party is to have the right to select cash or physical settlement just prior to final valuation.

The relationship of the delivery provisions to the actual requirements for transfer of the Deliverable Obligations are also crucial. To the extent that the delivery provisions of the agreement are not workable, protection may be illusory. If the seller of protection is only obligated to make payment against Delivery (as defined), and Delivery is not possible, the seller of protection may evade its obligation. The ISDA definition of "Deliver", which has become market standard, provides for transfer of a broad range of instruments, including negotiable securities and contracts such as loans, free of any liens or rights of set-off in respect of the Deliverable Obligations. The buyer of protection also makes a representation that it has conveyed all right, title and interest in the Portfolio free of claims, defences, liens and set-off. The buyer of protection will therefore wish to be comfortable that it will in fact be able to deliver (*e.g.* ascertain whether the underlying loan agreement prohibits or imposes conditions on assignments), that there is no risk of, *e.g.* a statutorily imposed lien arising regardless of any action or inaction of the buyer of protection or a contractually imposed lien in favour of a custodian or clearing house and that the Reference Entity has no contractual or statutory rights of set-off or counterclaims in respect of the Reference Obligations. The seller of

---

[31] It is not entirely clear which party has the discretion, but presumably discretion lies with the buyer of protection/seller of risk which is to deliver Deliverable Obligations. If the Deliverable Obligations are the Reference Obligations, any Stamp Tax is payable by the party customarily responsible; otherwise the buyer of protection is responsible for Stamp Tax.

protection will wish to be comfortable that it will in fact be able to take delivery and that there are no formalities or burdensome or expensive requirements with which it will be obligated to comply, such as the onerous requirements for holding for Russian GKOs. Satisfactory resolution of some of these concerns in advance may be difficult.

1.039 The ISDA credit swap confirmation addresses in a limited way the uncertainties posed by external problems in Delivery by establishing a 30-day period of delay if it becomes "impossible" or "illegal" to deliver or take delivery as a result of events which are beyond the control of the party affected and, if the buyer of protection is the affected party, do not reflect market conditions generally. Impossibility and illegality, it should be noted, present high legal thresholds. Neither term includes situations which could be described "merely" as extremely onerous, extremely expensive or commercially unreasonable. During this period, the affected party endeavours to deliver or take delivery as it is able against proportionate payment of the Physical Settlement Amount. Failing delivery after this period, the ISDA credit swap confirmation provides for an additional Termination Event with the party unaffected by the illegality or impossibility determining its loss or gain on termination. This follows the standard ISDA practice of putting the advantage of determining loss or gain on the non-Affected Party, presumably as an incentive to the Affected Party to sort the problem out. In a typical swap, the advantage to the non-Affected Party, reflected by the bid/offered spread, is relatively small. The parties may wish to consider the appropriateness of this approach in a credit derivatives context where the advantage to the non-Affected Party, and the corresponding disadvantage to the Affected Party, could be substantially larger.[32]

Other delivery issues to consider with respect to the ISDA credit swap confirmation include provision for a separate business day definition relating to days on which Deliverable Obligations can be delivered, for interest accruing on the purchase price if delivery is delayed, for allocation of the right to interest on the Deliverable Obligations paid during the period of delay and/or for reduction of the Fixed Rate Payer Calculation Amount proportionate to partial deliveries during the period of delay.

Calculation Agent and other discretion

1.040 The role of Calculation Agent in a credit derivative is far more important than its very limited ministerial role in the interest rate and currency swap market. In fact, as the derivatives market has expanded, the significance of the Calculation Agent's role generally has grown. In commodity derivatives, the Calculation Agent's discretion became significant with respect to disruption events. In the equity derivatives market, the Calculation Agent was given a crucial role with respect to capital or other types of events which required adjustments in numbers of shares and, often, in pricing and valuations. This trend continues with the credit derivative. In the ISDA credit swap confirmation, the Calculation Agent, albeit with limitations, makes a number of significant determinations.

The Calculation Agent not only performs the ministerial role in calculating Market Value, but it also determines whether or not accrued interest is included in the quotations, what dealers are to be approached and, if sufficient quotes are not obtained, alternative valuations. The Calculation Agent also determines Materiality,

---

[32] The parties may also wish to consider cash settlement, or a revised cash settlement procedure, as a fallback.

which means among other things selecting the formula to be used[33] and the fall-back rate if the Interpolated Swap Rate is not determinable from the specified screen rates. If a Downgrade Obligation ceases to exist, the Calculation Agent selects a substitute. If a Reference Obligation becomes illiquid by reason of the outstanding amount being reduced, ceases to be guaranteed by the Reference Entity, or is redeemed in connection with a mandatory obligation exchange, the Calculation Agent determines a substitute and, if necessary, may adjust its Reference Price. In the specially tailored forms of confirmation of various dealers, the Calculation Agent is often given discretion over a substantially wider range of determinations.

1.041   There is nothing intrinsically wrong with this discretion, as agreements should be drafted so that they do not fall apart over disagreements over procedure. Further, if a dealer is acting as Calculation Agent with respect to an end-user, it really must have some discretion. If a dealer had two similar mirror transactions, and it is Calculation Agent in neither, it would have direct exposure beyond its control to different selections made under the two transactions. Recognising the increased role of the Calculation Agent, the ISDA credit swap confirmation expressly imposes on the Calculation Agent general standards of good faith and commercial reasonableness and the obligation in certain of the above situations to consult with the other party.

Finally, the ISDA credit swap confirmation also provides a kind of third party arbitration if a party disagrees with a determination or failure to make a determination by the Calculation Agent or by the other party. In either case, the Calculation Agent selects the third party "arbiter" after consultation with the counterparty. It is not at all clear that a "determination" to which this dispute resolution clause would apply includes delivery of a Credit Event Notice or recitation therein of facts, allegations of satisfaction of subjective criteria or threshold amounts in Credit Events, accuracy of Publicly Available Information or selection of Deliverable Obligations.

Specialised products

1.042   Finally, certain types of products may by their nature require more revision to the ISDA form than others. In structured transactions in which credit derivatives are used among the participants and detailed attention is being paid to all other relevant documentation, it is advisable to make the extra effort to conform the derivative documentation specifically to the transaction. Total return trans-actions also tend to be documented less "notionally" and more tied in to actual payments on the Reference Obligation.[34]

The parties in these types of transaction may wish to pay particular attention to the provisions of the ISDA credit swap confirmation which correspond to pro-visions customary in risk and funded participations: representations as to each party making its own risk analysis and neither party being obligated to provide information to the other, each party being able to deal with the Reference Entity or Reference Obligations for its own account, clarification that no actual right to a

---

[33] There are several perfectly acceptable methods of calculating yield and the value of a security based on a yield, each of which results in different final values. The method selected is therefore significant.

[34] In addition, if the Reference Obligation is a fixed rate obligation, the ISDA credit swap confirmation would require further modification for the seller of protection/buyer of risk to pay a LIBOR floating amount and for the buyer of protection/seller of risk to pay a fixed amount, contingent on the corresponding Reference Obligation payment being made for it to become a total return product.

payment under a Reference Obligation is being assigned or transferred and no party being required actually to have exposure on a Reference Obligation. Other provisions customary in the sub-participation market may also be appropriate in certain situations depending on the nature of the credit derivative. If the buyer of protection is supplying information or underlying documentation, it may wish to impose confidentiality restrictions on the seller of protection.[35] The buyer of protection in a total return product may also wish to include a provision giving it a right to recovery of a payment under the credit derivative if it mistakenly believed that a Reference Obligation payment had been made or if the Reference Obligation payment must be returned to the Reference Entity or its representative. Where the parties anticipate the buyer of protection will be holding a Reference Obligation such as a loan, the seller of protection may wish to restrict the discretion of the buyer of protection to agree to actions in respect of the Reference Obligation which would prejudice the seller of protection. If a cash-settled total return product is based on amounts paid (or not paid) at maturity of the Reference Obligation coinciding with the Scheduled Termination Date of the derivative, the seller of protection may also wish to retain rights in respect of subsequent recoveries on the Reference Obligation. Similar concerns would arise in a physically settled trans-action if the seller of protection believes there is some risk it may not be able to take delivery of the Reference Obligations as a legal or practical matter. Both parties will also wish to consider the implications of external events set forth above which can result in the Reference Entity making a payment but the holder of the Reference Obligations not receiving the benefit of it.

On the other hand, if a party is matching or intends to match its exposure under a credit derivative with a reverse derivative, it would wish the greatest possible degree of standardisation in order to maximise the possibility that it will be able to exchange the risk with third parties in the credit derivative market and that its hedge will be complete. Consequently, there may be a tension between the desire of, for instance, a buyer of protection to fine-tune the documentation so that its risk is passed in its entirety and the desire of a seller of protection to standardise the parameters of the risk to improve the liquidity of its position.

Current documentation projects

1.043 ISDA has circulated draft 1999 ISDA Credit Derivatives Definitions. At the time of writing, the draft Definitions are in an advanced stage but a final version has not been published. It may, however, be useful as a progress report to describe certain features of the draft with the understanding that the final version is likely to differ.

Following ISDA's customary architecture, the structure is that of a definitions booklet (itself also incorporating the supplemented 1991 ISDA Definitions) which is incorporated into a short form confirmation entered into under an ISDA Master Agreement. Under the confirmation, various selections are to be made from a menu of choices which are substantively set forth in the Definitions. While "short form" may be something of a misnomer, the new confirmation will be substantially shorter than the current credit swap confirmation and will permit selection of a broad range of options through comparatively easy selections in the confirmation.

---

[35] Particularly in respect of a loan, the buyer of protection will wish to assure itself that it is not restricted under the Reference Obligation documentation in transferring the risk and in supplying information to the seller of protection, if it is doing so.

In addition to the architectural change, a number of changes are being made which reflect the market's experience with the current credit swap confirmation. Some changes expand the scope of possible transactions under the ISDA structure (although still limited to a credit default swap and not providing for a total return transaction) and others represent improvements following practical experience with the current confirmation.

Sovereign debt

1.044 Perhaps the most significant additional range of transactions results from the inclusion of definitions permitting transactions in relation to sovereign and supranational debt. There is a broad definition for sovereign, a broader definition for governmental authority and a definition for supranationals. In addition, certain Credit Events are adjusted to allow their applicability to sovereigns. For instance, Restructuring has been altered in several ways, including a modification to cover announcement of a restructuring, which has more significance in the context of sovereign debt than in relation to corporate debt.

Range of obligations

1.045 Another significant change is the greater flexibility and choice for specifying types of Reference Obligation, Obligation and Deliverable Obligation. These include a selection of obligations for payment of money, whether borrowed or not (*e.g.* lease payment or other types of receivables), and other possible characteristics (*e.g.* tradable, transferable, senior and pari passu) that may be selected to apply to otherwise unspecified obligations within one of those categories. In addition, there is an option to specify types to be excluded from a relevant category.

Currency

1.046 Other changes permit physical delivery with respect to Deliverable Obligations expressed in currencies different than the base currency of the Transaction. As drafted as of the time of writing, these provisions permit selection of Deliverable Obligations in different currencies but at no risk to the buyer of protection (*i.e.* the amount of the Deliverable Obligations is converted at spot rates current at the time of delivery). With some minor tinkering, these provisions could be adapted for cash settled transactions.

Failure to pay

1.047 The draft Definitions also effect some technical fine-tuning of several Credit Events in the long form confirmation. Notably, provision is made for a grace period in respect of Failure to Pay, where the maturity date of the Obligation is the Scheduled Termination Date of the Transaction. This avoids the risk, present in many outstanding confirmations, that failure to pay at maturity, given the grace period, does not constitute a Credit Event until after the Scheduled Termination Date and is therefore lost as a triggering event.

Market Value

1.048 Changes to the definition of Market Value provide that where the Calculation Agent is one of the parties and is unable to calculate Market Value, the other party will have the ability to obtain quotations. If neither party is able to obtain quotations, Market Value is specified as being zero (reflecting in particular experiences with Russian rouble debt).

Deliverable Obligations

1.049 Where Deliverable Obligations are not expressly designated in the confirmation, the parties may require the buyer of protection to deliver a notice specifying what obligations it intends to deliver on physical settlement. If Delivery is illegal or impossible beyond the control of the parties, the fallback under the long form confirmation was the occurrence of an Additional Termination Event with respect to all or part of the Transaction. The draft Definitions provide for Cash Settlement as a fallback, with appropriate changes to provide for its application under these circumstances. Tentative provisions also address inability to deliver because of contractual restrictions on Deliverable Obligations. If the buyer of protection fails to deliver for reasons not constituting impossibility or illegality beyond its control, the Transaction simply terminates and the other party is excused from performing.

Other changes

1.050 Provision is made for an Additional Termination Event to occur with respect to the Transaction if there is a merger or similar consolidation between the seller of protection and the Reference Entity.

Parties may select an option requiring the buyer of protection to give a notice that it wishes settlement to proceed, failing which settlement will not occur. This, as pointed out in Part II of this Chapter, may be important where there is the theoretical risk that value of Deliverable Obligations could be greater than the Reference Price as a result of market rate changes.

Provision is made for the ability to choose different Valuation Dates for the purposes of determining Final Price and Materiality.

Finally, the Calculation Agent provisions are pulled together and give, in one place, a summary of its functions in the Transaction. The dispute resolution clause from the current confirmation is still under substantial review and there is as yet no publicly proposed revised language. It is understood that the issue of dispute resolution in general is receiving broader attention within ISDA and may be addressed outside the scope of the final Definitions.

Part III: Selected Legal Issues

1.051 Legal issues finally resolved, or at least resolved on a commercially satisfactory basis, with respect to other derivatives, must often be reconsidered in regard to credit derivatives. Derivatives can be used consciously to replicate the cash flows of other types of financial transactions or they can inadvertently appear to be the economic equivalent of other types of financial transactions. Accordingly, categorising derivatives for purposes of applying laws relating to enforcement, regulation or taxation may be difficult. This has been one of the most intellectually stimulating challenges in the derivatives market since its beginnings in 1977, over which period many legal systems have gradually evolved to make a place for derivatives. Statutes, regulations and court decisions in many jurisdictions now provide guidance for the treatment of derivatives, in terms of enforcement, legality and tax.

The expansion of derivatives methodology throughout the system, however, provides further challenges, it still sometimes not being clear what fits into what place. Many of the laws relating to "derivatives" do not provide blanket treatment of all derivatives but relate to specified products, often providing for inclusion of other "similar" agreements. While an objective observer might class these specified products (or most of them) as derivatives, it does not necessarily follow that everything which is conventionally classed as a derivative fits within the relevant statutory or regulatory definitions. Thus, even though there are substantial reasons for classifying these credit products as derivatives, the classification does not by itself solve all legal issues. The issue is further complicated by the fact that there is a variety of different structures and economic functions within the "class" of credit derivatives. The appropriate treatment of individual credit products may be a significant legal issue. Calling a transaction a derivative, therefore, has increasingly little meaning. It is a beginning point and not an end in legal analysis.

Netting

1.052 Termination netting on a counterparty's default, or the ability of the other party to terminate all transactions (whether under a single agreement or otherwise), to value the relationship as a whole and to arrive at a single sum owing, is one of the most significant risk reduction techniques in the derivatives market. In many jurisdictions, the enforcement of termination netting of derivatives was legally uncertain, particularly where the defaulting party was insolvent. In order to make derivatives more readily available to residents of these jurisdictions and to protect the solvency of financial institutions in these jurisdictions, many legislatures have enacted laws which provide special protection for creditors in certain types of transactions set forth in the laws. Rarely, however, do these statutes give all-encompassing protection to "derivatives". The Irish netting statute (Netting of Financial Contracts Act, 1995), for instance, provides favourable treatment for a "netting agreement" for "financial contracts" in the insolvency of an Irish counterparty. Under that Act:

"financial contracts" means—

    (a) interest-rate contracts as follows—

        (i) single-currency interest rate swaps,
        (ii) basis swaps,
       (iii) forward-rate agreements,
       (iv) interest-rate futures,
        (v) interest-rate options,
      (vi) other contracts of a similar nature.

    (b) foreign-exchange contracts and contracts concerning gold, as follows—

        (i) cross-currency interest-rate swaps,
        (ii) spot foreign-exchange contracts,
       (iii) forward foreign-exchange contracts,.
       (iv) currency futures,
        (v) currency options,
      (vi) other contracts of a similar nature,.
      (vii) contracts concerning gold of a nature similar to sub-paragraphs (i) to (vi).

(c) (i) securities lending and securities borrowing contracts.
    (ii) sale and repurchase agreements, including reverse repurchase agreements, in relation to securities

(d) contracts of a nature similar to those specified in paragraph (a)(i) to (v) or paragraph (b)(i) to (v) concerning other reference items or indices relating to—

   (i) equities and bonds,
   (ii) precious metals except gold,
   (iii) commodities other than precious metals.

(e) contracts which are combinations of contracts specified at paragraphs (a) to (d),

(f) any contracts included by virtue of section 2 [regulations of central bank], and

(g) contracts of a similar nature, as specified by regulations under section 3.

1.053 There is no reference to credit derivatives. Arguably, a physically-settled total return swap or spread option, in either case with respect to a bond, would be covered under clause (d), but perhaps not a credit derivative involving a loan as a Reference Obligation or a digital-payout, credit default swap. If a credit derivative is not included in the protected category but is a Transaction under an ISDA Master Agreement along with protected Transactions, it is possible that the entire Master Agreement, since it was no longer an agreement applying solely to "financial contracts", would lose protection. If the court took a less draconian view, it is not clear how it would apply the provisions of Section 6(e) of the Master Agreement with respect to termination netting in relation to an insolvent Irish counterparty. Possibly, it would take a "two-pool" approach, contrary to the terms of the Master Agreement, and allow termination netting for the protected pool and separate treatment for the unprotected pool, followed by an analysis of whether the relevant set-off rules in Ireland permitted set-off between mutual claims arising under the two pools.

There are, therefore, still significant jurisdictions in which clear advice cannot be obtained as to the "nettability" of certain types of credit derivatives.[36]

Taxation

1.054 Many jurisdictions have integrated derivatives into their taxation system (at least to some extent). Of particular concern in the derivatives industry over the years, flowing from the fact that so many transactions cross national boundaries, has been the application of withholding taxes to derivative payments. Tax authorities struggled to provide appropriate solutions, generally desiring to exempt swap

---

[36] For example, there is substantial uncertainty in Italy as to treatment of credit derivatives under the Italian netting statute. On the other hand, the Czech Republic is considering legislation which provides protection for close-out netting for derivatives under a netting agreement with a Czech counterparty, specifies that this does not constitute set-off and provides a broad definition of derivatives not unlike that set out in the introduction to Part I of this Chapter. There is also provision for designation of specific contracts by the Ministry of Finance, the draft decree of which includes a range of credit products. A different approach is that of the French netting statute which, as noted in n.13, is not product specific but conditions its protection on the acceptability of the form of the netting or master agreement and the nature of the parties.

payments from withholding tax without opening up opportunities to use swaps to evade taxes in other situations or creating conflicts with traditional application of relevant tax principles to other products. Many jurisdictions, including the United States and the United Kingdom, have moved beyond the fictions[37] which they originally used to avoid withholding taxes in order to permit development of the markets in a cautious way and have either definitively or in practice addressed the issues squarely.

This has been accomplished in the United States by generally exempting cross-border payments under "notional principal contracts" from U.S. withholding tax if appropriate information or representations are obtained. The U.S. tax authorities have, however, expressed concern about the application of this exemption to equity swaps, given the potential to make cross-border payments of dividend equivalent amounts under equity swaps free of withholding tax. Although the Internal Revenue Service has been studying the issue for several years, to date no action has been taken that would exclude equity swaps from the general withholding tax exemption for notional principal contracts. In addition, detailed regulatory regimes govern the taxation of certain instruments, other than notional principal contracts, which have some similarities to certain types of credit derivatives: options, repos and securities loans. It is conceivable that the U.S. tax authorities might develop a similar concern with respect to payments under credit derivatives that are effectively substitutes for U.S. source interest payments that would otherwise be subject to withholding tax. Given, however, that interest payments on capital market transactions can generally qualify for the portfolio interest exemption from U.S. withholding tax, it would appear that any such concern should be limited to credit derivatives with respect to related party loans or bank loans. To date, no such concern has been expressed.

1.055 In the United Kingdom, the Finance Act 1994 exempted many derivatives, "qualifying contracts", from U.K. withholding tax. Equity-based products are clearly excluded from the definition of "qualifying contracts", as are derivatives with fixed rate flows on both sides and certain commodity products. Credit derivatives which are essentially options on debt are likely to be treated as qualifying contracts; total return swaps are unlikely to be treated as qualifying contracts. The withholding tax treatment of a derivative that is not a "qualifying contract" will be treated under general principles of U.K. tax law and Inland Revenue practice, including reference to any applicable double tax treaty. Although the Inland Revenue has stated that they would not "normally" seek to impose withholding taxes on derivatives which are not "qualifying contracts", different dealers take different views commercially on the soundness of the protection afforded by this position.

Again, the lesson is that, even though one can generally say that derivative payments are exempt from U.S. and U.K. withholding tax, it will be necessary closely to analyse the relevant laws in different jurisdictions with respect to their application to credit derivatives and, indeed, to different kinds of credit derivatives, with total return instruments raising the most serious issues.

---

[37] For instance, the U.K. Inland Revenue created a fiction as to the character of swap payments, saying they would treat them as interest if paid to or by a swap dealer. In the United States, the Internal Revenue Service created a source fiction, sourcing the payments overseas if made to overseas counterparties.

Recharacterisation

1.056 A court or regulator may ignore the derivatives structure and characterise the transaction in a manner adverse to the interests of one or both of the parties. A court could choose to re-characterise certain credit derivatives, *e.g.* a physically settled total return swap which is preceded by a sale of the Reference Obligation to the buyer of protection, as a secured loan to the seller of protection. If, then, there were registration or filing requirements or other formalities with respect to secured lending transactions of the seller of protection with which the buyer of protection had not complied, there would be a risk that other creditors of the seller of protection/buyer of risk might have recourse to the Reference Obligations.[38] Further, an interesting question, to which it is difficult to see a firm answer, is whether such a transaction might be prohibited by provisions in other contracts restricting the seller of protection in borrowing money or securing its debt.

Insurance

1.057 Most jurisdictions have substantial restrictions, enforced by regulatory bodies and judicial sanction, on offering insurance to residents, often limiting the offering of such products to closely regulated insurance companies. Breach of these laws and regulations may result in criminal penalties, fines or the invalidation of the agreement. In addition, there may be additional taxes, such as the U.K. insurance premium tax, imposed on payments deemed to be a premium. In the early days of the swap market, concerns were expressed as to whether or not swaps constituted insurance. This concern was most pronounced in relation to caps, some of the first manifestations of which were unfortunately entitled "interest rate insurance agreements". That designation rapidly disappeared from use and the legal concern, while never finally resolved, receded into insignificance as the market grew. A current concern in the credit derivatives market is whether or not a credit derivative constitutes insurance. First, the issue is not of primary concern with respect to a number of credit products such as a total return transaction or a yield option, whether cash or physically settled. The issue becomes more pronounced with a default product in which payment is triggered by a Credit Event. In one sense, to an uninformed layperson, it sounds like insurance: one party pays out on the occurrence of an external event. Further, the position is not helped by the use of credit derivatives to compete with monoline insurers with respect to financial guaranty insurance or to synthesise political risk insurance products.[39] The question then arises: why does a credit derivative of this type not constitute insurance?

In England, two approaches have been suggested. The Financial Law Panel has made a contextual argument in a position paper that there may be an overlap

---

[38] The issues here will be familiar to those who have analysed ISDA's Credit Support Annex (English Law — Transfer).

[39] For instance, a project sponsor in the People's Republic of China wished political risk insurance for a term of 15 years. The providers of such insurance would not provide protection for longer than 10 years. There was, however, 15–20 year PRC debt which traded in the international capital markets and for which there was a market. The solution was to create a special purpose vehicle, funded with U.S. treasuries and swaps, which issued a digital credit-linked note (synthetic PRC debt) with a 15-year term and a floating rate of interest plus a substantial margin appropriate for PRC debt of that maturity. Other terms of the debt were that it was payable in full at maturity, provided that if any of certain defined Credit Events occurred with respect to the People's Republic of China, the notes would be redeemable at half of par. The SPV issuer then wrote political risk insurance for the PRC project for a term of 15 years in return for a premium (which, of course, funded the spread on the synthetic credit-linked notes), callable on the occurrence of certain events (identical to the Credit Events) in an amount equal to the portion of the principal of the notes not being repaid.

between what is insurance business and what is financial business but, in that area of overlap, if the business is conducted by a regulated financial institutional it should not constitute insurance. This is in fact an "American" approach to analysing statutes, their purpose and the effect of the instrument in that context. More readily acceptable in the English market is the opinion of Robin Potts, Q.C., upon which ISDA members may rely, based on a transactional analysis. The opinion is predicated on the fact that the buyer of protection does not necessarily incur a loss on a default by the Reference Entity since it is not required to hold the Reference Obligation and might not in fact be holding it. Since the essence of insurance is payment to cover loss, a credit derivative, which is notional and under which payment is made by reference to external events and values rather than a party's loss, simply does not constitute insurance in this sense. This is a more "English" approach, looking at the letter of the law and regulation and applying it literally.

Needless to say, this issue must be analysed in any jurisdiction where a credit derivative is offered, regardless of the law selected to govern the contractual terms. In this analysis, the structure may be significant in some jurisdictions. For instance, a credit-linked note under which the seller of protection pays the purchase price up front and the buyer of protection may make a reduced payment of principal on a Credit Event may in some jurisdictions run a smaller risk of being characterised as insurance than a default swap in which the buyer of protection (insured?) pays a periodic fee (premium?) and the seller of protection (insurer?) makes a payment only if a specified event occurs.[40]

Regulation

1.058 In the second half of the 1980s, increasing attention was paid to regulatory issues in relation to swaps. In part, this attention was focussed on how, or if, swaps fitted into existing regulatory systems. In part, it was focussed on imposing regulation on these hitherto unregulated products.

Product regulation

1.059 There have been a number of interesting, and at times dangerous, issues arising in jurisdictions as to whether or not swaps are instruments which attract regulation or are prohibited under existing regulatory schemes. Often, however, the fears are allayed by statutes which clarify the status of defined types of instrument. For instance, there were questions as to whether or not swaps constituted futures within the meaning of the U.S. Commodity Exchange Act ("CEA") or securities within the meaning of the various U.S. securities laws. These regulatory frameworks have, to a limited extent, been adjusted by law and regulatory action to provide for various derivative products. Whether or not credit derivatives fall within those exemptive provisions must be analysed in each case.[41]

---

[40] On the other hand, the author is advised by Dr Claudi Rossell that in Spain section 1 of the Insurance Contract Act of October 1980 covers two types of contract, one providing for the grant of a quantity of money if a specific event takes place and the other providing for protection against loss. A digital default swap runs certain risks (subject to various counter arguments) in respect of the first type. A physically-settled default swap might be characterised as an insurance contract of the second type by reference to an insurer's right of subrogation and the implication of actual loss. The safest structure in Spain would appear to be a cash-settled default swap based on the value of the Reference Obligation at settlement.

[41] See S.K. Henderson *et al.*, "Equity Derivatives under U.S. and U.K. Law" (1992) 12 J.I.B.F.L. 555, which includes a discussion of the Commodity Exchange Act issues as well as the securities laws.

The purpose of the U.S. regulation of the futures market is protection of the investing public, control over speculation in basic commodities and preservation of the integrity of the relevant market, and is achieved in part through the prohibition under the CEA against transacting certain types of contracts other than on exchanges which are regulated by the Commodity Futures Trading Commission ("CFTC").

Between 1987 and 1989, the CFTC, encouraged by the futures exchanges, published proposals to define, indeed to restrict, the permissible limits of the swap market. Initially focussing on commodity swaps but eventually turning its attention to conventional swaps, the CFTC proposed several exemptive, but still rather restrictive, interpretations. Implicit in the CFTC actions, and reportedly explicitly held by the CFTC staff, was the belief that swaps in general constituted illegal off-exchange futures. The CFTC proposals were met with strenuous opposition from dealers, end-users and other governmental agencies, including the Federal Reserve Board, Department of the Treasury and Securities and Exchange Commission and in 1989 the CFTC promulgated a safe harbour ruling, acceptable in scope to the industry, with respect to most derivatives then being transacted off-exchange.

1.060 Concerns over the effectiveness of this safe harbour continued and, as a result of lobbying by ISDA and other interested persons on both sides of the issue, the Futures Trading Practices Act of 1992 (the "FTP Act") was passed and signed in 1992. The following are expressly exempted from the definition of futures under the FTP Act and CFTC regulations:

> a "rate swap agreement, basis swap, forward rate agreement, commodity swap, interest rate option, forward foreign exchange agreement, rate cap agreement, rate floor agreement, rate collar agreement, currency swap agreement, cross-currency rate swap agreement, currency option, any other similar agreement (including any option to enter into any of the foregoing)".

Not expressly included, and excluded from the exemption elsewhere, are equity swaps and options on securities such as bonds. If one cannot conclude that a given type of credit derivative is a "similar agreement", one must fall back on general principles and prior rulings of the CFTC. These would include positions that "credit" is not a "commodity" or index caught by the Commodity Exchange Act, that a credit derivative is a "forward contract" and not a futures contract, or that the CFTC safe harbour interpretation of 1989 applies to the credit derivative. Even if one (or all) of these fallback positions is correct, a determination that a given transaction is not statutorily exempted means that federal exemption from the state gambling laws is not available and those laws must be reconsidered.[42]

It is generally agreed, based on statutory analysis, judicially developed tests and regulatory practice that interest rate and currency swaps are not securities under U.S. securities laws. Options on securities, presumably including those the exercise of which is conditional on occurrence of a Credit Event, are, however, by definition securities. By reference to the current regulatory treatment of equity swaps and prevailing consensus among practitioners, one would argue that a credit default

---

[42] This is another issue which may require a fresh look generally in some jurisdictions. In Russia, for instance, courts held last year that non-deliverable forwards are unenforceable gambling contracts. While there is some hope that these decisions will be overturned or limited, they nonetheless highlight the legal risks which financial crises may generate, particularly with regard to products which are novel in a jurisdiction.

swap (to the extent it is not deemed an option) or total return swap involving debt securities as Reference Obligations were not "securities" within the meaning of the U.S. securities laws. If, however, the Securities and Exchange Commission were to take the view that equity swaps were in fact securities for particular purposes, one would have to analyse whether or not the same applied to credit swaps linked to a debt security and what the consequences would be in terms of registration of issuance, anti-fraud issues relating to offers and sales and broker/dealer registration requirements.[43] The result of such an analysis will have a significant impact on, among other things, the form and extent of disclosure with respect to these transactions, the nature of permissible counterparties, the jurisdictions in which the products may be offered and the identification of the entity in a particular dealer's corporate group which is the appropriate entity to offer the product.

Capital

1.061   The area in which the nature and treatment of credit derivatives has received most attention, at least between the industry and its financial regulators if not among day-to-day transactional lawyers, is the application of capital adequacy requirements to the risk relationship created by a credit derivative.[44] This is not surprising given the immediate requirement that a regulated financial institution must somehow include these instruments in its calculations for maintenance of capital and the different views as to the means of doing so between dealers, on the one hand, and regulators on the other. Generally, as might be expected, the position of the dealers has been to seek a framework for credit derivatives which minimises capital maintenance requirements and the position of the regulators is to require a framework which in their view preserves the financial soundness of the regulated institutions. While it would appear to be in the interests of both dealers and regulators to provide incentives for reduction of risk, from the dealers' perspective certain positions of some regulators would appear to penalise risk reduction activities by imposing inappropriate capital charges. These differences have substantially narrowed over the last several years. Indeed, industry/regulator discussions on credit derivatives are leading to a substantial overhaul of the international capital adequacy regime. Given the rapidity of change in this area, the balance of this Part will describe the parameters of the issues in their context rather than specific rules of particular regulators, which might well be obsolete by publication.

Capital was traditionally required to be maintained against on-balance sheet assets without discrimination as to debtor. In 1988, the Basle Accord required minimum capital adequacy charges which were more sensitive to credit quality, covered off-balance sheet exposures and would apply to regulated financial institutions in a relatively uniform manner in the G-10 countries.[45] In accordance with

---

[43] A typical credit-linked note, of course, is a security subject to the U.S. securities laws relating to registration and disclosure and exemptions therefrom. An interesting issue is the degree of disclosure which is required with respect to the underlying Reference Obligation, whether or not that constitutes a separate security and, if so, whether the separate security is deemed sold in the primary or secondary market.

[44] For a clear analysis of this complex area, see Das, "Credit Derivatives & Credit-Linked Notes — Regulatory Treatment — Parts One and Two", *Financial Products* (November 5 and December 3, 1998).

[45] What constitutes a regulated financial institution for capital purposes may vary from country to country. In the United Kingdom, this would include, in practice, all derivative dealers and, in the United States, banks but not other dealers such as affiliates of insurance companies or of securities houses. These latter institutions, of course, still have an interest in this subject since treatment of the regulated entities will affect market pricing and the capital costs of a regulated financial institution in dealing with them. References herein to banks will include regulated financial institutions which are not technically banks.

these principles, and the subsequent Solvency Ratio and Capital Adequacy Directives of the European Union, roughly similar capital requirements have been promulgated by national regulators, although differences in specific treatment at the national level remain[46]

1.062 The Basle Accord required financial regulators to prescribe the maintenance of capital of at least 8 per cent against credit exposures adjusted by broad risk weightings which varied by categories of debtors (*e.g.* 0 per cent for an OECD country, 20 per cent for an OECD bank and 100 per cent for a corporation or non-OECD bank). An asset which is guaranteed carries the lower of the risk weighting of the direct obligor and the guarantor.

The Basle Accord also required maintenance of capital against off-balance sheet items. A bank's commitment to lend or buy a security bears a 50 per cent risk weighting against what the funded exposure would be. The requirement that counterparty risk in swaps be included in calculating capital raised the issue as to the method of valuing counterparty risk. As the simple use of the notional amount in the swap would obviously not reflect credit risk, the swap must first be converted into a credit equivalent. The Basle Accord required a two-step credit conversion. First, the current mark-to-market or replacement value of the swap is calculated. Secondly, as there is a risk that external rates will change in the future and increase exposure, there as an "add-on" for potential exposure,[47] based on the product of the notional amount, number of remaining years and a percentage which varies by broad maturity categories and type of swap (in ascending order: interest rate, currency and gold, equity, other precious metals and other commodities). Given the generally high credit-worthiness of participants in the swap market, the maximum risk weighting for swap exposure was limited to 50 per cent, the effect of which is to reduce exposure to corporations and non-OECD banks from 100 per cent to 50 per cent of the credit equivalent.

1.063 A subsequent refinement of the capital adequacy regime, announced in 1996 and effective January 1, 1998, following developments under the European Directives, was the distinction drawn for larger financial institutions between assets held in the trading book and assets held in the banking book, based on the high credit quality and liquidity of the asset involved and the "trading intent" of the holder. Roughly, tradable securities issued by governments and investment grade (or equivalent) entities may be held in the trading book and are subject to two charges. First, is a specific charge (*e.g.* 0 per cent for governments, 0.25 per cent for OECD banks and 1.6 per cent for corporations and others) in respect of risk relating to the specific obligor (mainly its default risk, but also other event risk such as a leveraged take-over). The second is a market charge based on perceived risk from general market movements in interest and currency rates. Other assets, such as

---

[46] It should be emphasised that the regulators of the different countries do not constitute a unified front with respect to detailed application of the capital requirements. Discussions on credit derivatives have primarily been between ISDA and individual national regulators, including separate regulators in some countries (*e.g.* the SFA and the Bank of England, prior to their announced "merger"). That having been said, there is clearly consultation among the regulators and a trend towards a convergence of position among the U.K., U.S., French and Canadian regulators which, with the German regulators, have been the regulators most actively and publicly addressing the issues.

[47] A negative current value can reduce the add-on amount of the swap to zero but in the initial regulations, in practice, not below zero, *i.e.* to reduce exposure on another swap with that counterparty. Worded another way, termination netting was not in practice recognised. This was changed in 1996 if all swaps are documented under one agreement and appropriate opinions are obtained. The issues discussed above under "Termination Netting" are thus highly relevant to determination of capital in respect of credit derivatives.

securities of less creditworthy entities or loans to any party, are for reasons of low credit quality or illiquidity required to be held in the banking book and are subject to the full charge required under the initial Basle requirements.

In applying the market risk requirements for the trading book, the regulators have been responsive to industry needs and, in a first move away from use of broad and perhaps oversimplified categories, permitted dealers to use approved proprietary models to serve as the basis for calculating market risk requirements: Value at Risk ("VaR") models. These models measure the risk of an asset over a substantially shorter time horizon than that created by its maturity due to the institution's ability to alter its market risk profile rapidly (*e.g.* through sale of the asset) to varying degrees of confidence.[48] Some regulators also permitted use of approved VaR models in calculating specific risk.

Application to credit derivatives

1.064 The regulators have accepted characterisation of credit derivatives as derivatives, although there has been some discussion as to whether or not a credit default swap should be treated as a swap or an option. As noted throughout this Chapter, a credit derivative involves the transfer of risk in respect of a specific asset in addition to the counterparty risk between the parties to the derivative. An analysis of the application of capital adequacy requirements in respect of a credit derivative therefore involves treatment of the derivative in relation to both the underlying asset *and* counterparty risk. As will be seen, the treatment varies substantially depending on whether it is viewed from the perspective of the buyer or seller of protection and the nature of the Reference Obligation. The principal issues relate to whether or not the risk relationship should be part of the trading or banking book, the degree of offset between the derivative and an asset physically held and the avoidance of "double-charging" for risk, the treatment of credit derivatives with multiple Reference Entities, the level of "add-ons" for determining the potential exposure element of counterparty risk and the use of proprietary models for calculating credit exposure.

Allocation to trading or banking book

1.065 Generally speaking, the seller of protection will be considered as having direct exposure on the Reference Obligation, a long position, and the buyer of protection will be deemed to have a short position.[49] As will be noted from the different capital requirements listed above for banking book and trading book exposures, the trading book attracts substantially less capital, and thus allocation to the appropriate book has a significant effect on overall capital required to be maintained. ISDA's position is that all credit derivatives should be allocated to the trading book if there is trading intent and reasonable means of valuing the derivative, including of course the exposure in respect of the asset. The initial regulatory treatment was (and for the German regulators is) for the exposure on the Reference Obligation to be treated as part of the trading book or banking book as would the asset itself. A number of regulators have moved to a position permitting

---

[48] The principal areas of controversy between dealers and regulators with respect to VaR models are the length of the time horizon and degree of confidence.

[49] Where the credit derivative is hedged by another credit derivative, this position should, subject to sufficiently matching provisions, be disregarded and each derivative would bear a capital charge based on counterparty risk as discussed para. 1.068, below.

inclusion of a credit derivative involving a loan in the trading book if a combination (depending on the regulator) of the following conditions are met: the loan obligor would satisfy the rating test for inclusion, there is the requisite trading intent and compliance with the dealer's policies, the dealer is active in the credit derivatives market and there are acceptable means of valuing the asset.

Banking book

1.066 Where the derivative is allocated to the banking book, the seller of protection must maintain full capital against the asset and also in respect of counterparty risk. Where the seller has fully performed (*e.g.* a credit-linked note), the seller would have to hold capital based on the higher risk weighting of the Reference Entity and the buyer of protection.[50]

The principal issue for the buyer of protection under a credit derivative is the degree of offset between an asset held by the buyer of protection and a credit derivative under which it has bought protection in respect of that asset. If the asset is in the holder's banking book, ISDA's position is that there should be full or partial offset on the asset with a counterparty risk charge, *i.e.* no or reduced capital in respect of the asset and capital in respect of the counterparty risk. The logic is that, if the counterparty performs, there is in fact no risk on the asset. ISDA's fallback position is to recommend guarantee treatment. The regulators generally take the position that they would permit/require guarantee treatment, but only if the credit derivative "perfectly" matches the asset. In this case, if the protection is structured as a swap, the seller of protection will be treated as a guarantor and the asset will carry capital based on the category of the seller of protection.[51] By way of illustration, the holder of a corporate loan must maintain capital of 8 per cent against it. If it acquires protection under a matching credit derivative with an OECD bank (the risk weighting of which is 20 per cent), capital is reduced to an amount equal to 8 per cent of 20 per cent of the exposure, *i.e.* 1.6 per cent. On the other hand, if a perfect match is not recognised and substitution of risk weighting is not permitted, the holder buying protection could be required to maintain full capital against the asset and full capital for counterparty risk under the derivative. The buyer would in fact be penalised for undertaking a risk reducing activity, unless the regulators were to disregard the counterparty risk of the seller of protection.

Significant attention has thus been paid to what constitutes a mismatch, and to whether or not some relief and how much should be granted where there is a less than perfect match. As pointed out in Part I, the only credit derivative which provides complete protection is a total return swap in which the Reference Obligation is identical to the asset held and which has the same maturity as the Reference Obligation or, if a shorter maturity, provides for physical delivery or settlement based on precise market valuation. As noted in Part II, documentation structures, such as a credit default swap, also may create elements of basis risk (*e.g.* asymmetry of Credit Events, conditions to settlement, and timing and valuation of

---

[50] A credit-linked note can be replicated using a credit default swap confirmation under a Master Agreement in which the seller of protection maintains Credit Support in cash under an outright transfer Credit Support Annex in the agreed Independent Amount with an agreed Interest Amount payable by the holder of the Credit Support, the buyer of protection.

[51] If protection is obtained through issuance of a credit-linked note, there is, of course, no exposure to the holder and the buyer of protection/seller of risk ought to have no exposure in respect of the Reference Obligation held by it, subject to the discussion on mismatch, para. 1.068, below.

payments). Commercial elements of basis risk, as discussed in Part I, arise if the maturity of the asset is later than that of a related credit default swap, if the asset is a loan and the Reference Obligation is a tradable security of the loan obligor, if the Reference Obligations are otherwise different from the asset in terms of currency, seniority (*i.e.* the asset is subordinated and the Reference Obligation is senior) or if the Reference Entity is different than the obligor on the asset (even though there may be strong correlation between the different obligors). While a credit derivative with commercial or structural documentation mismatches still economically reduces credit risk to a greater or lesser extent (depending on the nature of the disparity and, where the issuers and/or assets differ, the validity of correlation analyses) the protection is clearly not absolute.

1.067 Though some regulators still require a "perfect-match", others are moving away from this approach in several ways. First, substitution of the seller's risk weighting for that of the loan obligor (*i.e.* on a guarantee basis) may be permitted by several regulators as long as the Reference Obligation and derivative match the asset in terms of issuer, seniority, currency and maturity, with appropriate cross-default provisions. Secondly, certain mismatches might result in partial relief. For instance, a currency mismatch may receive either a percentage reduction or a full reduction coupled with the maintenance of capital with respect to the foreign exchange exposure. A maturity mismatch may, for a total return swap, be disregarded or, for a credit default swap, be subject to a percentage reduction, treated as a commitment to lend or a combination of the two.[52] Third, with respect to mismatches resulting from documentation/structure (*e.g.* a credit default swap), some regulators will permit matching based on the institution's judgment, subject to particular scrutiny in this area on examination, *i.e.* on a case-by-case basis.

If there is a basket of Reference Obligations under a derivative allocated to the banking book, the buyer of protection may, subject to the matching rules, select one Reference Entity for offset from among those with the lowest risk weighting. The prevalent, and extremely onerous, position with respect to the seller of protection is that, at least in a first default structure, it must maintain additive capital in respect of all Reference Entities.

Trading book

1.068 If the derivative is included in the trading book, the capital treatment for the seller of protection would require a specific charge for the Reference Entity, a market charge in respect of the asset (if a credit default swap but not if a total return swap which mirrors the market risk) and a counterparty risk charge in respect of the buyer of protection. If the derivative is funded (*i.e.* a credit-linked note), the asset is risk-weighted to the higher of the Reference Entity or buyer of protection.

If the buyer of protection holds the asset in its trading book, full offset of specific and market charges may be allowed for a matching total return swap, leaving only the counterparty risk charge. Some regulators permit offset against the specific risk of the asset where there is a limited mismatch; and others do not. Where there is a

---

[52] A total return swap with a shorter maturity than the Reference Obligation will settle at current market value, reflecting deterioration in credit for reasons not constituting a Credit Event. A credit default swap with a shorter maturity than the Reference Obligation results in the buyer of protection reacquiring exposure at the original price. The shorter term credit default swap can thus be analogised to a commitment by the buyer of protection to repurchase the Reference Obligation at the original price at maturity of the swap and some regulators treat it accordingly (*e.g.* 70 per cent risk weighting; 20 per cent for the risk weighting of the OECD bank selling protection and 50 per cent for the commitment).

mismatch, there may in fact be two specific charges: the specific risk element in the asset or in the valuation of the derivative. Most regulators will require only that a capital charge be assessed against one leg, being the one with the larger exposure.

If the derivative involves a basket of Reference Obligations and is in the trading book, the buyer of protection may generally select which Reference Entity to use for offset, with some regulators requiring selection from among those with the lowest risk weighting. Treatment of the seller of protection ranges from the right to select the Reference Entity for inclusion in the trading book from among those Reference Entities with the highest risk weighting (if all Reference Entities are of sufficiently high creditworthiness), the use of models including correlation analysis of the Reference Entities (greater correlation equals lesser risk) to additive treatment.

Counterparty risk

1.069 Finally, there are issues as to valuation of counterparty risk in the credit derivative. First, current valuation of a credit derivative will, unless a Credit Event is pending, be substantially less than the face value of the asset. On entry of the derivative, the current valuation would in fact be approximately zero to both parties (unless one party has fully performed, as in an option or a credit-linked note, or a party has mispriced the derivative, subject, of course, to bid/offered issues), since the present value of the payments over the term from the buyer of protection, in theory, equals the present value of the protection over the term provided by the seller as of that time. From the perspective of the seller of protection, it has risk to the buyer of protection for payment of the fixed amount, which can be valued easily at any time (although there should perhaps be some adjustment in valuation for the probability of such payments ceasing, such as an occurrence of a Credit Event). This credit risk exposure is reduced by the value at such time of the protection the seller is providing. Under these circumstances, requiring a counterparty risk charge in addition to a charge in respect of the asset does not necessarily result in double-counting exposure. From the perspective of the buyer of protection, the situation is reversed but with different effects. If it is required to include a full counterparty risk charge with respect to the credit derivative in the banking book, it has not received the full benefit of guarantee treatment. In other words, it gets reduction of capital on the asset it holds to the seller's risk weighting, but then also has to maintain capital in respect of the seller's credit separately.

Secondly, the value of a credit derivative may change if the value of the buyer's payments decrease (*i.e.* market interest rates rise) or the credit of the Reference Entity changes. Potential future exposure is the likelihood of these occurrences. If the Basle Accord is followed, the potential exposure would be handled through the add-on approach. Current treatment of the "add-on" element for future potential exposure varies by the book to which the derivative is allocated. For instance, as noted above, interest rate swaps involve lower add-ons, equity instruments higher add-ons and commodity related instruments even higher. Credit derivatives are not specified. ISDA has recommended the use of interest rate add-on levels for credit derivatives involving Reference Entities with sufficiently high credit standing and equity level add-ons for others. Some regulators concur, and others require equity level or commodity level, differentiating by book or credit standing of the Reference Entity, with some providing more favourable treatment to the buyer of protection (*i.e.* interest or equity level based on the other factors).

Conclusions on capital

1.070 The use of credit derivatives and the analysis of their effects has in fact served to highlight some weaknesses in the international capital adequacy structure.

The use of arbitrary categories based on the type of obligor/counterparty, rather than its creditworthiness, with no sensitivity to maturity, may present disincentives to sound banking practice. For instance, a bank which is pushing up against its capital limits can, as noted above, purchase matching protection for a loan to a top rated corporation maturing in two years, against which it must maintain 8 per cent capital, from a lower rated OECD bank, thereby under current requirements substantially reducing its capital charge to 1.6 per cent. The cost of such protection is cheap. The capital-driven incentive is therefore to acquire protection for the *best* and *earliest maturing* assets, possibly from a seller of protection which itself is not terribly creditworthy (and is therefore perhaps charging a lower fee), rather than acquiring more expensive protection in respect of assets which present substantially greater risks from a highly-rated seller of protection which is not an OECD bank providing capital relief.

The regulators are sensitive to these issues. A perfect system would, in order to promote risk reduction, provide relief on the asset proportionate to the degree of protection obtained. Valuation of a credit derivative, if valid, in fact quantifies the credit risk involved. If there is an acceptable valuation model, valuation of the derivative should be the sole asset charge (subject to charges for potential exposure). Anything else is double-counting.[53] The regulators appear to be moving towards a model-based method of resolving this issue rather than an arbitrary all-or-nothing system or use of arbitrary categories coupled with specified degrees of reduction. In Part I,[54] a modelling approach to management of credit risk was discussed, based on the application of VaR techniques to credit. This is the most fundamental change occurring in banking at the moment. The dealer/regulator dialogue on credit derivatives is, as noted at the outset of this section, leading to a revolution of the capital maintenance system which reflects the revolution in the financial markets effected by derivatives technology.

Conclusion

1.071   As with many other novel and innovative types of transactions, a sensible lawyer will be hesitant to draw public conclusions on the numerous issues which may arise in numerous jurisdictions. The one safe conclusion is that selection of the derivative structure to replace traditional financial arrangements or to create new financial relationships does not necessarily result in the transaction falling within a specified legal pigeon hole with predictable consequences. The cautious lawyer will need to draw upon a wide range of legal specialities, probably from more than one jurisdiction, to identify and separate the troublesome issues from the irrelevant issues and then to deal with the former.

---

[53] In this connection, quantifying the degree of protection where the matching is imperfect will remain a troublesome issue, as will illiquidity of the Reference Obligation.

[54] See n.8, above.

Annex: ISDA Terms

1.072

Reference Entity: Entity or entities whose credit risk is being transferred or traded

Reference Obligations: Specified obligations or basket of obligations which are usually but not necessarily issued or guaranteed by the Reference Entity or Entities, which may be a loan, security or other type of obligation and which

(a) are used to price the payout on Cash Settlement or to determine the Materiality of a credit decline,

(b) may be used as a reference to determine existence of a Credit Event (in which case it is termed an Obligation) and/or

(c) in Physical Settlement, may be delivered on the occurrence of a Credit Event, on exercise or at the Termination Date (in which case it is termed a Deliverable Obligation)

Credit Events: Specified event with respect to a Reference Entity or Entities and/or an agreed Obligation, which may or may not be a Reference Obligation, which triggers the obligation to pay the Cash Settlement Amount or to Deliver Deliverable Obligations as reflected in a Credit Event Notice and, optionally,

(a) is confirmed by Notice of Publicly Available Information (which may be specified as coming from an agreed number of designated Public Sources) and/or

(b) has resulted in Materiality (a test as to whether or not a Credit Event is material, which is generally based on value of credit decline)

    (i) Price Materiality: the difference between the Initial Price (generally, an agreed amount) and the Market Value, after backing out any interest- related changes in value, exceeds the Price Decline Requirement or .

    (ii) Spread Materiality: the difference between the Initial Spread (generally, an agreed amount) and the Final Spread (the difference between Reference Obligation Yield and Interpolated Swap Rate) exceeds the Spread Widening Requirement

ISDA Credit Events are:

(a) with respect to the Reference Entity: Bankruptcy or Credit Event Upon Merger

(b) with respect to Obligations: Cross Acceleration with respect to debt in excess of an agreed Default Requirement, Cross Default with respect to debt in excess of an agreed Default Requirement, Downgrade with respect to specified Downgrade Obligations, Failure to Pay debt in excess of an agreed Payment Requirement, Repudiation, and Restructuring

Market Value:	For determining the Final Price for Cash Settlement or the existence of Materiality, the average of five dealer quotations (expressed as a percentage) for the Reference Obligations (which may be specified as bid, offered or mid-market), after discarding the highest and lowest, on the agreed Valuation Date or Dates
Cash Settlement Amount:	The product of (Reference Price − Final Price) and the Floating Rate Payer Calculation Amount
Deliverable Obligations:	For Physical Settlement, may be Reference Obligations, other specified obligations or obligations to be determined by one of the parties which are to be delivered against payment of the product of the Reference Price and the Floating Rate Payer Calculation Amount.

Chapter 2

The Legal Nature of Credit Derivatives

by John Jakeways *

Introduction

2.001 In the case of many new products in the derivatives and other markets, developments have occurred quickly and sometimes the legal, taxation and accounting analyses — or at least people's understanding of them and the issues they raise — have not quite kept pace. This has been particularly notable in the case of credit derivatives, and the aim of this Chapter is to identify and clarify some of the legal issues particularly relevant to credit derivatives.

The main issues raised in this context are:

(a) whether a credit derivative might fall foul of insurance laws;

(b) whether a credit derivative might be an unenforceable gaming contract;

(c) how issues of confidentiality and insider dealing impact on credit derivatives.

The nature of a credit derivative

2.002 As will be clear from the previous Chapter,[1] a credit derivative is, in simple terms, a contract that either pays out on the occurrence of an event which is linked to the creditworthiness of an unconnected third party, or attempts to compensate a party (regardless of the occurrence of any particular event) for changes in the value of a reference asset as a result of a real or perceived change in creditworthiness.

A credit derivative transfers, in one way or another, some or all of the credit risk attached to the notional holding of a particular asset (the **reference asset**), or something approximating to it, from one person (the **Buyer** of credit protection) to another person (the **Seller** of credit protection).

There are two basic types of credit derivative; the credit swap and the credit default option. An example of the former is the total return swap. A typical total return swap simply exchanges cash flows associated with the holding of a reference asset for cashflows associated with financing such a holding. The holder of the reference asset will pass over amounts equal to cash receipts on the reference asset — *i.e.* coupon or dividends — to the Seller of the credit derivative, together with an amount equal to any capital appreciation in relation to the reference asset over the period of the trade. The Seller will pay to the Buyer an amount equal to the notional financing cost of the reference asset, *i.e.* (usually) LIBOR plus a margin on

* Partner, Freshfields. *The information and expressions of opinion which this Chapter contains are not intended to be a comprehensive study nor to provide legal advice and should not be treated as a substitute for specific advice concerning individual situations.*
[1] Chap. 1 above.

the initial value of the asset, plus an amount equal to any capital loss on the reference asset over the period of the trade.

2.003 A credit default option, at its most basic level, provides that, in return for the payment by Buyer of an option premium, the Seller will make a payment to the Buyer if a certain event occurs in relation to a reference asset.

The size of the payment might depend on the nature or severity of the actual credit event. For example, the terms could be, if an event of default occurs in respect of the reference asset, Seller pays to Buyer the nominal amount of the reference asset in exchange for acquiring the reference asset. Alternatively, the terms may be that, if an event of default occurs, Seller pays the nominal amount of the reference asset minus its then current market value. The latter formula perhaps more closely approximates to the loss that an actual holder of the reference asset would have suffered as a result of the occurrence of the event in question.

Insurance

2.004 The market in credit derivatives has developed by stages. It is important to appreciate in understanding the legal issues that credit derivatives as a product developed over time as a natural extension of the types of risk that could be traded (or the speculation opportunities that could be offered) through derivatives.

It is also important to realise that there is nothing new in the trading of credit through various means — from simple sales and purchases of assets, to the giving of guarantees, the issuance of letters of credit and the entry into funded or unfunded subparticipations. On one level, credit derivatives are just another way of dealing in the same risks, their advantage is that they allow risk to be traded in a notional form without the Seller or Buyer holding the reference asset. This can be contrasted with other forms of credit risk transference, such as sub-participations or guarantees, which relate to a specific loan which needs to be held by the person buying the credit protection.

As the credit derivative market developed, however, it was perceived that credit derivative products were becoming more and more closely identifiable with protection against the risk of loss arising from the holding of a particular asset, including, at its most extreme form, the risk of issuer default. This is primarily because one use to which credit derivatives could be put is, it is true, guarding against the risk of actual loss arising from issuer default, or the risk of actual loss arising from a reduction in value of an asset as a result of weakening perceptions of credit quality, a risk for which credit insurance could often be purchased.

2.005 The focus on this particular use of credit derivatives does however seem slightly strange. They can equally well be used for other purposes, including speculating that a particular credit event might occur (*e.g.* a particular company might become insolvent), by buying the derivative without actually owning the underlying asset, or taking a long position in creditworthiness only (as opposed to the other features of the reference asset) by selling the credit derivative. Someone selling a credit derivative can be seen as using some of its appetite for a particular credit risk, and being paid for doing so. Indeed, the development of credit derivatives, enabling credit risk to be traded, reflects in large part the ability to trade interest rate risk or currency risk through the derivatives — it enables one part of the overall risk to the separated out and separately traded.

It may appear curious also that the attention applied to credit derivatives and their possible use as a hedge against actual loss is in contrast to the apparent lack of current comparable concern in relation to the other types of transaction (*e.g.*

subparticipations) with similar economic effect, and more direct linkage to actual losses, referred to above. However, the lack of concern in these latter situations is to an extent relatively recent. Some people did worry about the risk of, for example, sub-participations being characterised as insurance but have become comfortable over time that the insurance characterisation is not applicable.

It is important also to realise that credit derivatives are generally drafted in an objective, rather than a subjective, way. The occurrence of the relevant Credit Event is, generally speaking, simply a condition to the obligation to make payment and it is the occurrence of the event generally, rather than specifically in relation to assets held by the Buyer, that triggers a payment. Put another way, the occurrence of the relevant Credit Event is no more than part of the process of determining whether or not, contractually, the payment has become due. It is the trigger to the payment obligation, nothing more. There is no need for the Buyer actually to own the reference asset, and no need for the Buyer to suffer as a result of the occurrence of the Credit Event. The relevance of the reference asset is to provide a reference point as to whether the payment is due or not and, if so, as to the size of the payment that is due. The question is simply, "Has the trigger event to payment occurred and, if so, what is the amount of the payment due?"

2.006 As people focused on one of the possible uses of credit derivatives, *i.e.* protection against actual credit loss, the question was raised — what is the difference between a contract which pays out an amount which is economically equal to loss actually suffered as a result of issuer default, and an *insurance policy* taken out against such default risk?

And if the contract might be viewed as an insurance contract, does that raise any particular issues?

This aspect of a credit derivative — the possibility of using it for protection against an actual loss — was of course not entirely new: all investments and derivatives involve taking a long or a short position in a variable. That could mean that in any contract the taker of a long position is taking a risk (and protecting someone else against that risk), and thus "insuring" that other person against that risk. Therefore, it could by analogy be argued that something as straightforward as a fixed to floating interest rate swap, or a rate cap or floor, is an insurance contract.

In the case of a rate cap, the Seller is protecting the Buyer against interest rates going up. A Buyer which has borrowed £10 million at LIBOR, by buying the cap, is guarding against LIBOR going above the cap rate. The Seller will pay the Buyer LIBOR minus the cap rate. As a matter of law, is the Seller selling insurance against rates rising above the cap rate?

2.007 Such an argument was not commonly (if at all) raised. Nor was it argued that an interest rate swap, providing protection to end users against floating rates rising, was an insurance contract. The opposite argument was made in relation to interest rate swaps in the local authority swaps litigation (*Hazell v. Hammersmith & Fulham Borough Council*[2]). In that case it was argued that (at least in the way that local authorities were using them) interest rate swaps were pure speculative or gambling contracts — the opposite of insurance. In Lord Templeman's view this seemed to be the case even if the user's objective were to hedge a particular cashflow, an interest rate contract being "more akin to gambling than insurance". It doesn't seem to have been argued on behalf of the local authorities that the banks (or even, possibly, the local authorities) in those cases were wrongfully selling

---

[2] [1992] 2 A.C. 1.

insurance contracts — although on the facts it might have been difficult to argue that either party was hedging actual losses, and in many of the cases a statutory exemption to the Insurance Companies Act may have applied.[3]

Similarly, the insurance issue has not been commonly raised in the context of sub-participations, limited recourse loan agreements, guarantees and letters of credit. Certainly many, but by no means all, of the transactions over the years involving these features will have benefited from the exemption in the Insurance Companies Act 1982 which applies to general business of Classes 14 to 18 if it is carried on solely in the course of carrying on, and for the purposes of, banking business — yet the point has rarely been raised. The ICA provides no guidance as to when activities might be regarded as carried on in the course of, and for the purposes of, banking business, although the term "banking business" incudes those transactions "coming within the legitimate business of a banker" (*Tennant v. Union Bank of Canada*[4]).

The problem with insurance

2.008   If a contract comprises "insurance business" then it may only be entered into in compliance with the laws which regulate the conduct of insurance business. This leads to two questions:

(a) What is insurance business?

(b) What are those laws which must be complied with (and what are the consequences of breach of those laws)?

There is no clear definition of insurance business. The question has been considered in case law, and guidance is to be had from the Insurance Companies Act 1982, which regulates the insurance industry and which specifies certain categories of insurance business. Broadly, both the Insurance Companies Act and case law indicate that, generally, an insurance contract is one which protects the Buyer against actual losses suffered by it, in return for the payment of a premium. This idea, the concept of protection against loss, is important.

2.009   *Prudential Insurance Company v. IRC*[5] is often cited as authority for what the features of an insurance contract are:

"... what you do insure is that a sum of money shall be paid on the happening of a certain event. ... It must be a contract whereby for some consideration, usually but not necessarily for periodical payments called premiums, you secure to yourself some benefit, usually but not necessarily the payment of a sum of money upon the happening of some event ... that even should be one which involves some amount of uncertainty ... whether the event will happen or not, or ... as to the time at which it will happen. A contract which would otherwise be a mere wager may become an insurance by reason of the assured having an interest in the subject-matter — that is to say, the uncertain event ... must be an event which is prima facie adverse to the interest of the assured."

In essence, one party promises in return for a money consideration to pay to the other party a sum of money or provide him with some corresponding benefit, upon

---

[3] As considered below.
[4] [1894] A.C. 31, PC.
[5] [1904] 2 K.B. 658.

the occurrence of one or more specified events in which he has an interest, the events being outside the control of the insurer.

However, it seems that it is not possible to identify any single factor and treat it alone as the defining character of an insurance contract.

If a contract is insurance business, what is the consequence?

2.010 Broadly, unless an exemption applies, insurance business may only be entered into by a regulated insurance company. That is, the provider of the insurance — the person who is providing protection against the contingency or the specified risk of loss (being the Seller, using the terms adopted above) — must be authorised to carry an insurance business in the United Kingdom (or have "passported" into the United Kingdom under the Third Non-Life Insurance Directive (92/49 EEC) of the European Union). It must comply wth the rules laid out in the Insurance Companies Act 1982 and the regulations made thereunder.

It is a criminal offence to carry on insurance business in the United Kingdom unless authorised to do so. It follows that an unauthorised company entering into insurance contracts is likely to find itself and its directors facing the possibility of criminal sanction.

Further, if the provider of insurance is not regulated, the contract will be unenforceable by the insurer. This means that the insurer cannot sue for its premiums. In those circumstances, the insurance purchaser may be able to elect either to enforce the insurance contract, or to recover the premiums paid by him under the contract together with compensation for any loss sustained as a result of having paid the premiums.

2.011 This could potentially have serious consequences in the context of a credit derivative, where the Seller could not enforce its right to receive its premium or fee, and indeed might have to return it with interest. This could leave the Buyer free to enforce the contract if the relevant credit event occurs, or to recover its premium plus interest if the relevant Credit Event does not occur. If that were to occur the contract would become in effect a free option.

Additionally, and this is important in the context of the duties of the parties to each other, and possible actions along the lines of those taken against Bankers Trust, amongst others,[6] in an insurance contract the parties have additional duties to each other over and above those owed in normal contracts: in particular, the insured has a duty to act in the utmost good faith — generally, to provide all relevant information to the insurer — and if it fails to do so the "insurance contract" may be unenforceable by it. This duty of good faith is a common law duty which cannot clearly be contracted out of.

For example, if a credit derivative were an insurance contract, if the Seller could show that the Buyer had not complied with the elevated standards of utmost good faith required of a Buyer of an insurance contract, the Seller might not be required to perform.

These issues illustrate that there are serious potential pitfalls for both Buyer and Seller if a credit derivative is held to be an insurance contract.

Are credit derivatives insurance contracts?

2.012 The crucial question in this context then is: what is an insurance contract, and is a credit derivative an insurance contract? There is no definitive

---

[6] See Chap. 9 below.

answer to the second question — and indeed there could not be, as the answer in each case will depend on the terms of the contract. The fact that there is no definitive answer has in the past led some prudent or cautious lawyers to advise that in certain circumstances credit derivatives could be considered to be insurance contracts. This, in an absolute sense, is true, but it has resulted in a degree of anxiety over the question which is perhaps disproportionate.

Some assistance as to the meaning of insurance business is derived from the Schedules to the Insurance Companies Act 1982. These Schedules set out certain classes of insurance business, and the Insurance Companies Act does not apply to transactions which do not fall within these categories.

Schedule 1 relates to long term insurance business such as life and health insurance, and pension fund management. This is not relevant — credit derivatives do not fall within that description.

Schedule 2 however seems more relevant to credit derivatives, in particular classes 14, 15 and 16.

Class 14 includes:

> "effecting and carrying out contracts of insurance against risks of loss . . . arising from the insolvency of debtors of theirs or from the failure . . . of debtors of theirs to pay their debts when due".

2.013 This might appear to catch at least certain types of credit derivatives. That is because a credit derivative usually pays when a debt obligation (*e.g.* a bond) defaults. If the Buyer owns the bond, the issuer of the bond is its debtor and thus the credit derivative is protecting against default by a debtor. Therefore, if as a matter of fact the credit derivative purchaser holds the bond in question, the credit derivative might be taken to protect it against the risk of loss arising from its debtor not paying its debts.

Class 14 would not, however, catch derivatives such as interest rate swaps, where even if the Buyer is guarding against actual loss the risk hedged is not the risk of debtors failing to pay their debts.

Class 15 covers "suretyship". That is, amongst other things:

> "effecting and carrying out various bonds and similar contracts of guarantee."

If a credit derivative could be construed as a guarantee of performance of the issuer of the reference asset, that might lead it to be construed as insurance business — but a credit derivative drafted in such a way would be highly unusual.

Class 16 is a catch-all covering "miscellaneous financial loss" — and covers "effecting and carrying out contracts of insurance against any of the following risks, namely:

> (a) risk of loss . . . attributable to interruptions of the carrying on of business . . .
>
> (b) risks of loss attributable to . . . incurring unforeseen expense . . .
>
> (c) risks neither falling within (a) or (b) above nor being of a kind such that the carrying on of the business of effecting and carrying out contracts of insurance against them constitutes the carrying on of insurance business of some other class".

2.014 Class 16 bears close examination. Whilst (a) and (b) (and Class 14) refer to "risks of loss", sub-class (c) does not, and this is a curious omission. One might argue that the reference is effectively there as a result of the class description — "miscellaneous financial loss" — but the status of this wording is at best unclear (it might though be taken as a clear indication of legislative intent). The other point to note about sub-class (c) is that it brings within the ambit of the ICA "contracts of insurance" against risks not falling within the other classes in the ICA. This of course begs the question, what is a contract of insurance — to which the ICA therefore does not provide a clear answer.

Some guidance as to what is insurance business is to be drawn also from common law. Generally, the theme of the cases is to identify what comprises an insurable interest and whether the existence of an insurable interest is a prerequisite for an insurance contract. However, the case law is a little contradictory. While it is clear that protection of an insurable interest is generally required in order to have a valid insurance contract, it is not always clear whether any contract which could be characterised as insurance without an insurable interest is a void insurance contract under Life Assurance Act 1774, s.1, or not an insurance contract at all.

What is an insurable interest?

2.015 A contract which pays out if the Buyer suffers loss because his house burns down, and (usually) where the amount of the payment is determined by the size of the Buyer's loss, is an insurance contract — the Buyer has an "insurable interest" in his house. A contract which pays out when someone else's house burns down, where the Buyer has (and had, at the time the contract was taken out) no interest in that house, is not an insurance contract. The Buyer does not have an insurable interest in the house — he suffers no loss when the house burns down. Such a contract is more akin to a speculative contract (which might be unenforceable for reasons unrelated to insurance law).

A contract directly, rather than coincidentally, providing for payment to meet a loss or detriment to an insurable interest in something would frequently (but not always) be an insurance contract. However, a contract to make a certain payment upon the occurence of a specified contingency, but irrespective of whether actual loss occurs, is generally speaking not insurance business (although see the references to contingency insurance below, para. 2.018). This is because there is no requirement that loss be suffered (as generally contemplated in Schedule 2 to the Insurance Companies Act), and there is no requirement for the purchaser of the contract to have an insurable interest in the underlying asset. The simple fact that a party to a contract might coincidentally suffer the loss in question is not decisive. The contract is probably only insurance if as a term of that contract it only pays out if the Buyer has in fact suffered a loss.

The case law generally seems to establish the proposition that — for most types of insurance — the test is whether the contract compensates or indemnifies for loss in respect of an interest of the Buyer (see in particular the cases cited by Robin Potts Q.C. in his opinion referred to below: in particular, *Lucena v. Crauford*,[7] *Wilson v. Jones*[8] and *Re London County Commercial Reinsurance Office Ltd*[9]). The cases clearly support the proposition that the question is not one to be determined by reference to the economic effect of the contract. Instead, the question is one of construction of the terms of the contract as a whole (see *Fuji Finance Inc. v. Aetna Life Insurance Co. Ltd*[10]).

---

[7] (1806) 2 B.R.P. 269.
[8] [1867] L.R. 2 Exch. 139.
[9] [1922] 2 Ch. 67.
[10] [1995] Ch. 122.

2.016   The law has been scrutinised in some detail by many practitioners — most notably by Robin Potts Q.C. who was instructed by ISDA to consider the point.

As is intimated above, Robin Potts Q.C. carefully analysed the Insurance Companies Act and the common law, and concluded that, as credit derivatives within the scope he was considering do not provide an indemnity for loss, they are not within the categories of insurance business for the purposes of the Insurance Companies Act. The mere fact that the economic effect might in some cases be equivalent to insurance is not decisive.

This is a pragmatic, practical and sensible approach. It has the great advantage that it feels as if it is the right answer. As is frequently the case where one is trying to construe varied and in some cases old case law, there are however difficulties that one could raise in relation to it. Some of these are as follows:

2.017   *Class 16(c) does not in fact require there to be a loss*   As mentioned above, there is no direct mention of the risk of loss in the third column of sub-class 16(c), although the second column does refer to miscellaneous financial loss. Acordingly it can be argued that a loss is not necessary as a matter of construction of the ICA, if a contract is a contract of insurance as a matter of common law.

2.018   *A contract of insurance need not indemnify for loss*   There is a type of insurance called contingency insurance. It is possible for a contract to provide for the payment of a pre-determined amount on the occurrence of a contingency, without the need to show loss — for example life assurance, sickness, critical injury and personal accident insurance. Thus the statement that a contract is not an insurance contract if it does not indemnify for loss can be questioned. However, there remains a requirement for an insurable interest. It can be argued in some contingency contracts that the payment is, in effect, a pre-determined estimate of loss.

The general consensus is that there is a real difference between a credit derivative and an insurance contract, in that the obligation to pay under a credit derivative does not generally depend on the relevant party having an insurable interest (broadly, economic ownership) in the asset in question. A credit derivative will pay out regardless: the payment is not indemnity for loss, or a pre-determined payment in relation to something in which the Buyer has an insurable interest, but simply a contractual payment obligation which arises in certain defined circumstances and the size of which is calculated in a certain way. The Buyer might not continue to hold the relevant asset at the time of the Credit Event — and need never have owned it. The payment obligation will still arise even though the Buyer suffers no loss. This is the essential difference which allows one to conclude that the better view is that credit derivatives (properly drafted) are not insurance contracts.

In conclusion, although there may be certain similarities in certain factual situations between credit derivatives and insurance contracts, credit derivatives cover a much wider range of circumstances and are not restricted essentially to providing an indemnity against loss. For this reason they are not generally considered to be insurance contracts — athough if the parties genuinely intend to indemnify against actual loss, so that if no loss is suffered, no payment will be due, there is no reason why a credit derivative might not in some circumstances be an insurance contract.

Importance of wording

2.019   As has been seen above, the question of whether a contract may be insurance or not depends critically upon whether the contract provides protection against actual loss, or merely for a payment of a certain size to be made if certain conditions are met. Thus the drafting of the relevant contract is of critical importance, and careless cross references to assets actually owned by the Buyer, or "loss", should be avoided. In addition, in *Fuji Finance Inc. v. Aetna Life Insurance Co. Ltd* [1994] 4 All E.R. 1025, Nicholls V.-C. accepted the proposition that only where the principal object is to insure can the contract as a whole be called a contract of insurance. Robin Potts Q.C. in the work he did for ISDA suggested that it should be the object of both parties that the contract not be one of insurance. He suggested that, to bolster the argument that any individual credit derivative is not an insurance contract, there is merit in including wording in the relevant documentation to the effect that "*[the obligation] exists regardless of whether [the product buyer] suffers a loss or is exposed to the risk of loss upon the occurrence of [the event] and therefore the contract is not a contract of insurance*". Such a statement provides some useful evidence of the parties, intentions in entering into the contract. This statement cannot, however, alter the true nature of a contract if that intention was to create a contract of insurance.

Secured credit linked notes

2.020   An additional complexity arises if, for commercial reasons, it is necessary for an issuer of a credit linked note to give security for the performance of its obligations. This might easily be required, for example, in the case of a "CBO" (Collateralised Bond Obligation) where an issuing vehicle acquires a portfolio of bonds, financed by an issue of credit linked notes, where the obligation of the issuer to repay the notes (albeit at their reduced principal amount, if a Credit Event occurs) is secured over the same portfolio of bonds to which the Credit Events in the credit linked note relate. In this case, the issuer is issuing a credit linked note which, although not drafted precisely in such terms, will be written down in the case of Credit Events on a notional portfolio which matches the portfolio that the issuer actually owns.

In the absence of security, one can easily argue that a notional credit derivative will not become an insurance contract merely because the buyer happens to own an asset equivalent to the reference asset. However, where security is required to be given over assets which match the reference assets under the credit linked note, there may be a concern that the documents taken together require the issuer to own the assets and therefore to suffer a loss in circumstances where the principal repayable under the note is written down.

The concern may be partially allayed in that it is common in such circumstances for the reference assets in respect of the notes, and the assets subject to the security interest, not to be specific bonds, but instead to be a portfolio of unspecified bonds which individually and taken together satisfy certain portfolio eligibility criteria. In that case it can be seen that it is quite possible for the assets in the CBO bond portfolio to be different from those in the security portfolio, and thus the linkage is broken.

In any event, the better view seems to be that if the credit linked note on its own is not an insurance contract (because it is notional, with no requirement for actual loss) then the entry into an arrangement to provide an investor with additional credit protection should not affect the analysis. In the context of credit linked notes it is interesting to note that there are other practical arguments against such instruments being characterised as insurance contracts, namely (i) no premium is paid (even though economically this is factored into the interest rate payable, and

(ii) on the occurrence of a credit event payment still moves from the protection buyer to the protection seller (albeit in a smaller amount than would have been payable had the credit event not occurred).

The Financial Law Panel

2.021   The work of the Financial Law Panel in this area should be noted — in particular the Guidance Notice "Credit Derivatives — The Regulatory Treatment" published in May 1997. The FLP has made valuable comments, analysing the insurance question essentially as one of policy. This is perhaps in a sense a recognition that there is a material difference in quality or feel between what is meant by a derivative contract (or, more generally, investment business) and what is insurance, notwithstanding some similarities. The Financial Law Panel take the view that it is not appropriate to consider the issue on a transaction by transaction basis, but instead to consider whether the business of the company is in general an insurance business or an investment business, and depending on the answer to that question, to conclude that the business should be regulated either under the Insurance Companies Act or the Financial Services Act, as appropriate. They generally conclude that, as a matter of policy, credit derivatives are produced and traded between financial institutions generally within the ambit of the Financial Services Act 1986 and ought not therefore to fall within the Insurance Companies Act 1982.

Bearing in mind that, since January 1, 1999 insurance regulation has been the province of the FSA, the regulator of investment banks, it will be of interest to see whether this approach is adapted.

Gaming and wagering

2.022   A frequently asked question is — are derivatives, and, in this case more particularly, are credit derivatives, unenforceable gaming contracts?

Gaming and wagering contracts are unenforceable as a matter of public policy unless they fall within a statutory exemption to the Gaming Act 1845.

This is almost the flip-side to the question whether such contracts are insurance contracts. At one extreme, a contract might be providing an indemnity against actual loss and thus fall within the insurance regime. On the other hand, a purely speculative arrangement where no concept of actual loss is involved, and where another party may "win" or "lose" depending on whether the events specified in the contract occur, might be considered to be a simple wager. It should be noted, however, that Section 1 of the Life Assurance Act 1774 provides that "insurance . . . made by any person or persons . . . by way of gaming or wagering . . . shall be null and void". It cannot therefore be said that a contract cannot be one of both insurance and gaming.

A wagering contract is according to case law a contract involving two parties who profess to hold opposite views concerning the occurrence of a future uncertain event, mutually agreeing that on the occurrence of that event one shall win from the other.

The gaming question is of wider application than just credit derivatives — the question applies equally to, for example, interest rate swaps, which are as capable of being used for speculative purposes (see Hobhouse J. in *Morgan Grenfell v. Welwyn & Hatfield Council: Islington Borough Council (Third Party)*).[11] Derivatives generally

---

[11] [1995] 1 All E.R. 1.

fall within the class of contracts which may or may not be gaming contracts, depending upon the interests of the parties and their purpose in entering into the particular contract (Hobhouse J. drew the distinction in the *Morgan Grenfell* case between contracts which are inherently gaming contracts (such as bets on horses) and those which are not inherently gaming contracts where they can have a commercial justification).

2.023 Prior to the enactment of the Financial Services Act 1986 the better view was that a contract would not be considered to be a gaming contract and therefore unenforceable if it was entered into by one of the parties on arm's length terms for bona fide commercial reasons. In those circumstances it was felt that a party was not wagering but was carrying on a bona fide business. This view was confirmed in the *Morgan Grenfell* case. Accordingly, it is necessary to look at the purpose and interest of each of the parties, and ". . . it will only be if the purpose and interest of the parties to the transaction was to wager that the consequence of legal invalidity and unenforceability will follow. If either party was not wagering the contract is not a wagering contract".

Even an element of wagering in the action of a party would not affect the validity of the contract if it was "merely a subordinate element and was not the substance of the transaction" (*per* Hobhouse J. in *Morgan Grenfell*).

The debate is, at least in relation to certain contracts, now largely academic since the enactment of the Financial Services Act 1986 and in particular section 63, which exempts certain types of investment activity from the provisions of the Gaming Act.

That section provides that where one party enters into a contract by way of business (a different requirement to the ones imposed by common law) and the making or performance of that contract constitutes a dealing in an investment (as defined in the Financial Services act 1986), the Gaming Act is disapplied. The question usually therefore is whether the credit derivative in question is an investment within Schedule 1 to the Financial Services Act. Generally speaking, a credit default product, or a credit linked swap such as a total return swap, like other derivatives, is likely to be an option or a contract for differences and as such an investment. Such contract will not be unenforceable as a gaming contract provided that one of the parties is entering into the contract by way of business.

A slightly more difficult question arises in relation to some credit linked notes, where the amount lent and which therefore has to be repaid on maturity is reduced as a result of the occurrence of a Credit Event or series of Credit Events. A note as such will usually fall within paragraph 2 of Schedule 1 to the FSA, which includes debentures, including debenture stock, loan stock, bonds, certificates of deposit and other instruments creating or acknowledging indebtedness. The difficulty here arises from the fact that in certain circumstances the amount repayable under the credit linked note might be reduced to zero: can it be said that an instrument which by its terms contemplates that in certain circumstances no amount may be repayable under it, is a debenture or an instrument acknowledging indebtedness?

2.024 There is no conclusive answer to this and it is likely that the answer would vary from case to case (to the extent that an answer could be given). The best test seems to be to try to determine the "essential character" of the instrument, and whether that essential character is one of an instrument creating or acknowledging indebtedness. Whilst this may not seem to be very helpful or add much to the debate, an "essential character" test would discount a purely theoretical or extremely remote possibility of a zero redemption payment: this in itself would not prevent the instrument being a debenture if in reality it is highly likely that there will be some, even if very small, residual value in the asset. For example, a note which paid zero only if the aggregate value of the reference assets went down to zero would, it seems, be likely to be a debenture: in reality a defaulted asset is always likely to have some, albeit possibly very small, residual value. On the other hand, a note which could be exhausted — for example a note providing credit protection on an asset or portfolio of significantly greater value than the notional amount of the note — may well not be a debenture. If a credit linked note is not a debenture it could possibly be characterised as a contract for differences within paragraph 9 of Schedule 1 to the FSA as it is a contract the "pretended purpose of which is to secure a profit or avoid a loss by reference to fluctuations in the value or price of property of any description . . .". If, however, it is not a debenture or a contract for differences and is not within any of the other relevant paragraphs of schedule 1 to the FSA, the analysis will be the same as in relation to a credit linked loan agreement (a loan not being an instrument acknowledging indebtedness and thus not a debenture). In such circumstances it seems that the note will not be a gaming contract provided that, on the basis of pre-FSA case law, it was entered into on arm's length terms for bona fide commercial reasons.

Confidentiality

2.025 There are two important confidentiality issues that arise:

(a) A party may very well wish to keep the fact that it has entered into a transaction confidential.

(b) Information which demonstrates that a particular Credit Event has or might occur may itself be information held by one of the parties to a transaction on a confidential basis.

A common use of a credit derivative is for "relationship" bankers to lay off risk that they have undertaken in their normal dealings with their relationship clients. A client may, however, find it distasteful that its banker is seeking to reduce his exposure to that company, and accordingly the relationship banker is quite likely to want to keep that fact confidential.

Of course, the ability to do this may depend on the nature of the credit derivative. A "CLO" (Collaterlised Loan Obligation) issued into the public markets may not name the underlying credits which are being sold, but it will describe them by means of eligibility criteria, and it would be a naïve client of such an issuer who assumed that in no circumstances would the issuer want to lay off its risk to that client.

An OTC credit derivative, however, is different: there is no reason why the reference entity or any third party should become aware of the existence of the trade. For this reason, OTC contracts frequently require the fact that the trade has been entered into to be kept confidential.

2.026 The greater issue perhaps though is the difficulty that exists for parties to credit derivatives who also have some relationship with the reference entity, or some role in relation to a transaction involving the reference entity, which may give them information relevant to the question whether a Credit Event has occurred or is likely to occur, which information is however held on a confidential basis (and this may also give rise to other issues).

A way of addressing this (and one contemplated by ISDA) is to provide that a Credit Event can only be triggered by information which is "publicly available".

Thus, it may be known to a party that a reference entity has defaulted on indebtedness sufficient to trigger a cross default style Credit Event, but if that information is not publicly available it cannot trigger the Credit Event. Publicly available would usually be defined as published by, say, two public information sources (leading newspapers, screen information services, etc.) and derived from a source other than a party [or Affiliate] to the credit derivative (to prevent such party simply publishing the information). The publicly available information test might remove one dilemma, but it may also deprive a party of true credit protection — the Credit Event may have occurred, but unless the world at large is told of that fact, the credit derivative does not trigger. In practice, this provision has given rise to some problems in the context of real defaults which are not confidential but simply have not been reported as contemplated by the ISDA "publicly available information" provisions.

If a credit derivative does not require publicly available information, but the party with the information in question is able to use it to trigger a credit derivative, confidentiality issues may arise for the holder of the information and recipient of that information. The U.K. has no statutory code of banking secrecy or customer confidentiality. However, pursuant to principles established under the common law in *Tournier v. National Provincial and Union Bank of England* [1924] 1 K.B. 461, banks have a general obligation to maintain confidentiality of information relating to the affairs of customers. The principles in the *Tournier* case permit disclosure of information in certain limited circumstances, which include circumstances where disclosure is in the interests of the bank. Mere commercial benefit is insufficient grounds for invoking the "interests of the bank" rationale for disclosure. Accordingly, the original holder of the information may be prevented from disclosing the information as evidence of the occurrence of a Credit Event and the recipient of the information will probably be required to keep such information confidential and not, for example, to use it for its own business advantage.

Insider dealing

2.027   Another aspect related to confidentiality is insider dealing. Can a party by entering into a credit derivative, or exercising rights thereunder, whilst in possession of certain information as to the underlying reference entity, be infringing insider dealing laws by seeking to profit from such information? Potentially, the answer is yes in certain circumstances in relation to the entering into of a credit derivative. In relation to exercising rights thereunder, the answer will depend in part on the way in which such rights are exercised, and whether such exercise will lead to any dealing in the underlying asset, as would be the case for example if physical delivery were specified.

Under the Criminal Justice Act 1993 ("CJA") an individual is guilty of insider dealing if he has information as an insider and he deals in securities which are price-affected securities in relation to that information (the offence also catches those who possess inside information and who either encourage others to deal or who make an improper disclosure of the information). The definitions of "insider" and "inside information" are complex but are not considered in detail here since it will be assumed for this analysis that an individual does have inside information.

Dealings for these purposes are only caught if they are on a regulated market or the individual dealing is relying on a professional intermediary (or is himself a professional intermediary). It seems therefore quite possible that some dealings, whether in the derivative itself (dealings in the derivative are considered below) or in the underlying would fall outside the legislation altogether. However, it is assumed in the following analysis that any dealings are, prima facie, caught.

Securities are "price-affected securities" in relation to inside information, and inside information is "price-sensitive information" in relation to securities, if and only if the information would, if made public, be likely to have a significant effect on the price of the securities. It is clear that certain credit derivatives could be price-affected in relation to inside information, although it is also necessary to consider whether they fall within the definition of "Securities" for these purposes.

The insider dealing provisions in CJA apply only to "Securities" as specified in Schedule 2. This includes shares and stocks, debt securities, warrants, depositary receipts, options, futures and contracts for differences. However, the relevant provisions of the CJA only apply to such securities which satisfy the conditions applying to them under an order made by the Treasury for the purpose. The relevant order for these purposes is the Insider Dealing (Securities on Regulated Markets) Order 1994, as amended, which broadly speaking restricts the effect of the insider dealing provisions to securities officially listed in an E.U. Member State, or traded on a regulated market, and derivatives in relation to such securities. Thus the issue of a listed credit linked note could conceivably infringe insider dealing legislation, as could the entry into an OTC derivative (assuming it to be an option, future or contract for differences) referencing a listed bond, but the entry into an OTC derivative referencing an unlisted investment would not.

The definition of Securities includes contracts for differences which are defined as "Rights under a contract which does not provide for the delivery of securities but whose purpose or pretended purpose is to secure a profit or avoid a loss by reference to fluctuations in — (b) the price of particular relevant securities". Clearly certain credit derivatives could be construed as falling within this definition. Section 55(3)(b) CJA defines a disposal of relevant securities to include "bringing to an end a contract which created the security". It is possible that the exercise of a right to receive payment on the occurrence of a Credit Event could lead to the termination of the relevant credit derivative. Such termination could amount to a disposal for the purposes of the CJA and therefore fall foul of such legislation.

2.028 The insider dealing provisions apply, as we have seen, in relation to acquisitions and disposals of the relevant securities. In the context of derivatives this means entering into, or terminating, the derivative contract. They should not, however, automatically apply to the exercise of rights under a contract, although this will be affected by whether such exercise leads to a disposal of securities as discussed above. The fact that information enabling a party to designate the occurrence of a Credit Event is in fact inside information should not be caught by the insider dealing provisions, unless such designation leads to an acquisition or disposal of securities. This could be the case, for example, if physical settlement were to occur, involving the transfer of listed securities from one party to the other (although the equality of information defence might apply in such circumstances), or the acquisition or disposal of listed securities in the market. There is, however, a further defence which might apply. Section 53(1)(a) CJA provides that it is a defence for an individual to show that at the time of his dealing he did not expect:

> "the dealing to result in a profit [or avoid a loss] attributable to the fact the information in question was price-sensitive information in relation to the securities, . . ." (words in brackets added).

It can be argued that the loss avoided was primarily attributable to the exercise of rights under an instrument whose very purpose was the avoidance of that loss.

Accordingly, although the exercise was certainly dependent upon possession of the information, the avoidance of loss was not attributable to the fact that the information was price-sensitive. Furthermore, the holder of the derivative would presumably have been able to exercise his rights in the same way even if the information was public (and therefore incapable of being inside information).

The defence would seem in principle to be available to dealings either in the derivative itself or in underlying listed securities. However, it would not of course be available to the individual who, possessing the inside information, enters into a credit derivative. In these circumstances the individual does indeed seek to profit from his dealings based upon inside information.

On the question of dealing in the underlying securities, it is worth considering here the Financial Law Panel's views on insider dealing in the context of charges over securities ("Insider Dealing and Charges over Securities" published in April 1996). The paper considered the situation faced by lending banks who take security over assets including listed shares or bonds. The circumstances which give rise to the security becoming enforceable may comprise insider information, the possession of which prevents the security rights being exercised to the extent such exercise would involve the disposal of the listed assets.

Although this situation is analogous to physical settlement under a credit derivative, it may be possible to distinguish these circumstances. The disposal following the exercise of security rights would usually be a market sale at a time when the bank is in possession of price-sensitive information and where the defence discussed above clearly would not apply. Where the disposal under a credit derivative is by a transfer of listed securities from one party to the other, and provided that this transfer is at some pre-determined price (*i.e.* not related to market value) then it seems that the Section 53(1)(a) defence may be available. The defence should also apply where one party makes a payment to the other on termination of the contract. Where, on the other hand, there is dealing in the market, then the situation is identical to that faced by the bank in the example above. Accordingly, it should be possible to cash settle provided that the settlement was not calculated by reference to the amount realised by the buyer on a disposal of underlying listed securities in the market.

FSA guidance on the use of inside information

2.029 In December 1996 the Securities and Investments Board (whose role has now passed to the Financial Services Authority ("FSA")) issued a guidance release on the use of inside information in the context of equity related derivatives. The SIB stated that in order to comply with the SIB Principles, regulated firms should not:

(a) buy or sell an indirect stake where as a result of inside information it could not properly have bought or sold a direct stake in the open market; or

(b) enable a customer to buy or sell an indirect stake where the firm knows or has reason to believe that as a result of inside information the customer could not properly buy or sell an indirect stake on the open market.

In addition, the SIB stated that it considered that under the Principles a firm will not generally be able to rely on the "equality of information" defence to justify it so acting, even if such defence could be relied on in relation to criminal law.

The intention as explained in the guidance release is largely two-fold: first, to preclude firms from acting in circumstances in which individuals could not (the

CJA applies to individuals, not to firms) and, secondly, to seek to prevent an indirect dealing occurring that could not occur directly on the open market. The main circumstance in which this could occur (a dealing in a derivative on a listed security being prima facie within the insider dealing restrictions) would be if a defence applies to the derivative dealing that would not apply to an "open market" dealing. The main example of this seems to be the "equality of information" defence.

This guidance potentially presents more difficulty than the criminal law and indeed the SIB expressly states that the Principles may require firms to meet a higher standard than set out under the criminal law. The guidance might prevent a firm from dealing in any credit derivatives which reference listed securities where the firm could not properly deal in the reference assets on the open market (*i.e.* where it has inside information relating to those securities). This is because the "equality of information" defence, as we have noted, is not generally available to regulated firms and we have seen that the Section 53(1)(a) CJA defence would not permit market dealing in the reference assets. The guidance may therefore impose a wider restriction than the analysis above suggests might apply under the CJA.

It is fair to say that the SIB probably did not specifically have credit derivatives in mind when it issued its guidance release, although it does seem likely that the same principles would probably apply. There is perhaps a question however as to whether buying or selling an indirect stake would in this context extend to the termination of a credit derivative contract following an exercise of rights under the contract. So, although the position is not clear, even in circumstances where the entry into the derivative would not be caught by the insider dealing prohibitions, there are circumstances in which a regulated firm would not be able to proceed without breaching the SIB guidelines and care will need to be taken.

Financial Services and Markets Bill — Market Abuse

2.030   The Financial Services and Markets Bill was published in draft form in July 1998, and there has followed a detailed consultation and development process leading to the publication of a revised draft in June 1999. The draft Bill will have the function of reforming the regulation of financial services in the United Kingdom. Amongst many other things, it will include provisions to confer powers on the FSA to impose civil sanctions on persons who engage in market abuse on certain designated markets.

Clause 95 of the draft Bill defines market abuse broadly as behaviour which:

(a) occurs in relation to certain types of qualifying investment;

(b) satisfies one or more of the following:

    (i) it is based on information which is unavailable to informed participants in the market who are unaware of the behaviour but which, if available to such informed participants, would be likely to be regarded by them as relevant in deciding whether or not to enter into transactions involving investments of that kind;

    (ii) it is likely to give such informed participants a mistaken impression as to the supply of, or demand for, or as to the price or value of, investments of that kind;

    (iii) it is likely to distort the market so far as it relates to investments of that kind; and

(c) is likely, or (if the circumstances were publicly known or the behaviour became commonplace, or both) would be likely, to damage the confidence of such informed participants that the market, so far as it relates to investments of that kind, is a true and fair market.

The proposed statutory provisions are very general in nature and the Bill is therefore intended to empower the FSA to issue a code of conduct indicating the types of conduct expected to breach the statute. Breach of the code will be evidence (but not conclusive evidence) that the statutory provisions have been breached. In light of this, the FSA published its draft Code of Market Conduct (the "Code") and an associated consultation paper in June 1998. However, at the time of writing, the Code is being redrafted by the FSA, and accordingly the debate is here confined to the provisions of the Bill.

The market abuse provisions relate to investments which are listed or quoted on a Recognised Investment Exchange ("qualifying investments"). However, the Bill expressly deems behaviour in relation to derivatives based on qualifying investments to be behaviour which is subject to the market abuse provisions (clause 95(6)).

The second element of the test set out above (*i.e.* (b)(i)) may well be satisfied where a person knew of circumstances not in the public domain which could trigger the designation of a Credit Event.

This leaves the question as to whether the relevant behaviour (entering into, terminating or exercising rights under a credit derivative) would be likely to damage the confidence of informed participants that the market, so far as it relates to the derivatives or the underlying investments, is a true and fair market. It is hard to see how the exercise of rights and the termination of a credit derivative would damage market confidence in this way. Accordingly, such behaviour may fall outside the market abuse regime, although it will be necessary to see what bearing the revised Code might have on this argument. It is not even clear that entering into a credit derivative would be likely to damage market confidence if the circumstances (*i.e.* the Credit Event) were publicly known.

However, any market dealing in the underlying as a result of the entry into a termination of the credit derivative, or as a result of the designation of a Credit Event, could conceivably damage market confidence and therefore fall foul of the market abuse provisions.

Conclusion

2.031 There are a number of important legal issues that may arise in relation to credit derivatives, and this chapter attempts to address just some of the issues more frequently encountered.

The most frequently cited concern is the "insurance" issue, although in practice this has largely been laid to rest by, amongst other things, the opinion of Robin Potts Q.C. referred to above, at least in relation to ISDA style OTC non-loss linked transactions. The concern is one not to be forgotten though in creating bespoke credit linked structures and drafting the appropriate documentation.

Gaming, too, is usually unlikely to be a major concern, although again it is important not to lose sight of the issues raised.

The issues of more practical day-to-day concern are those relating to confidentiality, insider dealing and market abuse: these are areas which may have a real practical impact, and the framework in relation to market abuse is only now developing.

Chapter 3

Areas of Legal Risk in Sovereign-Linked Credit Derivatives

*by Martin Hughes**

Introduction

3.001 It is generally accepted that the economic crises which occurred in Asia and Russia during 1998 gave rise to serious legal problems in the derivatives markets, particularly in relation to credit derivatives. Specific areas of concern include the formulation of credit events, the concept of "publicly available information" and dispute resolution procedures. The crises also raise questions regarding the management of legal risk in the derivatives market and suggest the need to look afresh at the basis on which sovereign-linked credit derivatives are written.

The aim of this Chapter is to make a substantive contribution to the debate by identifying specific problem areas and possible solutions (with particular reference to sovereign-linked credit default swaps) and by seeking to draw some more generally applicable conclusions with regard to the management of legal risk in derivative transactions.

A credit default swap — assuming for the sake of convenience that it is one which requires cash settlement — is a contract whereby one party (the seller) agrees with another party (the buyer) that if any one or more of an agreed set of events (credit events) affects a specific debt obligation or set of obligations of an issuer, or the issuer itself (the reference entity), the seller will pay to the buyer an amount calculated by reference to the notional amount of the swap and any concomitant drop in value of one such obligation or a number of them (the reference obligations).

In return for this commitment, the buyer will agree to pay the seller a modest fee on a regular basis during the life of the swap, the duration of which will be agreed at the outset. Put in more straightforward, if slightly inaccurate, terms, the seller will compensate the buyer for a notional loss suffered by reason of a deterioration in the creditworthiness of the issuer. (There need not, probably will not, be any actual loss; it is for this reason that it is generally accepted that credit default swaps are not contracts of insurance.)

The specific areas which will be considered in this Chapter are:

(a) the formulation of the credit events;

(b) the use of "publicly available information" as a means of determining whether or not a credit event has occurred; and

(c) the type of provision which is made for the resolution of a dispute as to whether or not a credit event has occurred.

---

* Partner, Weil Gotshal & Manges, London.

Credit Events

Market practice

3.002 Although the credit derivative market is, in relative terms, in its infancy, the market has developed a fairly standard approach to the scope of the Credit Events in a credit default swap, at least where the reference entity is corporate and not sovereign. The Credit Events in a conventional, corporate issuer swap would include bankruptcy, payment default, merger, "cross acceleration", "cross default", credit downgrade, repudiation and restructuring. Box A contains draft, market-standard ISDA Credit Events as in circulation in 1998, provisions which may well have formed the basis for many swaps written in respect of sovereign risks in Asia and Russia.

In practice, the precise wording of a swap is always a matter for negotiation; and market practices, and thus ISDA's approach, have been constantly changing since the inception of the market. As a result, the ISDA terms are no more than an indication of the Credit Events which a particular swap might contain.

Despite the continuing move towards standardisation, a process spearheaded by ISDA, many sovereign-linked swaps will have been documented not in an ISDA format but in the house style of one party or the other, or, just as likely, in a manner which represented a compromise between the parties' preferred approaches on a variety of important issues.

Whatever the form of document used, the ISDA approach to Credit Events is very likely to have been adopted or, at least, to have influenced the parties' thinking. As a result, many of the sovereign-linked credit default swaps with which we are concerned will have contained Credit Events which originated in a corporate context. This is one of the sources of the problems which have been encountered.

Sovereigns are different

3.003 Corporate issues of public debt are almost always subject to a domestic insolvency regime. In addition to this, the assets of a corporate issuer in some other jurisdiction can often be made subject to a local insolvency or bankruptcy procedure. There will be procedures under which creditors may file claims and procedures for the valuation of claims. There will be provision for a tribunal of one sort or another to determine who gets paid what and, in due course, to wind up or terminate the existence of the corporate entity the subject of the proceedings.

It is very different where an issuer is sovereign. (It is also likely to be more or less different where the issuer is quasi-sovereign, for example, a legally distinct entity which is owned by a sovereign, but this chapter confines itself to sovereigns as such.) A key distinguishing feature of a sovereign debt default is that there is no applicable insolvency regime.

This is one of the reasons why a sovereign debt restructuring is very different from a corporate restructuring. There is always pressure on a distressed corporate debtor either to develop a viable workout programme under protective bankruptcy legislation, for example "administration" in the U.K. or "Chapter 11" in the U.S., or to reach agreement with its creditors. If a solution is not developed or agreement is not reached, a corporate debtor can be wound up, its existence terminated and its management's jobs lost (if the original management has survived that long).

3.004 As has been said before, countries do not go bankrupt and the pressures to reach agreement with creditors are very different. It is usually said by external creditors to recalcitrant sovereign debtors that a voluntary solution needs to be agreed so that the country can return to the international capital markets. The truth is that a country can remain absent from these markets almost indefinitely. The need to have access to the international markets is a political one, not an economic one, and the management (in the form of the Minister of Finance) is more likely to lose its jobs through offering terms which are perceived to be too generous than by failing to reach agreement with external creditors.

Thus, a restructuring event taken from a set of corporate events may well fail to catch a deterioration in a sovereign's creditworthiness which it was intended to. Worse than this, from the perspective of a market which needs certainty in these areas if disputes are not to impede its operation, ill-suited restructuring events may make it impossible to be sure whether a credit event has or has not occured. This is what happened in 1998.

A case study

3.005 What follows is a hypothetical case study which is closely based on real life experiences, but in which the names and circumstances have been altered to protect the innocent. Suppose the following:

- A sovereign issuer (the Republic of San Seriffe) experienced economic problems which led to massive capital outflows, the imposition of capital controls, devaluation and a debt crisis.

- Six months earlier, two financial institutions, Shortbank and Longbank, had entered into a pair of credit default swaps in respect of which the reference entity was the Republic of San Seriffe and the reference obligations were the U.S. $750 million 9 per cent Republic of San Seriffe bonds due June 3, 2006.

- Shortbank was the seller in the first of the swaps to mature (which was of one year's duration). Longbank was the seller in the other swap, which matured four years later. In each case the seller was the "calculation agent".

- Within three months of the onset of its debt crisis, the Republic of San Seriffe contacted one of its core relationship banks, HelpyouBank, and indicated that it could not pay the coming year's maturities on its commercial bank debt.

- HelpyouBank quickly arranged for the formation of a creditor committee which met the Republic's Minister of Finance a month later.

- The press reported the meeting and quoted the Minister as saying that the Republic was seeking a rescheduling of its commercial bank debt and meanwhile was going to stop servicing current maturities.

- Both Longbank and Shortbank contacted their lawyers. Longbank asked its lawyers to demonstrate that a credit event had occured. Shortbank asked its lawyers to demonstrate that no credit event had taken place.

Conflicting contracts

3.006 The lawyers were confronted with a not wholly unprecedented problem. The swaps had been documented under non-standard, ISDA based contracts but, unfortunately, the two banks had sent each other their preferred forms (which had quite different Credit Events) and there was a dispute as to which form governed the swaps. Both banks' lawyers decided to analyse both forms to see which favoured their clients. Paragraphs 3.007 to 3.009 contain three Credit Events. The first is Longbank's restructuring event, the second is Shortbank's restructuring event and the third is a "payment event", which was the same in both forms.

In this context the expression "Payment Event" refers to a failure to pay. Failure to pay means, after giving effect to any applicable grace period (under any terms in effect at the trade date), the failure by the reference entity to make, when due, any payments equal to or exceeding the default requirement under any obligations of the Republic.

Many swaps would contain both forms of event, but the pretence that one bank wanted to rely on one of them and one on the other serves to underline how a particular phrase may be seen as supporting a commercial aim even though an objective analysis would suggest otherwise.

Longbank's restructuring event

3.007   In the context of Longbank's Restructuring Event, restructuring means that a moratorium is proposed or a suspension of payments is declared in respect of any indebtedness or obligation of the Republic. The first event could be said to describe quite accurately the early stages of a sovereign debt rescheduling. Whatever words are used by the sovereign and its creditors (be they London Club, Paris Club or others) at the beginning of a sovereign debt rescheduling (or restructuring — the two words have the same meaning in this context), one of the first steps is almost always a cessation of payments of principal. However, Shortbank argued that since no formal declaration had been made, the *de facto* moratorium or suspension of payments imposed by the Republic did not constitute a credit event.

Given that Longbank's exposure as seller had three years to run, it had a hard decision to make. Should it declare an event where it was seller (knowing that it could not force Shortbank to do likewise) or should it sit on its hands and hope that no formal declaration was made after the expiry of the shorter term swap but before the expiry of the longer one? (The reason Shortbank could not be forced to declare an event is that it was the Calculation Agent and, in accordance with usual practice, was entitled to make that determination in its sole discretion.)

Shortbank's restructuring event

3.008   The second event posed a different problem which arose a few weeks later when the Republic announced it had reached agreement with the Paris Club for a rescheduling of the current year's maturities. In the context of Shortbank's Restructuring Event, restructuring means that a waiver, deferral or rescheduling of any obligation of the Republic, the effect of which is that the terms of such obligation are materially less favourable from an economic, credit or risk perspective to a holder of such obligation. Leaving aside for the moment the difficulties posed by the materiality requirement, when does a Paris Club rescheduling happen? Is it when an outline agreement is struck in Paris and evidenced by a "minute" or "procés-verbal" or is it when bilateral agreements, which implement the terms of the outline agreement, are signed between debtor and creditor countries?

Longbank's lawyers argued that, because immediately after the meetings in Paris the Republic's Minister of Finance had announced that the Republic had "agreed a rescheduling with the Paris Club", there had been a rescheduling within the terms of the Shortbank restructuring event. They pointed out that the parties to the Paris Club discussions, the Republic of San Seriffe and its governmental creditors, all regarded a rescheduling as having been agreed at those discussions and that the IMF had publicly referred to the Republic's Paris Club rescheduling as being an important step in the Republic's progress towards achieving the economic objectives which had been agreed with the IMF. If these parties think there has been a rescheduling, there must have been one, Longbank's lawyers said.

However, Shortbank's lawyers took the view that no rescheduling could be said to have occured until at least one bilateral agreement had been signed. They argued that what had been achieved in Paris was no more than an agreement to agree. In any event, they added, even if there were a rescheduling as a result of what was agreed in Paris, the "materiality" requirement of Shortbank's restructuring event was not satisfied. The requirement was that the new terms of the rescheduled obligations are less favourable (than the previous terms, presumably) from a risk perspective to a holder of such obligations. This was not the case, the lawyers argued. Since the Republic had agreed to payment terms which it could comply with, as the IMF confirmed, the risk, that is the risk of default, was reduced by the rescheduling.

An unresolved dispute

3.009 Not surprisingly, Longbank did not think much of this argument and, anyway, regarded its restructuring event as the one the parties had agreed on. Shortbank, for its part, disagreed and invited Longbank to invoke the swaps dispute resolution procedures (which, fortunately, were the same in both parties' preferred forms). Since the payment event was also identical in both forms of contract, why was the dispute between Longbank and Shortbank not resolved by reference to this event? To answer this question, we need to look at the concept of publicly available information.

Publicly available information

3.010 The difficulties arising out of the need to apply the typically brief description which constitutes a credit event to a complex set of circumstances is compounded by the use of the concept of "publicly available information". This concept, an established market practice, embodies the idea that circumstances can only constitute a credit event if information which reasonably confirms the occurrence of such credit event has been published in (usually) not less than two internationally recognised sources of published information.

When a sovereign reschedules its debt, the economic reality is readily apparent and the process is well understood by those involved. It is, however, a matter of chance whether a rescheduling will take a form, or be described in terms, which neatly and unarguably fit within a three or four line credit event. It is also a matter of chance whether the media will find relevant the same specific characterisations of the process as may be singled out in that credit event.

With regard to the payment event in a credit default swap, the usual requirement is that a payment default is relevant only if in excess of a specified amount (the default requirement). However, when a sovereign default is reported, it is likely that the amount of individual non-payments will not be information that ever reaches the public domain. Why would the amount of a single missed payment be of interest where a country is defaulting on the totality of its current debt obligations?

3.011   In practice, the effect of the "publicly available information" requirement is that what will trigger a conventionally written credit default swap will be the media's perception of what needs to be reported rather than what is actually going on. It is not clear that this is what the parties to a swap intend or what the market wants.

To exaggerate only slightly, there is a real risk that the market may adopt documentation practices the result of which will be that credit default swaps are not triggered by a deterioration in creditworthiness but simply by accident. Whether or not provisions of the sort we have looked at will trigger payment depends, amongst other things, on how a sovereign chooses to announce the reality of a crisis-driven rescheduling and how the media choose to report that reality.

A slight sense of unease about this as a basis for a significant financial market is not reduced by the inclusion in swap contracts of dispute resolution provisions which are calculated to deny reality the victory it deserves.

Before taking a look at the dispute resolution provisions which will have applied to many swaps which came under the spotlight in 1998, it is important to note that ISDA credit derivative documentation has been receiving a great deal of attention in the media at the time of writing, particularly sovereign related provisions and dispute resolution procedures. No doubt some, if not all, of the issues raised in this paper will be addressed through this process.

Dispute resolution provisions

A disinterested third party

3.012   The central problem with dispute resolution provisions of the kind used in the swaps entered into by Longbank and Shortbank (see paragraphs 3.013 and 3.014) is the requirement that a dispute should be resolved by a disinterested third party which is itself, or is the affiliate of, a dealer in obligations of the type represented by the reference obligation. Not surprisingly, experience has shown that in a time of crisis there are no such dealers or, if there are, they do not want to get involved. As a result, it is likely that the next generation of dispute resolution provisions will take a different approach. Meanwhile, there are lessons to be learnt from attempts which have been made to utilise the disinterested dealer approach.

The effect of the provisions we are considering is to make it difficult to find any forum in which a dispute may be resolved. The English courts would be reluctant to get involved where contracting parties have chosen their own dispute resolution procedure and, in any event, one or both parties might be reluctant to have the dispute resolved through judicial proceedings. This poses a dilemma for both parties: if the courts are not to be used, but the agreed procedure fails, what is to be done? The answer, in practice, is that the parties will need to agree on an alternative forum for resolution of the dispute or to reach agreement between themselves. Thus, ironically, the one thing the disinterested dealer approach does not do is to resolve the dispute. What it does is to create another level of disagreement. An alternative approach is urgently required.

Time limits

3.013   By market standards, the time given to the disputing party to invoke the dispute resolution procedure — 10 London business days — is generous; less time would be allowed in many cases. More critically, the provisions require that a determination of the dispute be made within five London banking days of the exercise by the disputing party of its right to invoke the procedure. Again, experience has shown that five working days is not even enough time in which to establish the absence of a disinterested dealer, let alone to resolve a dispute over whether or not a sovereign has defaulted or is in the process of restructuring.

This was particularly true where discussions were based on the sort of provisions described earlier in relation to "payment event". However, even if more appropriately worded provisions are used, it is arguable that the timetable is far too compressed. The adoption of a compressed timetable is based on the view that the market will not function efficiently if weighed down by unresolved disputes. The problem with this approach is that in difficult cases compressed timetables do not resolve disputes, instead they force one or other disputing party to find ways of delaying the process so as to procure a means of establishing an acceptably objective and informed dispute resolution process.

Where large sums of money are at stake and most, if not all, market participants face the same set of issues, speedy but potentially clumsy dispute resolution is not what the market needs. On the contrary, what is critical is that, as already suggested, decisions are taken (and seen to be taken) on an informed basis by an impartial tribunal. Decisions taken in any other way, decisions which may set market-wide precedents, will operate to the detriment of the market and will serve to increase legal risk rather than assist institutions in its management.

Dispute resolution provision and calculations

3.014 In terms of drafting a dispute resolution provision in relation to calculations, the following form of wording would address the issue:

> "In the event that a party (the 'disputing party') does not agree with any determination made (or the failure to make any determination) by the calculation agent or the other party (the 'determining party'), the disputing party shall have the right to require that the determining party have such determination made by a disinterested third party that is a dealer of derivative obligations and that is, or whose affiliates are, dealers in obligations of the type of bonds but is not an affiliate of either party. Such dealer shall be selected by the calculation agent in its reasonable discretion after consultation with the parties. Any exercise by the disputing party of its rights hereunder must be in writing and shall be delivered to the determining party no later than the tenth London banking day following the London banking day on which the determining party notifies the disputing party of any determination made (or of the failure to make any determination). Any determination by a disinterested party shall be binding in the absence of manifest error and shall be made as soon as possible but no later than within five London banking days of the disputing party's exercise of its rights hereunder. The costs of such disinterested third party shall be borne by:
>
> (i) the disputing party if the disinterested third party substantially agrees with the determining party's determination, or
>
> (ii) the non-disputing party if the disinterested third party does not substantially agree with the determining party.

Determinations as to any amounts due shall (if possible) be calculated retrospectively with reference to the actual amount that was due on any cash settlement date and shall not account for subsequent changes with respect to the bonds. Interest on any amounts due that are subject to dispute shall be paid from (and including) the date of non-payment to (but excluding) the date such amount is paid, at the termination rate. Such interest will be calculated on the basis of daily compounding and the actual number of days elapsed."

"Derivative obligation", in this context, means any privately negotiated forward, swap or option on one or more rates, currencies, commodities, equity securities, debt instruments, economic indices or measure of economic or credit risk or value, or any similar transaction.

Management of legal risk

3.015 It is clear from the foregoing analysis that in 1998 legal risk in the derivatives market manifested itself in at least three ways: key concepts (payment default and restructuring) had been defined inappropriately or unhelpfully; an established technique (publicly available information) produced results at odds, it would seem, with the purpose of the contracts in which it was employed; and procedures designed to resolve disputes (the disinterested dealer and the compressed timetable) produced the opposite result. The consequences of the events of 1998 also suggest that there is a more general area of legal risk which deserves attention.

Simplicity and complexity

3.016 The drive towards standardisation has led to the existence of a surprising, if not dangerous, relationship between form and substance with respect to a wide range of derivative contracts, particularly credit derivatives such as credit linked notes. Very many derivative transactions are very simple, straightforward swaps, forward contracts and the like. Despite this, the market standard documentation continues to grow in complexity (although this does not trouble the market professionals who view a mastery of the intricacies of ISDA as simply a starting point).

At the same time, one of the virtues of the ISDA approach is that it can handle very complex transactions. Thus, traders, lawyers and transaction management teams have become used to using a relatively complex set of contractual rules and provisions to handle both the simplest and the most complex transactions.

This has unforeseen consequences. Simple transactions are documented in a complex fashion, which may be unnecessary but this is not a fundamental problem. Worryingly, however, very complex transactions are processed as if they were simple just because the complex documentation they require is structurally identical to that which is used for things that really are simple. As a result, complex transactions involving genuinely difficult documentation are handled inappropriately. The time allowed by the market for institutions to prepare and review documentation of this kind is often no more than the time allowed in the context of very simple trades.

3.017 A group of associated risks, for example, sovereign risk, transferability, regulatory risk, counterparty risk and delivery risk may be very easily described in commercial terms. It may then seem that it is correspondingly straightforward to prepare or review the confirmation or contract which is to document a trade based on an assessment and pricing of these risks.

In fact, as lawyers and transaction managers working in these areas are well aware, it can be very difficult to pin down these types of risk in a contractual document. If asked to prepare or review such a document in the space of two or three hours, the likely response will be to the effect that "that is impossible, but if you insist . . ." Causing the complex to be treated in this way and to be processed as if it were simple is probably not the best way to manage legal risk.

This is a conclusion suggested and supported by the events of 1998. Are there other inferences which might be drawn from those events in relation to sovereign-linked credit derivatives?

Seeing the wood for the trees

3.018 The earliest credit default swaps were documented by contracts which were no more than two pages in length, the operative provision being along the following lines: "if [sovereign] defaults on any public bond issue or reschedules all or part of its external debt, Party A will pay to Party B . . ."

It is not certain that any credit default swap was written in quite such simple terms, but why not? If traders can discuss a trade in plain (and simple) English, why cannot the resulting contract be written in similar terms? The answer, as every finance lawyer knows, is that simple concepts and everyday phrases contain a wide multitude of risks which it is the lawyer's job to identify, analyse and eliminate (or if not eliminate, pass on to the other side).

Why cannot this be done, an outsider might ask? Why not document trades in the simple terms in which they are made? The answer, of course, is that to do so would be to encourage uncertainty; the result would be a multitude of disputes and this would impair the efficient operation of the markets.

At this point déjà vu looms: the circle has turned. The certainty which was sought through detailed, lawyer-written documentation has been lost, perhaps only temporarily, through the use of intricate, market standard documentation and this in turn has lead to an increase in legal risk, an increase which threatens to overwhelm the commercial risks which the parties intended to assume.

An alternative approach

3.019 If a fundamental objective is to preserve an active market in which disputes are infrequent and for the most part easily settled, it may be that a different approach should be taken. One basis for an alternative approach is to be found in the disinterested dealer approach (and, incidentally, is supported by the concept of "publicly available information").

Perhaps what the market wants is a system under which the existence or absence of a sovereign credit default is determined not by the facts but by the market's perception of the facts. If the only credit event in a credit default swap stated that a credit event is to be regarded as having occurred if and only if the market believes the relevant sovereign to have defaulted or to have commenced restructuring, disputes might be few and far between.

Stated in this way, the idea seems rather outlandish, but if restated to refer to a sovereign's standing on a credit deterioration index, the appearance of normality returns. All that is needed is for the market to agree to how the index should be constituted and who should maintain it.

This may or may not provide a solution to the problems faced by participants in the sovereign-linked credit derivatives market. But one way or another, a middle way needs to be found between the simplicity of the concept of sovereign default and its elusiveness in contractual terms.

Annex: Glossary of Terms

3.020

Bankruptcy:	(Extensive corporate bankruptcy/insolvency provisions).
Credit event upon merger:	The reference entity consolidates or amalgamates with, or merges with or into, or transfers all or substantially all its assets to, another entity and the creditworthiness of the resulting, surviving or transferee entity is materially weaker than that of the reference entity immediately prior to such action.
Cross acceleration:	The occurrence of a default, event of default or other similar condition or event (however described), other than a failure to make any required payment, in respect of the reference entity under one or more obligations in an aggregate amount of not less than the default requirement (if any) which has resulted in such obligations becoming due and payable before they would otherwise have been due and payable.
Cross default:	The occurrence of a default, event of default or other similar condition or event (however described), other than a failure to make any required payment, in respect of the reference entity under one or more obligations in an aggregate amount of not less than the default requirement (if any) which has resulted in such obligations becoming capable at such time of being declared due and payable before they would otherwise have been due and payable.
Downgrade:	The credit rating is lower than the specified rating or the downgrade obligation is no longer rated by any rating agency.
Failure to pay:	After giving effect to any applicable grace period (under any terms in effect at the trade date), the failure by the reference entity to make, when due, any payments equal to or exceeding the payment requirement (if any) under any obligations.
Repudiation:	The reference entity disaffirms, disclaims, repudiates or rejects, in whole or in part, any obligation or challenges the validity of, any obligation in any material respect.
Restructuring:	A waiver, deferral, restructuring, rescheduling, standstill, moratorium, obligation exchange or other adjustment occurs with respect to any obligation of the reference entity and the effect of such is that the terms of such obligation are, overall, materially less favourable from an economic, credit or risk perspective to any holder of such obligation.

Chapter 4

Seller Liability for Credit Derivatives

by Dr Alastair Hudson[*]

Introduction

4.001   This Chapter considers the liabilities which may befall those financial institutions which sell or market credit derivatives structures. In particular, it is concerned with the possibility of developing well-understood English law claims to present a further dimension in the appropriate regulation of derivatives. It is contended that extensions made both to existing restitutionary common law and to equitable causes of action by the courts in recent years may come to constitute that new dimension, providing empowerment for buyers in the over-the-counter derivatives markets.[1]

The nature of seller liability

4.002   By the expression "seller liability" is meant the range of legal claims which may obtain against either an individual trader or a financial institution which sells a financial instrument to a buyer. Clearly, therefore, such legal claims could be available in relation to retail banking business as well as in relation to the corporate derivatives business, which will be focused on in this chapter. The legal claims vary between personal tortious remedies connected to the manner in which products are sold, equitable proprietary remedies connected to the fiduciary obligations involved with the manner of selling complex financial products, and the contractual and tortious liabilities connected with the nature of the financial products sold.

There have been great changes in English law in respect of these forms of claim. Therefore, this Chapter will consider the changing environment in which sellers of financial products have to operate. Of particular importance is the development of forms of constructive fraud, such as undue influence, and the broadening of categories of negligence in connection to professional advisors.

The inter-action of law and credit derivatives

4.003   Credit derivatives are the latest star in the derivatives firmament. They combine all of the commercial strengths and weaknesses of more established derivatives products, and, because they are based on established structures, they give rise a number of similar legal issues. What is different about credit derivatives is that they involve the use of an intangible, almost chimeral, indicator (credit

[*] Barrister, and Senior Lecturer in Law, Queen Mary & Westfield College, University of London.
[1] The arguments that make up this Chapter are the subject of extended contextual discussion in A. Hudson, *The Law on Financial Derivatives* (2nd ed., Sweet & Maxwell, 1998). 450pp. A version of this Chapter was presented to Cambridge Symposium on Economic Crime, on September 15, 1998.

worth) as an underlying pricing mechanism. The introductory part of this chapter re-visits some of the issues dealt with elsewhere in this book[2] in order to place them in the discussion of seller liability.

This Chapter examines the potential liabilities which credit derivatives raise for those financial institutions which deal in them and which sell them to corporate clients. The conundrum is this. The professional adviser faces potential liability for advising a client to follow a particularly risky course of action. Therefore, the adviser will also advise the client to seek independent advice, or will seek some representation from the client as to the client's own competence to evaluate that advice. In the case of complex derivatives products, the details of the transaction will be secret because the pricing structure will be commercially sensitive information. Therefore, the client will not be permitted, under the terms of the transaction, to seek external advice. Even if the client were able to seek such advice, that advice would be procured from a professional adviser which would seek to install its own funding structure. Where the seller is also "house bank" to the client, that is the bank which provides most of the ordinary borrowing and other financial requirements of the client, it would be expected that the client would rely entirely on the advice given to it by the house bank.

Consequently, the seller of derivatives products will occupy a unique position in relation to the client which increases the risk of potential future liability to the client in the event that there is any loss resulting from the derivative product sold.

The nature of the credit derivative

4.004 The "credit derivative" is a collective term for a group of products which use familiar financial derivative techniques: the option, the forward and the swap. The aim of the credit derivative is to provide the buyer with an entitlement to receive a cash flow which varies in size according to the movement in the credit worth of a "reference entity". For example, where the buyer has lent money to a reference entity, perhaps by subscribing for a public debt issue, and is concerned that a deterioration in the credit worth of the reference entity will decrease the value of its own investment, the buyer will seek a cash flow which will make good the difference between the value it would have received if the credit worth had not deteriorated and the actual value it does receive. Therefore, the credit derivative offers a neat risk management tool to preserve the effective value of an investment to the investor.

Alternatively, the credit derivative might be used for speculative purposes. Where the credit worth of a reference entity is volatile, it would be possible to receive a cash flow sensitive to the fluctuating credit worth of the reference entity but with the intention of making speculative profit on the size or direction of such a movement. The only difference between a hedging and a speculative position in this context would be the existence or non-existence of an underlying exposure to the credit worth of the reference entity which pre-dates the credit derivative.

The mechanics of the creation of the product are also significant. A number of issues arise: *calculation, valuation, materiality,* and *representations*. Many of these issues are covered in the documentation. However, all of them will be effected by the discussions between the individual trader and other agents acting on behalf of the seller and those acting on behalf of the buyer, and are considered at paragraph 4.019.

---

[2] Principally in Chaps 1 and 3 above.

4.005   There are three basic structures governing the payment that is made by the seller of the derivative, subject to what is said below about each form of transaction. The first mechanism is the total return structure in respect of which the seller provides the cost of funding the underlying debt obligation periodically to the buyer; the buyer pays a fixed rate periodically and on maturity of the underlying debt obligation to the seller. Typically this is a swap or embedded security structure. It is on the happening of a credit event that the seller is required to pay an agreed amount to the buyer representing the value of the underlying security. Given the use of payment netting, the seller is generally only required to make payment after a credit event.

The second structure is a fixed payment by the seller on the happening of a credit event. This second structure is usually provided for in an option or barrier structure. The third payment structure is related to the scale of the movement in the credit deterioration of the reference entity's credit worth whereby the seller pays an amount which fluctuates according to the spread against the market value of the underlyer.

The Credit Event

4.006   As set out above, the credit derivative will operate to make payment to the buyer on the happening of an event connected to the credit performance of the reference entity: "the Credit Event". The precise phrasing and structuring of the Credit Event is therefore central to the operation of the derivative transaction. A number of the concerns set out in the master agreement will apply to the credit derivative in respect of the performance of the counterparty buyer and seller in any event. What is specific to the credit derivative is the range of credit events and termination events which will trigger payment obligations under the transaction.

As considered above,[3] the Credit Event may be in relation to the entity which issued the underlying obligation (or reference entities) itself, or may be priced in relation to other reference entities or indicators. The first form of Credit Event may therefore relate to a specified level of performance of the reference entity in relation to the specified underlying obligations. The precise framing of that type of Credit Event would therefore be an issue to be decided between the seller and buyer of the credit derivative. The more technical the Credit Event, the more the seller's expertise will be relied upon. The issue of the seller's liability is considered in detail below.

The remaining types of Credit Event are more generic in nature and form: the majority being similar to those for the master agreement. The most significant form of Credit Event in this context is the insolvency of the reference entity. The definition of insolvency would seek to extend beyond actual insolvency to events which are expected to indicate the impending insolvency of the reference entity: the presentation of a bankruptcy petition, a vote taken by the entity in a general meeting to wind the entity up, or where the company is unable to meet its public debt or ordinary bank debt obligations.[4]

---

[3] By Schuyler K. Henderson in Chap. 1.
[4] The last category as to the inability to meet debt obligations contains the same issues as to sufficient financial knowledge about the reference entity on the part of the contracting parties. As with a credit downgrade clause, the parties require access to information about the reference entity which will enable it them to isolate the occurrence of such an incident.

Failure to perform

4.007   The most fundamental form of Credit Event is the failure to pay category where the reference entity fails to make payment on an underlying obligation. The underlying obligation requires specification, as would any other transaction in relation to which failure to pay is to constitute a Credit Event.[5]

The issue in relation to failure to pay or to deliver is then whether that failure is defined as being a failure under the terms of the underlying obligation itself or in relation to terms set out specifically in the credit derivative. Failure to pay would include a failure to make payment as required by the contractual obligations of that underlying obligation, or in relation to a specified number of business days in any event. The failure to pay may be made subject to a *de minimis* level. Alternatively, failure to pay may include failure to make delivery of assets. In the context of delivery, the issue would arise whether or not the delivery of a similar assets to the delivery obligation could be valid performance under the underlying obligation but not under the derivative. Further, an obligation to pay interest in relation to late performance might constitute a default under the credit derivative. The final category of failure to pay or deliver would encompass the more general category of the reference entity's repudiation, by litigation, termination or straightforward default under the underlying obligation.

Cross default and cross acceleration

4.008   The further set of provisions are the cross default and cross acceleration provisions. Where failure to pay or deliver occurs in relation to the specified underlying obligation, the concern of the buyer of the derivative will be to receive payment in circumstances where the reference entity has failed to meet payment or delivery obligations under other specified transactions. In relation to cross accleration, where the reference entity is required to make payment under specified transactions sooner than was contractually required, would cause there to be a Credit Event under the derivative. Cross default would also cover similar defaults under specified transactions by entities which are affiliated to the reference entity. The scope of these two clauses broadens the range of transactions and entities which bear on the performance and potential, future insolvency of the reference entity.

Credit downgrade clauses

4.009   The core of credit default clauses is the credit downgrade clause. In relation to master agreements, it is the credit worth of the counterparties which is at issue; in relation to a credit derivative it is the credit worth of the reference entity which is at issue.[6] Where the reference entity has its credit rating reduced by one or more recognised ratings agencies,[7] then a credit derivative must deal with the alteration required in the payments under the derivative transaction. In the case of a barrier arrangement, for example, this may lead to the first time a payment is required from the seller.

The issue is therefore as to the ratings agencies which are acceptable for the purpose of credit rating. There may be policies within the ratings agencies which

---

[5] Subject to what is said below, para. 4.008 in relation to cross acceleration and cross default.
[6] In contracting a master agreement for a credit derivative, there may be a tier of credit worth language which relates solely to the counterparty, and not to the reference entity, in the usual way.
[7] Or by some other mechanism set out in the contract.

the parties may wish to discount in the calculation of pricing structures under the agreement. It is possible that the ratings agency may alter its policy. The credit rating may alter in relation to a corporate restructuring which the parties to the derivatives transaction may wish to attach a different weighting to that attaching to the rating agency's rating decision. The credit derivative documentation may account for this, as considered by Henderson in Chapter 1. In circumstances where the ratings agency's published downgrade is based on factors outwith their commercial concerns, the parties may prefer to reach their own decision. Evidently, the role of the calculation agent in respect of the credit calculation process becomes more important than simply in relation to the size of payments to be made between the parties.

In relation to the credit profile of the reference entity, it is assumed by the contracting parties that the reference entity will retain the same corporate structure throughout their transaction. Therefore, any events of restructuring will typically be expressed to constitute Credit Events. The principle concern, relating to the credit performance of the reference entity in this context, is the impact of the credit worth of the resultant entity after the corporate restructuring. A material reduction in the credit worth would constitute a Credit Event. Similarly, a repudiation by the resultant entity of the contractual obligations of the former reference entity would similarly constitute a Credit Event.

Issues under publicly-issued securities

4.010   There are a number of issues which arise in connection with securities which are held under global notes or which are held by a custodian either as a trustee or bailee. Therefore, there are issues as to the custody of the securities making up the underlying obligations as well as the performance of the reference entity in respect of them. Consequently, the documentation is required to deal with a number of issues relating specifically to the custody process of global notes issued as part of the public debt securities process. The first is the risk of the insolvency of the trustee and the ability of rights holders to enforce their title against the underlying securities. The second is the performance of the custodian in relation to the underlying obligations, particularly in relation to any potential negligence in its performance of the custody task or in the efficacy of the clearance system in relation to the securities.

Other than custodian risks are a parcel of risks relating to the performance of the reference entity in respect of its publicly issued debt. The question of corporate restructuring in respect of the derivative has been considered; however, there is also the question of the restructuring of the reference entity under the terms of its securities. The issue arises of mismatches in the termination provisions across the different forms of documentation. Similarly, there is the question of the covenants and credit support elements of the debt documentation. Where those provisions fail under the securities documentation, the parties must provide for the failure under one agreement to constitute an event of default under the other.

Other regulatory contexts

4.011   A number of miscellaneous other issue arise in relation to taxation and regulatory risk. The taxation issues are considered by Richard Collier in Chapter 6, relating primarily to the potential applicability of withholding taxes, double tax treaties, and the varying tax regulation of foreign exchange in each jurisdiction.[8]

Credit options

4.012 The credit option entitles the buyer to receive a one-off payment on the occurrence of some specified event which triggers payment under the option. The option may be settled either in cash or by physical delivery of a specific security. The buyer pays a premium to the seller in the ordinary way. The option becomes in-the-money in circumstances in which the underlying obligation decreases in value according to the price fixed in the option documentation. A cash-settled option then requires the seller to pay an amount of money, or a physically-settled option may require the seller to deliver securities in return for the underlying obligation. As with standard option structures, the option may have an exercise period which arises within specified time periods or on a specific maturity date. The exercise mechanism may be an automatic one, or be reliant on notification between the parties.

The buyer's right to exercise the option may arise in the event of a straightforward decline in the performance of the underlying obligation in the market beyond a level specified in the strike price of the option. In this instance a barrier structure is created whereby the option is exercisable only where that limit has been crossed. The barrier structure may also specify a further limit beyond which market movements are outwith the expectations of the parties and therefore the transaction will be deemed frustrated. However, the right to exercise may, alternatively, be restricted to the happening of a Credit Event. That Credit Event itself may be subject to the materiality of the Credit Event or the publication of information as to the condition of the underlying obligation.

Total return swaps

4.013 The credit swap provides for the seller to provide protection against the risk bound up in the buyer's exposure to the underlying obligations. In effect, as considered above, the seller provides the cost of funding the underlying debt obligation periodically to the buyer. Therefore, the seller will pay a floating rate including a contractually agreed amount on the maturity of the underlying obligation or in relation to a Credit Event under the transaction. Reciprocally, the buyer pays the return received by it from the underlying obligation. On the maturity of the underlying debt obligation, the buyer pays the final value on maturity to the seller.

Seller	Buyer	Underlying obligation
Seller pays floating rate linked to LIBOR plus an amount on maturity or Credit Event	Buyer pays floating rate plus value on maturity or Credit Event	Underlying obligation pays floating rate linked to LIBOR plus principal on maturity

---

[8] The outline of tax regulation is considered, the detail of each tax code outside the U.K. being beyond the scope of this work.

Therefore, the swap element of the transaction relates to the exchange of cash flows between the seller and the buyer which are closely related to the return generated by the underlying obligations. The fixed rate which the buyer is effectively paying is the contractually agreed spread over the return on the underlying obligations. The position risk accepted by the parties is that a Credit Event is triggered which requires the seller to make a higher level of payment to the buyer: it is this contingent obligation from the seller which constitutes the floating rate element under the classic swap structure. It is this element which insures the buyer against a loss from the underlying obligations. Otherwise, the application of payment netting between the parties will ensure that it is effectively only the cost of funding relating to the buyer's exposure to the underlying obligation until a Credit Event occurs. It is on the happening of a Credit Event that the seller is required to pay an agreed amount to the buyer representing the value of the underlying security or another amount specified in the documentation.

4.014 The swap structure, linked in nature to forward contracts, requires payment to be made in a manner which is contingent on the extent of market movements. As a result it is possible that market movements will exceed the expectations of the parties, thus requiring payment by the seller in excess of its largest expectations. A barrier structure might then be used. The inception of the requirement to make payment would arise where the barrier level of market movement or the happening of a Credit Event, as required by the transaction, is satisfied. Similarly, to cap the exposure of the parties, and to express their contractual expectations as to the largest possible market movements, a barrier level would then be activated to place a maximum on the size of payment made by the seller.

The aim of the credit swap is to generate reciprocal cash flows such that the buyer is paying a fixed rate spread in relation to which the seller bears the risk of paying an amount which floats according to the happening of the Credit Event. This is primarily attractive to the buyer who requires a cash flow return to hedge its exposure to the underlying obligations. A similar cash flow structure is generally used in relation to embedded derivatives. This fluid, cash-flow-orientated situation is to be contrasted with other commercial situations where the buyer seeks a one-off payment under a credit option.

While the foregoing analysis considers swaps generically, the credit swap is usually structured either as a total return swap or as a credit default swap. The credit default swap aims to provide protection against credit losses associated with a default on a specified underlying obligation. The buyer swaps its credit risk on the underlying obligation with the seller, as indicated above. The buyer is therefore paying a fee in return for which the seller makes a payment on the happening of a Credit Event. Under a total return swap the buyer pays the seller the "total return" on the reference asset including any increase in its market value.[9] The seller is therefore paying a floating rate of interest to the buyer in return for this income stream. The "guarantee" element for the buyer arises where there is some depreciation in the market value of the asset which requires payment from the seller, on a payment netting basis.

---

[9] Thus, the seller is occasionally said to have "synthetic ownership" of the reference asset because the seller receives all the accretions and disbursements associated with absolute beneficial ownership of the reference asset from the buyer.

Performance under the credit derivative

4.015 The credit derivative will require performance or payment in circumstances in which a Credit Event, considered above, occurs. The requirement is that, further to the happening of the Credit Event, the necessary differential between the market value and the contractually agreed threshold has been reached. Alternatively, the pricing structure will be orientated around a differential between the market spread on the underlying obligation and the reference yield on the underlying obligation as defined in the derivative agreement. The requirement would be that the Credit Event is material as required by the derivatives transaction.

As considered above in relation to total return swaps, there are three basic structures governing the payment that is made by the seller of the derivative. The first mechanism is the total return structure[10] in respect of which the seller provides the cost of funding the underlying debt obligation periodically to the buyer; the buyer pays a return from the underlying obligation periodically and on maturity of the underlying debt obligation to the seller. Typically this is a swap or embedded security structure. It is on the happening of a Credit Event that the seller is required to pay an agreed amount to the buyer representing the value of the underlying security. Given the use of payment netting, the seller is generally only required to make payment after a Credit Event.

The second structure is a fixed payment by the seller on the happening of a Credit Event. This second structure is usually provided for in an option or as part of a barrier structure. The third payment structure is related to the scale of the movement in the credit deterioration of the reference entity's credit worth whereby the seller pays an amount which fluctuates according to the spread against the market value of the underlyer.

The specific payment provisions in relation to credit derivatives are considered separately, depending on the type of structure at issue, below.

The embedded structure

4.016 As part of the documentation of the underlying obligation, an embedded structure enables the issuer to control its own exposure to the performance of the security. The payment structure is related to the scale of the movement in the credit deterioration of the reference entity's credit worth whereby the seller pays an amount which fluctuates according to the spread against the market value of the underlyer. The aim for the issuer, who buys the embedded credit derivative, is to receive payment from the seller equal to any increase in the principal amounts to be made at maturity of the security. Alternatively, payment may be required to be made earlier than maturity where a Credit Event had occurred.[11]

The insurance issue

4.017 One issue which arises in relation to the credit derivative is that it is a form of insurance. This is particularly the case in relation to those contracts which pay out a lump sum equal to the lost underlying security or loan on the happening of a Credit Event. If a derivative is properly classified as an insurance contract, the

---

[10] Considered above, para. 4.013, in relation to total return swaps.
[11] This structure is similar to a fully-funded loan participation where it is structured as a total return obligation, as considered in Chap. 1 by Schuyler K. Henderson.

seller will be liable for prosecution and the contract will be avoided if it is sold outwith any registration under the insurance legislation. In the context of credit derivatives such as credit default options, this would mean that the seller would be unable to sue for its premium and unable to enforce its contract more generally. Further, it is not clear how the seller would comply with the insurer's general obligation to act in the utmost good faith in a situation where it is seeking to make profit out of the contract. For the buyer, it means it is able to avoid the contract and recover its premium plus interest, or seek specific performance of the contract. The definition of "insurance business" is most clearly defined in the Insurance Companies Act 1982, under which an insurance contract emerges as a contract to protect the buyer against losses suffered by it in consideration of the payment of a premium.

The 1982 Act carries definitions of types of insurance business in its Schedules. Schedule 2, class 14 come closest to a definition of insurance business which seems most akin to the effect achieved by complex derivatives:

> "effecting and carrying out contracts of insurance . . . against risk of loss . . . arising from the insolvency of debtors of their or from the failure . . . of debtors of theirs to pay their debts when due"

4.018   For example, the effect of a credit default option would appear, at first blush, to fall within this definition on the basis that the option would be a hedge against the reference entity's failure to make payment on some obligation. This class does not appear to catch swap structures, for example, which are not orientated around the credit default of a reference entity but rather are concerned with mutual obligations to make payments of cash flows. However, a swap which created a nexus between the floating rate amount and the credit default of the reference entity would appear to fall within this definition.

Class 16 covers "miscellaneous financial loss" dealing with risks of loss not captured by other provisions in Schedule 2. What is not clear is the breadth which would be lent to this provision. It would appear that a credit derivative designed to provide a payment only on the eventuality of an actual loss to the investor would appear to be close to an insurance contract. However, a product which required payment to that investor in any event, or in the case of a swap by that investor on a reciprocal basis in any event, would not be akin to an insurance contract because a payment obligation under it would not be tied to realisation of an actual loss. In an area as subtle as this there is clearly room for manoeuvre and interpretation. All that is open to the financial engineer structuring the derivative product is to design a payment mechanism which carries the reciprocal and obligatory nature of the swap, as opposed to a condition precedent orientated around compensation for some specified loss.

Founding claims

4.019   The nature of the credit derivative is therefore that it, in terms, provides a form of insurance policy for the buyer. However, the insurance policy only works if the derivative product performs in the manner expected by the parties. Therefore, the seller is required to make a number of representations as to the performance of the product and as to the likely credit performance of the reference entity. As highlighted above, there are four key issues with reference to a credit derivative: *calculation, valuation, materiality,* and *representations.*

The core of credit default clauses is the credit downgrade clause. In relation to master agreements, it is the credit worth of the counterparties which is at issue; in relation to a credit derivative it is the credit worth of the reference entity which is at issue.[12] Where the reference entity has its credit rating reduced by one or more recognised ratings agencies, then a credit derivative must deal with the alteration required in the payments under the derivative transaction. In the case of a barrier arrangement, for example, this may lead to the first time a payment is required from the seller.

Calculation

4.020   The first issue is therefore as to *calculation* and in particular the policies of the ratings agencies which are used for the purpose of assessing the credit rating of the reference entity. There may be policies within the ratings agencies which the parties may wish to discount in the calculation of pricing structures under the agreement. Similarly, the ratings agency may alter its own policy. The credit rating may alter in relation to a corporate restructuring which the parties to the derivatives transaction may wish to attach a different weighting to that attaching to the rating agency's rating decision. Alternatively, the parties may construct their own mechanism by which the credit worth of the reference entity is to be calculated. In circumstances where the ratings agency's published downgrade might happen too far after the Credit Event complained of, the parties may prefer to reach their own decision. Evidently, the role of the calculation agent in respect of the credit calculation process becomes all the more important than simply in relation to the size of payments to be made between the parties.

Valuation

4.021   Having decided on a mechanism for calculation, the calculation agent will then be required to reach a *valuation* of the credit of the reference entity. In relation to the credit profile of the reference entity, it is assumed by the contracting parties that the reference entity will retain the same corporate structure throughout their transaction. Therefore, any events of restructuring will constitute Credit Events. The principle concern, relating to the credit performance of the reference entity in this context, is the impact of the credit worth of the resultant entity after the corporate restructuring. A material reduction in the credit worth would constitute a Credit Event. Similarly, a repudiation by the resultant entity of the contractual obligations of the former reference entity would similarly constitute a Credit Event.

Materiality

4.022   The core of the documentation for a credit derivative is the *materiality* provision which provides that the credit downgrade in relation to the reference entity must be sufficiently material to require payment under the credit derivative itself. As part of the structuring role of the seller, this provision requires the making of further representations by means of assurances as to the performance of the transaction. Furthermore, the calculation agent, typically the seller in accordance with standard market practice, will be required to assess the materiality of the alteration in credit worth. The calculation agent's own decisions as to credit,

---

[12] In contracting a master agreement for a credit derivative, there may be a tier of credit worth language which relates solely to the counterparty, and not to the reference entity, in the usual way.

involving a necessary degree of subjectivity as to the projected cash flows of the reference entity, require the making of, in effect, ongoing representations as to the performance both of the reference entity and of the credit derivative itself.

Representation

4.023   In the context of *representation* the seller will not only represent the performance of the product in relation to the credit of the reference entity, but will also represent the suitability of the product to meet the insurance (hedging) or speculative commercial purpose of the buyer. Litigation has commenced in a number of contexts in the United States relating to the suitability of derivatives products provided by financial institutions both to corporate clients and to public authorities. In the English jurisdiction there is also now a decided case on the liability of derivatives sellers to a less experienced buyer.[13]

The specific context of seller liability

Rogue trader

4.024   For the derivatives markets, the most important scandal of recent years is probably the Joseph Jett mortgage bonds farrago at Kidder Peabody in the early 1990s. It is important precisely because it has nothing to do with derivatives. More to the point, it has nothing to do with derivatives but bears all the hallmarks of the derivatives-related scandals. As with Leeson, and other rogue traders at NatWest Capital Markets, Sumitomo, etc., Jett was a single trader who was unchallenged by internal control systems as he fraudulently rolled over loss-making transactions and booked them as profitable ones. This was similar to Leeson's technique for hiding his losses on SIMEX by rolling them over.

In short, the problem is that internal control systems do not want to challenge profit-making traders. Furthermore, internal controllers often do not understand the detail of complex products like derivatives and are therefore unable to supervise their use efficiently.

4.025   The rogue trader cases therefore revolve around the activities of one "star" trader who is not challenged by the internal supervision mechanisms of his employer. In the headline cases, such as Leeson, this leads to a large loss for the employer institution, or perhaps the bankruptcy of that entity. However, the rogue trader cases go further. Rather that being limited to spectacular crashes, aggressive traders who are outwith the effective supervision of their employers will frequently deal with clients in a way that is not in the best financial interests of that client or which are not in the best interests of the employer.

In terms of the client, over-the-counter derivatives, being privately negotiated transactions executed between two parties off-exchange, necessarily put the knowledgeable seller at an advantage over the inexpert buyer. This theme is taken up in the "mis-selling" section below, para. 4.026, however, what is clear is that the financial institution will have both the expertise to devise complex hedging or speculative strategies for a corporate client and a desire to market and sell those strategies to clients rather than the high-volume, low-complexity products which have been used for a long time.[14] A rogue trader at this level will pocket the profit

---

[13] See the discussion of *Bankers Trust International plc v. PT Dharmala Sakti Sejahtera* [1996] C.L.C. 518, para. 4.026 below.

[14] See perhaps the product used in *Bankers Trust International plc v. PT Dharmala Sakti Sejahtera* [1996] C.L.C. 518, considered in Hudson (1998) at Chap. 5, "Seller Liability and Suitability".

rather than fret about the impact on the client. Indeed, in terms of the employer, aside from the possible financial loss in respect of transactions which may subsequently have to be terminated because they transgress a standard of integrity in dealing or a substantive law norm, is the reputation and relationship loss of losing a client as a result of the impact of having sold an unsuitable product too aggressively.

Mis-selling

4.026 The other form of mis-use (to deploy a neutral term between "use" and "abuse") has been the selling of derivatives products to end-users which are not suitable for their purpose, for the particular end-user, or not suitable simply in the level of risk inherent in them. Litigation has commenced on both sides of the Atlantic against institutions like Bankers Trust in a number of mis-selling claims brought by different clients.[15] The various categories of contractual, tortious, equitable and restitutionary liabilities to which Bankers Trust became defendant in actions brought by its clients have been discussed elsewhere.[16]

What has been considered less is the availability of private law claims which could be brought either by the shareholders of Bankers Trust against the board of directors for failing to supervise effectively its Treasury department, and by shareholders of Bankers Trust for the loss ensuing to the company as a result of defending claims for mis-selling derivatives to end-users. From a regulatory stand-point, or from the stand-point of ensuring economic stability, it is important that the selling and buying institutions are maintaining suitable supervision over their own employees. For the selling financial institution, this requires effective super-vision of the manner in which traders conduct business with clients and the products which are sold to them. For the non-financial, buying institution, this means that the company must ensure that its treasury and finance departments only use financial products which they understand. To achieve both of these goals it is not enough to rely on monolithic, quasi-governmental regulatory bodies. Rather, it is necessary to empower those who have a stake in those corporate bodies to bring their agents to account. It is necessary to consider the possible liabilities of those agents one to another.

Classifying claims

4.027 In English law there are distinctions to be made between types of claims and remedies which are available in the financial derivatives context for some misfeasance by the seller of a product.[17] Those claims can be analysed as falling into three categories: claims arising out of contract (consent), claims arising out of tort (wrongs), and claims arising on the basis of some unconscionable act by one or other of the parties (unjust enrichment). The tri-partite division between consent, wrongs and unjust enrichment is a modish one, commanding the particular support of restitution lawyers.[18]

---

[15] *The Proctor and Gamble Co. v. Bankers Trust Company and BT Securities Corp*, Civil Action No. C-1-94-735 (S.D. Ohio); *Gibson Greetings v. Bankers Trust Co.* Civil Action No. C-1-94-620 (S.D. Ohio, filed September 12, 1994); *Bankers Trust International plc v. PT Dharmala Sakti Sejahtera* [1996] C.L.C. 518 — in truth this last claim was a counter-claim against Bankers Trust.
[16] Hudson above, n.2.
[17] See perhaps Cranston, "Banks, Liability and Risk" in *Banks, Liability and Risk* (Cranston ed., Lloyds of London Press, 1995), pp. 1–14.
[18] See perhaps Birks, "Trusts Raised to Reverse Unjust Enrichment: The *Westdeutsche* Case" [1996] R.L.R. 3, 26.

The "consent" category deals with issues which have arisen from the contractual or pre-contractual agreement of the parties. Typically such claims will arise out of the law of contract. As considered in the discussion of the confirmation process in creating derivatives documentation, there will be a number of situations in which there is an issue as to whether or not the parties have formed any sort of enforceable agreement, whether there is sufficient documentary evidence of such an agreement, or whether the parties have reached agreement on all the terms which were vital to the formation of a viable contract. Claims based on this category would therefore tend to revolve around factual issues as to agreement and remedies based on common law, such as damages for breach of contract, or in equity such as specific performance, injunctions, equitable accounting or compensation.

4.028 For the most part, claims based on consent will tend to settle in the marketplace, unless one of the parties has become insolvent. Where transactions are cash-settled the parties will tend to come to some accommodation as to an amount which would settle their differences. This is particularly the case between two financial institutions. Rather than suffer the legal cost of litigation and the reputation cost of unperformed transactions, most market counterparties will tend to opt for settlement. In situations involving non-market users of the products, such as local authorities, the scope for litigation is greater. In particular, market-makers in derivatives products will tend to favour the implementation of their contractually agreed means of termination and settlement, or to rely on market standard procedures (principally because the standard market forms of settlement were agreed between the financial institutions under the ISDA umbrella in any event).

The claims based on "wrongs" will generally revolve around a claim which, in the context of derivatives, is based on the suitability not only of the product sold for the client and for the purpose, but also the suitability of the method by which it was sold and structured. Generally, it could be anticipated that a claim in suitability would be brought by a non-financial institution seeking a remedy from a bank which wrongly sold it a particular derivative product.[19] The wrong complained of might fall into one of a number of factual categories:

(a) that the seller made a misrepresentation or misstatement as to the intrinsic nature and structure of the derivative;

(b) that the seller ought to have given fuller advice as to the effect and risk-profile of the derivative;

(c) that the derivative itself was unsuitable for the purpose for which it was sold and acquired;

(d) that the derivative itself was simply unsuitable for that buyer in all the circumstances; or

(e) that some error was made in the course of selling, describing, analysing, pricing, constructing or implementing the derivative which caused the derivative to be unsuitable.

---

[19] As in the best known of the U.S. cases in this area: *The Proctor and Gamble Co. v. Bankers Trust Company and BT Securities Corp*, Civil Action No. C-1–94-735 (S.D. Ohio) and in England the decision in *Bankers Trust International plc v. PT Dharmala Sakti Sejahtera* [1996] C.L.C. 518.

Evidently, a number of well understood claims in the law of tort emerge from this list: misrepresentation, negligent misstatement, negligence, or potentially fraud. Similarly, some other claims may emerge on these facts which are not necessarily based on tort: mispredictions, breach of fiduciary duty, or failure to comply with regulatory standards as to client business rules. The issues of mistake, whether mistakes of law or fact,[20] form part of the law of contract or unjust enrichment depending on the circumstance.[21]

4.029 The claim in unjust enrichment[22] would be a claim mounted on any one or more of the following factual bases:

(a) to recover specific property lost as a result of the supply of some unsuitable financial derivative product;

(b) to acquire specific property in satisfaction of a claim concerning other specific property lost as a result of some supply of an unsuitable financial derivative product;

(c) to order payment of money in compensation for some loss suffered as a result of some unsuitable financial derivative product; or

(d) to impose financial or fiduciary responsibility on the defendant in respect of some loss suffered as a result of some unsuitable financial derivative product.

There is some potential overlap between the factual basis of some of the claims in wrongs and these claims in unjust enrichment. The basket category "unjust enrichment" itself would appear to classify as exclusively restitutionary those remedies and claims which are properly equitable — particularly in the light of the attitude of the majority of the House of Lords in *Westdeutsche Landesbank v. Islington*.[23] The claim to recover specific property relies on there being some proprietary right to trace or claim against that property. To a restitution lawyer this claim achieves restitution of that property[24]; to the trusts lawyer it is the assertion of a common law or equitable tracing claim against that property.[25]

The category "unjust enrichment" is therefore intended to cover the broad range of equitable claims and those restitutionary claims which are concerned with the buyer of a derivative seeking to recover property or value from the seller of that derivative. This new category is, it is contended, the one most appropriate to be developed in future to permit one entity to recover profits made as a result of

---

[20] It is accepted that English law does not currently accept the possibility of an action for mistake of law (*Bilbie v. Lumley* (1802) 2 East 469) although a large body of academic commentary and judicial obiter dicta suggest that the principle may yet be overturned: *Woolwich Equitable Building Society v. Inland Revenue Commissioners* [1993] A.C. at 70, 154, 199, *per* Lord Keith and Lord Slynn; *Restitution: Mistakes of Law and Ultra Vires Public Authority Receipts and Payments* (1994), Law Comm. No. 227; J. Beatson [1995] R.L.R. 280; G. Virgo, "Striking the Balance in the Law of Restitution" [1995] L.M.C.L.Q. 362; *Air Canada v. British Columbia* (1989) 59 D.L.R. (4th) 161; *David Securities Pty Ltd v. Commonwealth Bank of Australia* (1992) 175 C.L.R. 353.

[21] And also the reader's point of view about the ubiquity of the law of restitution.

[22] The term "law of unjust enrichment" is preferred to "law of restitution" in the wake of the House of Lords' decision in *Lipkin Gorman v. Karpnale* [1991] 2 A.C. 548.

[23] [1996] A.C. 669.

[24] See Smith, *Law of Tracing* (Oxford, 1997), p. 1 *et seq.*; Birks, *Introduction to the Law of Restitution* (Oxford, 1989), pp. 358 *et seq.*

[25] *Westdeutsche Landesbank Girozentrale v. Islington LBC* [1996] A.C. 669; *F.C. Jones & Sons v. Jones* [1996] 3 W.L.R. 703.

mis-selling or the actions of a rogue trader by another entity. Thus, classes 1 and 2 above refer to the recovery of some specific property from the seller, where that seller or some other person has been enriched by the receipt of property from the buyer in connection with the unsuitable provision of that financial derivative. Classes 3 and 4 refer to some unconscionable act on the part of the seller or some other person which results in an award of monetary compensation or the imposition of financial obligations based on constructive trusteeship.

4.030   In attempting to reach a catch-all standard for claims in this area, a test of "suitability", it is submitted, would be the most apposite. Suitability is described by some of the commentators as an "emerging standard"[26] derived from U.S. financial regulation and as emerging from U.K. regulation.[27] In the Conduct of Investment Business rules there is specific mention of suitability. The SIB's conduct of business rules[28] deal with derivative transactions under which private customers have a contingent liability to make payments at some time in the future, there is a requirement that a two-way customer agreement is put in place. The policy aim of the regulatory principles is to protect customer rights by ensuring the suitability of seller's product recommendations and discretionary transactions. The regulation of such agreements requires that there is no restriction on the part of the advisor to restrict its liability in respect of its obligations to advise without negligence and with due skill, care and diligence. With reference to complex financial products, which may involve derivatives, the advisor is required to ensure that the investment is suitable for that particular customer.

Suitability, as considered in the context of this section, is in the form of the collective term for a group of common law, statutory and equitable claims to do with the liability of the derivatives dealer. There has been some debate as to the need for a concept of suitability within the English common law to protect unsophisticated users of financial derivatives from the dangers inherent in the products and also to protect them from the attentions of experienced sellers.[29] Much of the argument circulates around the issues which typically arise in the debate as to the need to regulate financial derivatives because they are risk-laden time-bombs in the hands of the unwary. The principle argument for the development of a distinct category of liability on grounds of suitability is that derivatives constitute a new risk which is deserving of a specific, tailor-made remedy. The counter-argument is that there is a sufficiency of common law and equity able to deal with these claims.[30] This argument is capable, at its edges, of running into the anti-regulation argument that existing regulatory safeguards ought to be sufficient to protect the unwise or unwary on entering into derivatives agreements.

The other sense in which the term "suitability" is frequently used in the financial services context is in the regulatory field. As a point of re-emphasis, the point of view of this section is that English law does have enough common law and equitable forms of action to cater for the needs of the inexperienced buyer — but that the term "suitability" is a useful collective term for their application and motivation in this context.

---

[26] Cranston, *Principles of Banking Law* (Oxford, 1997), p. 212.
[27] See Blair, *Financial Services: The New Core Rules* (Blackstone, 1991), p. 94.
[28] SIB Rules, Chap. III, Pt 2.
[29] *e.g.*: Greene, "Suitability and the Emperor's New Clothes" (1996) 3 E.F.S.L. 53; and Little, "Suitability, the Courts and the Code" (1996) 3 E.F.S.L. 119.
[30] See especially Greene, above, n.30.

Derivatives dealer liability under English law

4.031 In the context of derivatives there has been one reported decision which has considered the specific liability of the sellers of financial derivatives in the decision of Mance J. in the case of *Dharmala*.[31] This case summarises precisely the issues which are specific to the selling of financial derivatives in general and interest rate swaps in particular.[32] There are indications in the judgment that the relationship between the parties is of a particular nature that it needs to be considered on its own facts. By extension then, the circumstances of all sellers and buyers of financial derivatives need to be considered on their own facts. In particular, Mance J. held that not all statements made by BT are necessarily to be considered to be representations if DSS is to be expected to exercise its own skill and judgment as to the content of that statement. To this extent the Bank of England's London Code is cited with approval in its approach to each individual client and an evaluation of that client's level of knowledge and expertise in the requisite field.

In relation to one of the two swap transactions at issue, Mance J. was more critical of BT because the seller's marketing material tended to emphasise the likelihood of gain rather than the risks of the loss, and further that that material might have given a misleading impression of the effect of the product. Mance J. found expressly that such a transaction would have founded liability for the tort of misrepresentation in respect of an inexperienced counterparty. On the facts, however, DSS appeared to be suitably experienced and diligent to form its own, independent assessment of the effect and risk of the swaps proposed by BT. Mance J. thus emphasised the relativity involved in assessing potential liability in this context. A counterparty which was demonstrably incapable of ascertaining the risks involved, or a counterparty which had not been as pro-active as DSS in pursuing these particular structures and relying more on the seller, would appear to have good grounds for a claim based on misrepresentation.

4.032 As to the general claim based on "breach of duty", Mance J. found that many of DSS's requirements for the swaps had not been communicated fully to BT to the extent that the were alleged by DSS to have existed in any event. Further, economists' predictions of the future movement of the U.S. economy which had been supplied by BT were reasonably made and based on detailed research. As such, it was held, BT ought to have no liability based on the outcome of those economic predictions which had not, in themselves, caused DSS to enter into the transactions.

Importantly, in general terms, there was no duty on BT to act as general advisor to DSS. Furthermore, Mance J. was explicit in his finding that the courts should not assume such duties in all cases. A duty of care, under any of the heads sought be DSS, should be inferred only where it was justified on the particular facts. DSS were experienced in financial matters and as such should be expected to understand the partially speculative nature of the transactions. On these facts, it was held, there was no reason for BT to be saddled with a responsibility to advise DSS generally in the manner suggested by DSS's counter-claim.

Contrary to the risks associated with mis-selling derivatives, there are the personal risks taken by the officers of the buyer in entering into these products. In

---

[31] *Bankers Trust International plc v. PT Dharmala Sakti Sejahtera* [1996] C.L.C. 518; see also Picarda, "Interest Rate Swap Agreements in the Courts" [1996] B.J.I.B.F.L. 170.

[32] For a particularly useful summary of the decision, see the Financial Law Panel's *"Bankers Trust v. PT Dharmala Sakti Sejahtera*: Case Summary" (London, Financial Law Panel, January 1996).

one decided U.S. case, directors have been held liable by shareholders for failing to protect the company against market movements by means of hedging derivatives.[33] Alternatively, those directors also run the risk of litigation where their use of derivatives causes loss to the company.[34]

Dealers' representations

4.033 In the context of a financial derivative product, it is the uncertainty of future market movement that forms the rationale for the entire transaction. That is so whether the transaction is constructed around speculative gain or prudent risk management. There are two potential categories of issue: resultant loss caused by unanticipated movements in market rates (*"failure of model"*) and loss caused by a reckless level of risk being taken by the buyer on the advice of the seller (*"suitability failure"*).[35] In the context of "failure of model" the allocation of risks lies with the advisor in seeking to match market volatility with the forecasts and assessments set out in the pricing model. Failure to anticipate all of the resultant movements may, of course, stem straightforwardly from negligence and thereby be actionable in tort. The issue would arise as to the foreseeability of the loss actually suffered. Alternatively, the buyer could seek restitution on the basis of a failure of basis: that is, the movement of the appropriate markets in a way and to an extent which the parties had not expected. In reference to options on equity markets, for example, it would be advantageous to the commercial parties to specify a maximum volatility which they anticipate in the market, such that excess volatility (outside their expectations or common intentions) would be discounted. It is submitted that volatility outwith those boundaries would give rise to a claim founded on failure of basis.

The claim based on "suitability failure" would arise where the risk which the buyer sought to manage was not met by the return provided by the product bought. For example, the use of an interest rate swap which did not pay an interest rate to the buyer equivalent to the size of risk inherent in its existing debt portfolio (a rate equal to x), but rather one which contained an element of speculation (thus specifying a rate equal to $x + y$). The element that equalled y would be unnecessary for the purposes of debt management. The factor to be proved by the buyer claiming suitability failure would be that the element y constituted an unsuitable addition of risk which went beyond the basis upon which the transaction was created. It may be that the element y arises from market disruption which the parties had not foreseen but which was not covered by the contract. Alternatively, y might be an element which was knowingly added to the transaction but which constituted an unacceptable increase in the risk incumbent on the buyer.[36]

Shareholder remedies

4.034 The future of private law in relation to the use and abuse of derivatives will depend upon the ability of shareholders to control the use of derivatives by

---

[33] *Brane v. Roth* 590 N.E. 2d 587 (Ind. App. 1 dist, 1992).

[34] See Henderson, above, Chap. 1 who explains that shareholders in Proctor and Gamble brought litigation against directors of that company in the wake of litigation with Bankers Trust: *Elaine Drage et al. v. Proctor & Gamble et al.*, Court of Common Pleas, Hamilton County, April 1994.

[35] At this level there is a potential claim, as considered above with reference to reckless risk-taking.

[36] It was this latter, factual category which founded Proctor and Gamble's claim against Bankers Trust in relation to a claim for a loss of approximately U.S. $160 million caused by the selling of "high octane swaps" for the corporate party's debt management which had an in-built exposure to speculative movements in the underlying markets. The corporate party brought the action on the basis of the bank's allegedly negligent advice in selling the product without recognising its unsuitability both for the purpose and the particular buyer.

banks or their clients, the obligations of the fiduciary to control the use of derivatives and the concomitant obligations of any fiduciary to provide information as to the use of derivatives. In short, this revolves around the power of the shareholder to hold the director to account for mis-use of derivatives in her fiduciary capacity. Those matters are, however, outwith the scope of this chapter.

Fiduciary duty to control

4.035 It appears that there are two contexts in which liability for breach of fiduciary duty might be important. The first is where a seller is advising an institution as to its derivatives investment strategy in circumstances where it occupies a fiduciary relationship in respect of its client. As with the facts of the leading cases, often the use of information acquired from the fiduciary relationship to make profit is itself grounds for liability. The second situation is where a market-making seller provides a structure to its client in relation to which it makes a profit for itself. There is straightforwardly a conflict between the fiduciary obligations of protecting the beneficiary and the need to make profit.

The further issue is the nature of the remedy against the fiduciary.[37] If the fiduciary had used trust property to generate a profit, then that profit would be said to derive from that property. Therefore, it would appear that in relation to the rule against profit-making by fiduciaries, the profit ought to be held on proprietary constructive trust for the trust by the fiduciary.[38] In *Boardman v. Phipps*, Lord Cohen held that the fiduciary should be "accountable to the respondent for his share of the net profits which they derived from the transaction": it is not clear whether that accounting is on a proprietary or a personal basis.[39] The reference to "net profits", presumably, refers to profits made after deducting the expense of making them. However, Lords Hodson and Guest hold affirmatively that the confidential information obtained by Boardman was the property of the Phipps trust. Therefore, the profits generated by the fiduciary ought properly to be considered to have been in equity the property of the Phipps trust throughout.

4.036 The other possible approaches would be simply to make good the amount lost to the trust in money terms. This does not amount to a proprietary remedy necessarily. In *Target Holdings v. Redferns*,[40] Lord Browne-Wilkinson identified three possible remedies in connection with a breach of trust. The first was compensation; the second was the reinstatement of the trust fund, a proprietary remedy; the third was a payment of money to the trust equal to the value of the amount lost by the trust fund. This final approach is reminiscent of a remedy for unjust enrichment being equal to the value subtracted from the trust fund by the enrichment of the fiduciary.

The amount of interest to be paid by the constructive trustee will differ according to the trustee's honesty. As a result of the decision in *Westdeutsche Landesbank v.*

---

[37] For a fuller discussion of this issue see Hudson, *Principles of Equity and Trusts* (Cavendish, 1999).
[38] In *The Law on Restitution*, Burrows argues that in the context of unjust enrichment, this award is restitutionary, although this form of constructive trust is more usually proprietary.
[39] The nature of the remedy in *Boardman* is, however, somewhat problematic (see Underhill & Hayton, *Law Relating to Trusts and Trustees* (15th ed., Butterworths, 1995), p. 356 discussing particularly *Regal v. Gulliver* [1942] 1 All E.R. 378, [1967] 2 A.C. 134n). Therefore, it is not impossible for personal rights to be translated into proprietary rights on the happening of a suitable event. The distinction between *Reid* and *Westdeutsche* would be said to be, on Lord Browne-Wilkinson's terms, the knowledge Reid had that his receipt of the payments was a breach of the trust held in him by his employers.
[40] [1996] 1 A.C. 421.

Islington LBC,[41] where the trustee knew of the unconscionability of his actions, he will hold any trust property on trust from the time when he first has that knowledge. Such a proprietary right under constructive trust principles will then give the trust a right to receive compound, rather than merely simple, interest. Where the constructive trustee had no such knowledge, no proprietary claim arises and only simple interest will be payable.

Fiduciary duty to provide information

4.037   Information is the key to control of the use and abuse of derivatives. As considered above, all derivatives debacles have been caused by fraudulent, rogue trades or a straightforward lack of expertise and information in the derivatives field. In relation to boards of directors or agents, the question arises as to the obligation to inform their members as to derivatives policies. The shareholders of end-users of derivatives require information as to the treasury department's policies in relation to speculation and risk management. The shareholders of financial institutions similarly need to be informed as to the compliance procedures of the bank and the suitability of transactions with end-users.[42]

Dealer's unconscionable profit

4.038   Where a dealer makes a profit from an unsuitable product that would appear to be an unjust enrichment remediable by a restitutionary remedy. In the wake of the decision in *Westdeutsche Landesbank v. Islington LBC*[43] where one party receives the property of another with knowledge of some factor in that transaction affecting its conscience, then the property so received is to be held on constructive trust by the recipient. By extension, where that property is received but then passed on by the recipient, it will attract personal liability to account to the payer under the doctrine of knowing receipt[44]; or, if there is no receipt of the property but simply some action as an intermediary in setting up the transaction, the intermediary will face personal liability to account as a dishonest assistant where the transaction takes some reckless risk as to suitability of the product for the context.[45]

As considered with reference to the *Dharmala* case above, the issue of undue influence may also turn on the relationship between the buyer and the seller. In circumstances where the buyer would typically rely on the seller for advice without recourse to any other expert, perhaps as its house bank which provided all its finance requirements, and where the client has no particular financial expertise of its own, the seller must be particularly careful in marketing complex products. In *Dharmala* itself, DSS argued that BT owed it a duty to suggest more straightforward products which would have achieved its objectives. Mance J. found that DSS had been involved in and eager for the particular product created. However, where a more risky and complex product is foisted on the buyer by the seller, in circumstances where vanilla, less risky products would have achieved the same goals, it is suggested that the seller is at risk of a claim for undue influence brought by the buyer.

---

[41] [1996] A.C. 669.
[42] For a fuller discussion of this topic see Hudson, *Principles of Equity and Trusts* (Cavendish, 1999), p. 212 *et seq.*
[43] [1996] A.C. 669.
[44] *Polly Peck plc v. Nadir No. 2* [1992] 4 All E.R. 769.
[45] *Royal Brunei Airlines v. Tan* [1995] 2 A.C. 378.

A claim for undue influence, if successful, permits the victim to set aside the transaction which has been created as a result of that undue influence.[46] That liability would lead to the contract being set aside in toto, leaving the seller to put the parties back in the position which they had previously occupied (if the seller had received net payments) or to write off the loss (if the buyer had received net payments). This action is categorised as a form of "constructive fraud".[47] The victim will be able to set aside a transaction on the basis that there has been some form of undue influence but not as a means of protecting itself from the result of its own folly or failure to act.[48] Furthermore, the victim will not be able to establish undue influence simply because there is inequality of bargaining power between transacting parties; rather, the buyer must show some undue influence over and above that.[49] This issue is considered in detail at the end of this Chapter in *Undue influence*.

4.039 The issue is this: if equity will respond to a fiduciary who takes unacceptable levels of risk with the trust fund, what is it that will lead to a person being made a fiduciary? In a fiduciary relationship[50] although, it is suggested, there are circumstances in which the advising seller so inter-meddles with the affairs and risk management objectives of the buyer that the seller must come to occupy a fiduciary relationship in respect of its counterparty and client.[51]

The role of the equitable doctrines of undue influence, constructive trusts to give effect to the settlor's intentions and of common intention constructive trusts, were not issues raised by Lord Browne-Wilkinson in *Islington*.[52] In *Barclays Bank v. O'Brien*[53] the House of Lords established the need to take independent advice. The issue arises then: what advice will dispel the undue influence? Further to *Crédit Lyonnais v. Burch*,[54] it is not clear whether there is the possibility of undue influence in OTC derivatives market or whether these multinational organisations are simply arm's length parties. However, where the buyer is a non-financial institution which typically relies on the seller for all or most of its financial information and advice, then it would appear that there is an increased likelihood of liability for undue influence.

The decision in *O'Brien*[55] as to the application of the principle of undue influence in the provision of guarantees in respect of domestic mortgages, could be extended to cases of commercial guarantees or collateral agreements which are obtained in respect of derivatives transactions. It is possible to argue that *O'Brien*[56] is a decision

---

[46] *Allcard v. Skinner* (1887) 36 Ch.D. 145; *National Westminster Bank v. Morgan* [1985] A.C. 686; *Barclays Bank v. O'Brien* [1994] 1 A.C. 180; *TSB Bank v. Camfield* [1995] 1 All E.R. 951.

[47] See *Snell's Equity* (29th ed., Sweet & Maxwell, 1990), p. 550.

[48] *Tufton v. Sperni* [1952] 2 T.L.R. 516.

[49] *National Westminster Bank v. Morgan* [1985] A.C. 686; although it is perhaps unclear how this doctrine is to be applied in the wake of *O'Brien*.

[50] *National Westminster Bank v. Morgan* [1985] A.C. 686.

[51] *Lloyds Bank v. Bundy* [1975] Q.B. 326, a decision which concerned advice given by a bank to an old man who relied entirely on the advice of the bank's manager: *cf. National Westminster Bank v. Morgan* [1985] A.C. 686.

[52] [1996] A.C. 669.

[53] [1994] 1 A.C. 180; [1993] 3 W.L.R. 786.

[54] [1997] 1 All E.R. 144. See also *Barclays Bank v. O'Brien* [1994] 1 A.C. 180; *CIBC Mortgages v. Pitt* [1994] 1 A.C. 200; *Massey v. Midland Bank* [1995] 1 All E.R. 929; *Midland Bank v. Serter* [1995] 1 All E.R. 929; *Bank of Boroda v. Reyerel* [1995] 2 F.L.R. 376; *Banco Exterior Internacional v. Mann* [1995] 1 All E.R. 936; *Halifax Mortgage Services Ltd v. Stepsky* [1996] Ch. 1; [1995] 4 All E.R. 656; *Banco Exterior International SA v. Thomas* [1997] 1 W.L.R. 221; [1997] 1 All E.R. 46; *Barclays Bank v. Thomson* [1997] 4 All E.R. 816.

[55] [1994] 1 A.C. 180; [1993] 3 W.L.R. 786.

[56] [1994] 1 A.C. 180; [1993] 3 W.L.R. 786.

which is also about risk allocation. In compiling a test for equity in commercial situations, a test of "commercially suitable conduct" may be better than "unconscionable conduct". As with *Tan*,[57] it is likely that there would be an establishment of an objective standard of probity.

Tortious liability: fraud and negligence

4.040 Further to what has been said above in relation to unconscionable profits from unsuitable derivatives transactions, the more straightforward common law claims will revolve around dealer fraud or negligence. The fraud-based claims would involve matters of fact, deduced usually from tapes of conversations between the parties, which are not susceptible to much legal analysis. The issue of one more of regulatory control in relation to the activities of traders or in the hands of shareholders seeking to control the affairs of the company as to the observance of conduct of business requirements.

A further issue then arises in relation to bribes and unlawful acts, which takes a much tougher and clearer line on the appropriate remedy. Where a person committing an unlawful act and/or receiving a bribe is in a fiduciary position during the commission of such an act, the fiduciary is required to hold any property comprising the bribe on proprietary constructive trust for the beneficiaries of the fiduciary duty. That proprietary constructive trust requires that any profits made are similarly to be held on constructive trust. Similarly, any losses made as a result of investing the bribe will be required to be made good by the constructive trustee.[58]

4.041 The core rule was set out by the Privy Council in *Att.-Gen. for Hong Kong v. Reid*.[59] The former Attorney-General for Hong Kong had accepted bribes in relation to the prosecution of individuals within his jurisdiction. The bribes which he had received had been profitably invested. Lord Templeman held that a proprietary constructive trust is imposed as soon as the bribe is received on the recipient of the bribe. This means that the employer is entitled to any profit generated by the cash bribe received from the moment of its receipt. Similarly, Lord Templeman held that the constructive trustee is liable to the beneficiary for any decrease in value in the bribe and also for any increase in value in the bribe.

Negligence is a slightly more difficult concept in this context. The ways in which sellers and buyers can be negligent in relation to derivatives products are numerous. For the seller the fundamental issue would be making an error in the creation of the product by means of mis-pricing, or mis-documenting the transaction. This problem could be dealt with most straightforwardly by means of an action in relation to mistake, or for rectification of the contract. The more difficult forms of negligence would relate to a mis-allocation of the type of product to the commercial circumstances of the buyer. This might arise from a negligent appraisal of the risks involved in the product, or a negligent mis-understanding of regulatory, legal or capacity risk. The common thread, again it is contended, is the unsuitability of the product for the circumstances.

From the perspective of the negligence of the buyer's agents (in particular its finance director, treasury department, professional advisers, and board of directors) the categories of negligence are similar to those for the seller. The action brought

---

[57] *Royal Brunei Airlines v. Tan* [1995] 2 A.C. 378; [1995] 3 W.L.R. 64.
[58] See also *Reading v. Att.-Gen.* [1951] A.C. 507.
[59] [1994] 1 A.C. 324; [1994] 1 All E.R. 1.

on behalf of the buyer's shareholders (subject to what is said above about the availability of an action for negligence) would be in pursuance of negligent mistakes or mis-appraisals of the nature of the obligations acquired. For the buyer the mis-appraisal would be orientated around either the acquisition of an obligation which becomes unacceptably large or around the failure to hedge adequately a commercial risk.

Personal liability to account

Dishonest assistance

4.042 Dishonest assistance is considered to be a category of wrong because it does not depend on the assistant receiving some unjust enrichment.[60] Rather, the wrong of assisting in some breach of a fiduciary duty or trust is sufficient to ground personal liability as a constructive trustee. Where a person dishonestly assists another in a breach of duty, that dishonest assistant will be personally liable to account to the beneficiary of that duty for the value lost to the trust. "Dishonesty" in this context is a broad concept requiring that there be some element of fraud, lack of probity or even reckless risk-taking. It is not necessary that any fiduciary is dishonest; simply that the dishonest assistant is dishonest. The distinction from liability for "knowing receipt", considered below, is that there is no requirement for the imposition of liability that the stranger have had possession or control of the property at any time.[61]

The core of this area are contained in the speech of Lord Selborne L.C. in *Barnes v. Addy*[62] where his Lordship held:

> "strangers are not to be made constructive trustees merely because they act as the agents of trustees in transactions within their legal powers, transactions, perhaps, of which a Court of Equity may disapprove, unless those agents receive and become chargeable with some part of the trust property, or unless they assist with knowledge in a dishonest and fraudulent design on the part of the trustee".[63]

The core notion is therefore knowledge of a "dishonest and fraudulent design". The categories of knowledge which are required in this context have been the subject of much debate in the caselaw. In there were five categories of knowledge. The applicable categories of knowledge are those set out in *Baden v. Société Générale*[64] and reduced in number in the wake of the decision in *Re Montagu*[65] to actual knowledge, wilfully shutting one's eyes to the obvious, and wilfully and recklessly failing to make inquiries which an honest person would have made. Before the decision of the Privy Council in *Tan*, dishonest assistance required that there be

---

[60] While there is debate among the commentators, many have doubted whether or not this form of liability should really be described as a "constructive trust": see Oakley, *Constructive Trusts* (3rd ed., 1997), p. 186 *et seq.*

[61] *Agip (Africa) v. Jackson* [1991] Ch. 547; *Polly Peck International v. Nadir (No. 2)* [1992] 3 All E.R. 769; *Westdeutsche Landesbank v. Islington* [1996] A.C. 669.

[62] (1874) 9 Ch.App. 244 at 251–252.

[63] Similarly, as Lord Browne-Wilkinson held in *Westdeutsche Landesbank v. Islington*: If X has the necessary degree of knowledge, X may himself become a constructive trustee for B on the basis of knowing receipt. But unless he has the requisite degree of knowledge he is not personally liable to account as trustee: *Re Diplock* [1948] Ch. 465 and *Re Montagu's Settlement Trusts* [1987] Ch. 264.

[64] (1983) [1993] 1 W.L.R. 509.

[65] [1987] Ch. 264.

some fraud in the misapplication of trust funds (see *per* Vinelott J. in *Eagle Trust plc v. SBC Securities Ltd.*[66]; Scott L.J. in *Polly Peck International v. Nadir (No. 2)*.[67]

4.043 The liability in respect of deposit-taking banks can be difficult to conceptualise. For example, where X Bank allows a cheque drawn on A's account to be paid to a third party's account, the bank may be liable for dishonest assistance. Where the third party's account was overdrawn, the credit of the cheque will make the bank potentially liable for knowing receipt where the funds are used to reduce the overdraft because in the latter instance the bank receives the money in discharge of the overdraft loan. Similarly, where the bank charges any fees in connection with the transfer, it may be liable for knowing receipt of a part of that money.[68]

The leading case on dishonest assistance is the decision of the Privy Council In *Royal Brunei Airlines v. Tan*.[69] In describing the nature of the test for liability for dishonest assistance, Lord Nicholls held the following:

> "acting dishonestly, or with a lack of probity, which is synonymous, means simply not acting as an honest person would in the circumstance. This is an objective standard."[70]

It is therefore sufficient that the assistant fails to live up to an objective standard of probity, whether that be establishing on the facts or by reference to a regulatory standard (such as the SIB core principles). This is to be contrasted with the action for knowing receipt which, in the judgement of Scott L.J. in *Polly Peck*,[71] sets out a form of subjective test of whether or not the recipient ought to have been suspicious and thereby have constructive notice of the breach of trust in those particular circumstances.

4.044 It is also not required that the assistant be proved to have been acting fraudulently, as indeed it could not be shown that Tan was because he had aimed to return the money to the trust fund. Indeed, Lord Nicholls expanded his discussion of "dishonesty" to consider the taking of risk by that assistant. Risk is expressly encompassed within the new test. Lord Nicholls says:

> "All investment involves risk. Imprudence is not dishonesty, although imprudence may be carried recklessly to lengths which call into question the honesty of the person making the decision. This is especially so if the transaction serves another purpose in which that person has an interest of his own."[72]

Therefore, the issue arises of the advisor who stands to profit from the transaction proving unprofitable to the buyer in circumstances where the advisor recommends the taking of a large investment risk. The basis of this form of liability is that a third party "takes a risk that a clearly unauthorised transaction will not cause loss . . . If the risk materialises and causes loss, those who knowingly took the risk will be accountable accordingly."[73] There is a difference where there is doubt whether

---

[66] [1992] 4 All E.R. 488 at 499.
[67] [1992] 4 All E.R. 769 at 777.
[68] See Oakley, *Constructive Trusts* (Sweet & Maxwell, 1997) p. 186 *et seq.*
[69] [1995] 2 A.C. 378.
[70] *ibid.*
[71] *Polly Peck International v. Nadir (No. 2)* [1992] 3 All E.R. 769.
[72] [1995] 2 A.C. 378 at 387.
[73] *ibid.*

the risk is authorised or not. In situations where an investment advisor retained by the trustees is unsure whether or not an investment is encompassed by the investment powers of the trust, the issue arises whether or not the investment advisor is acting dishonestly.

The test for dishonesty is therefore a level of risk which the court considers to be too great. Therefore, an accessory may be liable where the risk taken, for example in respect of an interest rate swap, is done in furtherance of a contractual obligation to invest property and manage its level of risk. The court might consider that risk to be too great. Whereas the market might consider a plain interest rate swap to be standard practice and even advisable in many circumstances.

4.045 Therefore, the role of a derivatives advisor is problematic. In terms of transactions such as that in *Dharmala*[74] where the losses generated are very large in cash terms, it will appear *ex post facto* that the risk taken could have been unacceptable. This is particularly so where the derivative is being used as part of a portfolio investment strategy but then generates a loss which is large in terms of the total size of the portfolio, or which is disproportionate to the losses generated by the other assets making up the portfolio.

On the basis that it is the court's decision on the level of risk that counts, it is therefore difficult to counsel an advisor as to the approach to be taken to the investment of trust property. It is not a failure to ascertain whether or not the investment is in breach of trust which is decisive of the matter, but rather whether or not the *level of risk* assumed is in breach of duty. "[H]onesty is an objective standard". Therefore it is for the court to measure the level of risk and, consequently, the honesty of the third party. The outcome would seem to depend upon "the circumstances known to the third party at the time". However, recklessness as to the ability of the trust to invest must similarly be a factor to be taken into account in deciding on the honesty of the third party investment manager.

Knowing receipt

4.046 In contradistinction to dishonest assistance, knowing receipt requires that there have been some receipt of property, whether cash or non-cash assets, which has been paid away in breach of duty. Where a person receives trust property in the knowledge that that property as been passed in breach of fiduciary duty, the recipient will be personally liable to account to the trust for the value of the property passed away.[75] It is a defence to demonstrate the receipt was authorised under the terms of the trust or that the recipient has lawfully changed his position in reliance on the receipt of the property.[76]

Whether or not there has been receipt will generally be decided in accordance with the rules for tracing claims.[77] In the decision of Millett J. in *Agip v. Jackson*,[78] his lordship held that:

". . . there is receipt of trust property when a company's funds are misapplied by any person whose fiduciary position gave him control of them or enabled him to misapply them."

---

[74] [1996] C.L.C. 518.
[75] *per* Scott L.J. in *Polly Peck International v. Nadir (No. 2)* [1992] 3 All E.R. 769.
[76] *El Ajou v. Dollar Land Holdings* [1993] B.C.L.C. 735.
[77] *El Ajou v. Dollar Land Holdings* [1993] B.C.L.C. 735.
[78] [1989] 3 W.L.R. 1367 at 1389.

The categories of knowledge applicable in this context are those set out by Peter Gibson J. in *Baden v. Société Générale*[79] as follows:

(a) actual knowledge;

(b) wilfully shutting one's eyes to the obvious;

(c) wilfully and recklessly failing to make inquiries which an honest person would have made;

(d) knowledge of circumstances which would indicate the facts to an honest and reasonable man;

(e) knowledge of circumstances which would put an honest and reasonable man on inquiry.

4.047 As Scott LJ held in *Polly Peck*,[80] these categories are not to be taken as rigid rules and "one category may merge imperceptibly into another". Indeed, the fourth and fifth categories are the most interesting given that they are potentially the broadest. The first three categories of knowledge are taken to indicate actual knowledge of the circumstances. The actual knowledge categories encompass situations in which the defendant knew the material facts, regardless of whether he tried to ignore them. The last two are indicators of constructive notice.[81]

The case of *Polly Peck*[82] concerned a claim brought by the administrators of the plaintiff company against the Central Bank of Northern Cyprus. It was alleged that the Central Bank had exchanged the sterling amounts for Turkish lire either with actual knowledge of fraud on the plaintiff company or in circumstances in which the Central Bank out to have put on inquiry as to the source of those funds. As such, it was said on behalf of the plaintiff that the Central Bank had been the knowing recipient of the funds taken from it in breach of the director's fiduciary duty, when the money had been under the control of the Central Bank, and that the Central Bank was therefore liable to account as a constructive trustee for those sums which had passed through its hands.

The Court of Appeal held that there was no requirement to prove a fraudulent misapplication of funds to found a claim on knowing receipt. It was enough to demonstrate that the recipient had had the requisite knowledge both that the funds were trust funds and that they were being misapplied. In deciding whether or not the Central Bank ought to have been suspicious, Scott L.J. preferred to approach the matter from the point of view of the "honest and reasonable banker"[83] although he did express some reservations that this should not be considered to be the only applicable test in this context.[84] The only available defences against a claim for knowing receipt are bona fide purchaser for value without notice,[85] change of position,[86] or (potentially) passing on.[87]

---

[79] [1993] 1 W.L.R. 509.

[80] *per* Scott LJ in *Polly Peck International v. Nadir (No. 2)* [1992] 3 All E.R. 769.

[81] *per* Millett J. in *Agip v. Jackson* [1989] 3 W.L.R. 1367 at 1389.

[82] *Polly Peck International v. Nadir (No. 2)* [1992] 3 All E.R. 769.

[83] *op cit.* at 778–780.

[84] It does appear however, that the reasonableness of the recipient's belief falls to be judged from the perspective of the recipient itself.

[85] *Westdeutsche Landesbank Girozentrale v. Islington LBC* [1996] A.C. 669.

[86] *Lipkin Gorman v. Karpnale* [1991] 2 A.C. 548, considered above.

[87] *Kleinwort Benson v. Birmingham C.C.* [1996] 4 All E.R. 733, considered above.

Mispredictions

4.048 The process of selling financial derivatives is necessarily bound up with making predictions as to future market movements. Both counterparties will have a view as to the indicators of one market or another. In the structuring of speculative derivatives products both buyer and seller will be taking positions based on their expectations of future market movements. Where the buyer is acquiring a hedge for some identified market risk, the seller will have a view on likely market movements which will inform the decision as to the pricing of that hedge. Similarly, the buyer will have an understanding of the risk which makes the hedge desirable in the first place. In both speculative and hedging situations the seller will rely on materials generated by its economists and market analysts in deciding the appropriate spread to be built into the pricing structure. The more complicated the product and the less expert the buyer, the more likely it is that the seller will communicate some of this analysis to the buyer. Frequently, market analysis will operate as an inducement to the buyer to acquire the structure. As considered above, this may give rise to tortious liability if the materials are found to constitute a representation rather than a mere statement of opinion. Alternatively, the materials may be found to form a contractual inducement or a material term. In any event, the marketing materials will form a prediction as to future market movements. In *Dharmala*[88] it was held that such materials would not found any contractual or tortious liability where the buyer would be expected to form its own opinion of those materials and their statements of opinion.

In considering the suitability of products, and the potentially available remedies, a further question arises as to liability for "mispredictions" in restitution. There are two possible issues in that context: first, where there has been a misprediction which would lead to an unjust enrichment and, second, a claim arising out of estoppel.

In the context of unjust enrichment a misprediction would be analysed as a misjudgment as to material events impacting on the financial derivative which were to happen in the future. The case of *Barder v. Caluori*[89] deals with the potential availability of restitution in this situation. In that case a wife killed her children and herself in destroying the home which was to have been passed to her former husband as part of their divorce settlement. As part of the divorce settlement, a value had been arrived at for the value of the property. The question arose whether there was a remedy based on restitution available for misprediction of the value and condition of property in these circumstances. Liability in that case would not be imposed. Birks' general view is based on the principle that a claim for restitution cannot be founded on a misprediction. However, he refined the general principle such that it applies strictly in cases of mistake.[90]

4.049 It would appear that where the misprediction arises in the situation where an advisor specifies the circumstances in which it is anticipated that certain events will take place, liability might well be imposed. Birks suggests in that context that, while an action based on failure of consideration is more likely, the claim would be a viable one if it were founded on failure of basis.[91] A failure of basis is a restitutionary action based on the assertion that the very basis of the parties'

---

[88] [1996] C.L.C. 518.
[89] [1988] A.C. 20.
[90] Birks, *Introduction to the Law of Restitution*, p. 451.
[91] Birks, p. 219.

agreement has failed, such that it should be unwound and value restored to each counterparty. As Birks suggests, this restriction on action to failure of basis rather than a general action for failure of consideration is important "[o]therwise it would be difficult to explain to anyone why restitution should not always follow when any risk turns out badly".[92]

From the perspective of a credit derivative it is the uncertainty of future movement in credit worth that forms the rationale for the entire transaction. That much has already been said, whether seeking speculative gain or prudent risk management. There are two potential categories of issue: resultant loss caused by unanticipated movements in the reference entity's credit ("*failure of model*") and loss caused by a reckless level of risk being taken by the buyer on the advice of the seller ("*suitability failure*").[93] In the context of "failure of model" the allocation of risks lies with the advisor in seeking to match market volatility with the forecasts and assessments set out in the pricing model. Failure to anticipate all of the resultant movements may, of course, stem straightforwardly from negligence and thereby be actionable in tort. The issue would then arise as to the foreseeability of the loss actually suffered. Alternatively, the buyer could seek restitution on the ground of a failure of basis: that is seeking recovery for loss caused by the movement of markets in a way which the parties had not expected. In reference to options based on credit, for example, it would be advantageous to the commercial parties to specify a maximum volatility which they anticipate, such that excess volatility (outside their expectations or common intentions) would be discounted. It is submitted that volatility outwith those boundaries would give rise to a claim founded on failure of basis.

4.050   The claim based on "suitability failure" would arise where the risk which the buyer sought to manage was not met by the return made by the product bought. For example, the use of a credit swap which did not pay an interest rate to the buyer equivalent to the size of risk inherent in its existing debt portfolio (a rate equal to x), but rather one which contained an element of speculation (thus specifying a rate equal to $x + y$). The element that equalled y would be unnecessary for the purposes of debt management. The factor to be proved by the buyer claiming suitability failure would be that the element y constituted an unsuitable addition of risk which went beyond the basis upon which the transaction was created. It may be that the element y arises from market disruption which the parties had not foreseen but which was not covered by the contract. Alternatively, y might be an element which was knowingly added to the transaction but which constituted an unacceptable increase in the risk incumbent on the buyer.[94]

Restitution on a ground similar to this was illustrated in *Muschinski v. Dodds*.[95] That appeal concerned a joint venture between a man and a woman to build a house on a plot of land. The woman was to provide the money for the purchase. The man was to provide some value by dint of his work on the property. He would also put forward some money to the project when his divorce was settled. The venture failed

---

[92] Birks, p. 451.

[93] At this level there is a potential claim, as considered above with reference to reckless risk-taking.

[94] It was this latter, factual category which founded Proctor and Gamble's claim against Bankers Trust in relation to a claim for a loss of approximately U.S. \$160 million caused by the selling of "high octane swaps" for the corporate party's debt management which had an in-built exposure to speculative movements in the underlying markets. The corporate party brought the action on the basis of the bank's allegedly negligent advice in selling the product without recognising its unsuitability both for the purpose and the particular buyer.

[95] (1986) 60 A.L.J.R. 55.

when planning permission for construction on the site was refused. The ensuing strain brought an end to the joint venturers' personal relationship. The majority saw the case as one of failure of basis. The dissenting judges (Brennan and Dawson JJ.) considered the case to be one of constructive trust in which property should be distributed according to the agreed shares between the parties. The former approach is based on the restitutionary response to the change of anticipated circumstances.

On failure of basis, in the High Court of Australia in *Muschinski v. Dodds*[96] Deane J. held that:

> "The circumstances giving rise to the operation of the principle were broadly identified by Lord Cairns, L.C., speaking for the Court of Appeal in Chancery, in *Atwood v. Maude*[97]: where 'the case is one in which, using the words of Lord Cottenham in *Hirst v. Tolson*[98] a payment has been made by anticipation of something afterwards to be enjoyed [and] where . . . circumstances arise so that the future enjoyment is denied.'[99] Those circumstances can be more precisely defined by saying that *the principle operates in a case where the substratum of a joint relationship or endeavour is removed without attributable blame* and where the benefit of money or other property contributed by one party on the basis and for the purposes of the relationship or endeavour would otherwise be enjoyed by the other party in the circumstances on which it was not specifically intended or specially provided that the other party should enjoy it. The content of the principle is that, in such a case, equity will not permit that other party to assert or retain the benefit of the relevant property to the extent that it would be unconscionable for him to do so."[1]

4.051 It is interesting to note that the principle is stated to be without attributable blame, whereas its application in the financial context is as likely to be in cases where the contention is based on the fault of the seller rather than redressing the impact on the buyer. However, it is suggested that where the financial institution realises a substantial profit under the transaction, by analogy that profit would be restored to the buyer where it would be unconscionable to retain it. In accordance with the discussion above, that unsuitability should be considered to be an unjust factor, it is submitted that the better ground for this approach in commercial cases would be where the product created by the seller is unsuitable for the purpose desired by the buyer and communicated to the seller, that unsuitability should give rise to a restitutionary remedy.

There is no proprietary claim against a dishonest assistant[2]; *i.e.* one who does not receive trust property.[3] Therefore, a personal liability to account as a constructive trustee would attach to a financial institution, in connection with a misprediction that was held to be "dishonest", which arranges or brokers a derivatives product

---

[96] (1986) 60 A.L.J.R. 55 at 67.
[97] (1868) 3 Ch.App. 369 at 375.
[98] (1850) 2 Mac. & G. 134; 42 E.R. 52.
[99] In *Atwood* the court allowed an order for repayment of a proportionate part of premium where the plaintiff had paid towards the establishment of a partnership which was then dissolved without the fault of either partner.
[1] (1986) 60 A.L.J.R. 55 at 67.
[2] Considered above, para. 4.042.
[3] Hanbury and Martin *Modern Equity* (13th ed., Sweet & Maxwell, 1993), p. 666; Oakley (1995) 54 C.L.J. 377, 383; Hudson (1999), p. 410 *et seq.*

without acquiring any of the property. Thus, in the context of a credit derivatives or some warrant issues or swaps embedded in bond issues, there would be liability on the broker for taking "reckless risks" even where that person does not receive any of the underlying property.[4]

The nature of that restitutionary response is considered in more detail above, para. 4.038 in connection with the availability of proprietary remedies.

Undue influence

4.052 The issue of "suitability" clearly imports notions of unconscionable behaviour on the part of the seller of financial derivatives. As has been considered, the relationship of banker and client will not necessarily import a fiduciary relationship, although there are a number of situations in which a fiduciary relationship will arise: where the bank induces business by agreeing to become financial advisor,[5] where the bank advises a customer to enter into a transaction,[6] and where the advises a person to enter into a transaction which is to their financial disadvantage without ensuring that they have taken independent advice.[7]

In the case of derivatives, liability potentially arises for advice given to a client with respect to selling financial derivatives. Where the client is reliant on the expertise of the advisor, there is a liability for the advisor not to exert undue influence over that client by selling them products which are to their financial detriment in situations where they have reposed trust in the advisor. The application of this principle in the recent mortgage cases has revolved around the relationship of "special tenderness" between husband and wife in securing borrowings over the family home. In those circumstances, the bank has been held to have a responsibility to ensure that the spouse who is acting to their financial disadvantage (as surety or co-mortgagor) must have received independent advice.

There is a different relationship between parties in the OTC derivatives market. The clients are sophisticated corporate entities or financial institutions, rather than ordinary members of the public.[8] Therefore, the clients are expected to be able to procure their own legal and accountancy advice. The advice given by the seller of the derivative is likely to be the only advice received by the buyer; either because the seller is the "house bank" to the buyer or is a specialist in the particular product sold. In either case, the client can properly rely on the advice that is given to them.[9]

---

[4] This liability is different from the liability of a trustee in a eurobond transaction, for example: see Tennekoon, *Legal Aspect of International Finance* (Butterworths, 1992).

[5] *Woods v. Martins Bank Ltd* [1959] 1 Q.B. 55; *Standard Investments Ltd v. Canadian Imperial Bank of Commerce* (1985) 22 D.L.R. (4th) 410.

[6] *Lloyds Bank v. Bundy* [1975] Q.B. 326; *Royal Bank of Canada v. Hinds* (1978) 88 D.L.R. (3rd) 428.

[7] *National Westminster Bank plc v. Morgan* [1985] A.C. 686; *Barclay's Bank v. O'Brien* [1993] 3 W.L.R. 786; *CIBC v. Pitt* [1993] 3 W.L.R. 786.

[8] With the exception of some occasional retail business done with the private clients of investment banks.

[9] There is an overlap here with the tort of misstatement (and the principle in *Hedley Byrne v. Heller*) considered in para. 4.028. However, tortious remedies will not extend claims *in rem* where the plaintiff is seeking to recovery specific property provided as part of the transaction. This desire for a proprietary claim may arise in respect of a physically-settled transaction or a transaction in which securities are provided as a premium or fixed rate payment, or where compound interest is sought in respect of cash-settled transactions.

4.053 The finding of undue influence should, it is suggested, provide a further unjust factor to found a claim in restitution.[10] Where the seller profits from some unconscionable pressure applied to the client, those profits would constitute an unjust enrichment at the expense of the buyer, remediable by some restitutionary response. The appropriate response to remedy the enrichment would be a proprietary claim to recover the full amount of gain made and the full, potential loss to the buyer connected with the seller's use of the property.

It is submitted that another possible claim under the umbrella of suitability would arise where there was some undue influence on this model. The appropriate form of remedy would be the imposition of a constructive trust in line with the unconscionable nature of the transaction. Whether there is sufficient knowledge in the seller may not be apparent from the assertion as to whether or not the product sold was considered to be suitable at the time when it was sold. It is possible that the creation of a product which negligently exposed the buyer to an unforeseen risk, would be an unsuitable product. Where the seller had advised the use of that structure and had prepared a pricing model and a risk model in connection with the transaction, it is submitted that that would be sufficient to constitute undue influence in circumstances where the client would naturally rely on the advice given to it by the seller.

4.054 As considered with reference to the *Dharmala* case above,[11] the issue of undue influence may also turn on the relationship between the buyer and the seller. In circumstances where the buyer would typically rely on the seller for advice without recourse to any other expert, perhaps as its house bank which provided all its finance requirements, and where the client has no particular financial expertise of its own, the seller must be particularly careful in marketing complex products. In *Dharmala* itself, DSS argued that BT owed it a duty to suggest more straightforward products which would have achieved its objectives. Mance J. found that DSS had been involved in and eager for the particular product created. However, where a more risky and complex product is foisted on the buyer by the seller, in circumstances where vanilla, less risky products would have achieved the same goals, it is suggested that the seller is at risk of a claim for undue influence brought by the buyer.

A claim for undue influence, if successful, permits the victim to set aside the transaction which has been created as a result of that undue influence.[12] This action is categorised as a form of "constructive fraud".[13] The victim will be able to set aside a transaction on the basis that there has been some form of undue influence but not as a means of protecting itself from the result of its own folly or failure to act.[14] Furthermore, the victim will not be able to establish undue influence simply

---

[10] While this appears doctrinally heretical, given that undue influence is an equitable doctrine, the purpose of undue influence appears straightforwardly to be one in which the victim of that influence recovers value unjustly acquired by the defendant. The exception to this general rule might be the doctrine set out in *Barclays Bank v. O'Brien* whereby a mortgagee who does not necessarily have to carry out the undue influence either itself or through an agent, may be held to have had constructive notice of it, thus being bound. However, it would appear that this too is a form of unjust enrichment in the hands of the mortgagee if that mortgagee is entitled to take possession of its security: see Hudson, *Principles of Equity and Trusts* (Cavendish, 1999), Chap. 18.

[11] para. 4.031.

[12] *Allcard v. Skinner* (1887) 36 Ch.D. 145; *National Westminster Bank v. Morgan* [1985] A.C. 686; *Barclays Bank v. O'Brien* [1994] 1 A.C. 180; *TSB Bank v. Camfield* [1995] 1 All E.R. 951.

[13] See *Snell's Equity* (29th ed., Sweet & Maxwell, 1990), p. 550.

[14] *Tufton v. Sperni* [1952] 2 T.L.R. 516.

because there is inequality of bargaining power between transacting parties; rather, the buyer must show some undue influence over and above that.[15]

In *Barclays Bank v. O'Brien*[16] Lord Browne-Wilkinson identified two forms of undue influence: actual undue influence[17] (where there has been demonstrable undue influence practised on the victim) and two categories of presumed undue influence.[18] The forms of presumed undue influence included relationships where there would be reliance by one party on another necessarily, such as the relationship between doctor and patient or solicitor and client, and also where there was a relationship of trust and confidence between the parties.[19] It is contended that such categories of presumed undue influence would obtain in many circumstances between an experienced seller and an inexperienced buyer of financial derivatives, where the seller induces the buyer to execute a particular form of transaction.

In general circumstances, the relationship of banker and customer will not give rise to a fiduciary relationship[20] although, it is suggested, there are circumstances in which the advising seller so inter-meddles with the affairs and risk management objectives of the buyer that the seller must come to occupy a fiduciary relationship in respect of its counterparty and client.[21]

4.055   The role of the equitable doctrines of undue influence, constructive trusts to give effect to the settlor's intentions and of common intention constructive trusts, were not issues raised by Lord Browne-Wilkinson in *Islington*.[22] In *Barclays Bank v. O'Brien*[23] the House of Lords established the need to take independent advice. The issue arises then: what advice will dispel the undue influence? Further to *Crédit Lyonnais v. Burch*,[24] it is not clear whether there is the possibility of undue influence in OTC derivatives market or whether these multinational organisations are simply arm's length parties. The decision in *O'Brien*[25] as to the application of the principle of undue influence in the provision of guarantees in respect of domestic mortgages, could be extended to cases of commercial guarantees or collateral agreements which are obtained in respect of derivatives transactions. It is possible to argue that *O'Brien*[26] is a decision which is also about risk allocation. In compiling a test for equity in commercial situations, a test of "commercially

---

[15] *National Westminster Bank v. Morgan* [1985] A.C. 686; although it is perhaps unclear how this doctrine is to be applied in the wake of *O'Brien*.

[16] [1994] 1 A.C. 180.

[17] See also *Williams v. Bayley* (1866) L.R. 1 H.L. 200; *Bank of Montreal v. Stuart* [1911] A.C. 120; *Re Craig* [1971] Ch. 95.

[18] See also *Allcard v. Skinner* (1887) 36 Ch.D. 145; *Tufton v. Sperni* [1952] 2 T.L.R. 516.

[19] On trust and confidence see also *Goldsworthy v. Brickell* [1987] Ch 378 at 401 *per* Nourse L.J. "the party in whom [confidence] is reposed, either because he is or has become an adviser of the other or because he is or has become entrusted with the management of his affairs . . .".

[20] *National Westminster Bank v. Morgan* [1985] A.C. 686.

[21] *Lloyds Bank v. Bundy* [1975] Q.B. 326, a decision which concerned advice given by a bank to an old man who relied entirely on the advice of the bank's manager: *cf. National Westminster Bank v. Morgan* [1985] A.C. 686.

[22] [1996] A.C. 669.

[23] [1994] 1 A.C. 180; [1993] 3 W.L.R. 786.

[24] [1997] 1 All E.R. 144. See also *Barclays Bank v. O'Brien* [1994] 1 A.C. 180; *CIBC Mortgages v. Pitt* [1994] 1 A.C. 200; *Massey v. Midland Bank* [1995] 1 All E.R. 929; *Midland Bank v. Serter* [1995] 1 All E.R. 929; *Bank of Boroda v. Reyerel* [1995] 2 F.L.R. 376; *Banco Exterior Internacional v. Mann* [1995] 1 All E.R. 936; *Halifax Mortgage Services Ltd. v. Stepsky* [1996] Ch. 1; [1995] 4 All E.R. 656; *Banco Exterior International SA v. Thomas* [1997] 1 W.L.R. 221; [1997] 1 All E.R. 46; *Barclays Bank v. Thomson* [1997] 4 All E.R. 816.

[25] [1994] 1 A.C. 180; [1993] 3 W.L.R. 786.

[26] [1994] 1 A.C. 180; [1993] 3 W.L.R. 786.

acceptable conduct" may be better than "unconscionable conduct". As with *Tan*,[27] there would be an establishment of an objective standard of probity.

The issue is this: if equity will respond to a fiduciary who takes unacceptable levels of risk with the trust fund, what is it that will lead to a person being made a fiduciary? In commercial cases there are a number of established examples of bankers in relation to their clients. With reference to more sophisticated corporate clients, the test must revolve some notion of *suitability*. That is, suitability of advice given and suitability of the financial product used in any given situation. In the context of derivatives, this standard of suitability is more likely to be of greater importance than with reference to established and comparatively risk-controlled forms of product (such as share issues or bond issues). In arranging a bespoke derivative facility, the client is peculiarly in the hands of the advising institution. Where that institution takes unacceptable risks, that should be considered to be a breach of the duty owed to the client.

4.056 Similarly, any analysis of commercial law and the availability of proprietary claims in equity will have to confront the *Re Goldcorp*[28] issue as to whether or not there is identifiable property to be held subject to the trust. There, despite a representation to the contrary in the detail of the contractual agreements, there could not be a proprietary right in any property held by the other contracting party. This approach would appear to be preferable from the point of view of avoiding systemic risk because all losses are netted rather than allowing some unsecured creditors to escape with proprietary rights and thus leaving less in the pot for the remainder of the creditors.

One issue which arises in this context is whether a test for suitability would give rise to a claim in restitution for a wrong committed by the bank or to a claim in restitution based on a personal claim in restitution (money had and received) or a proprietary claim in equity. The former claim, related to the commission for a wrong, would arise under negligence, breach of contract or negligent misstatement. The latter claims are the business of the decisions in *Westdeutsche Landesbank v. Islington*.[29]

Too little knowledge is the dangerous thing

4.057 In the information age, it is ironic that the most hi-tech industry in the global trading village has generated scandal, deceit and loss by means of a lack of communicated information. Derivatives-related scandals at institutions like Barings and Kidder Peabody have arisen due to a lack of information being supplied to senior management, and inertia among senior management to seek more information from traders who were turning in extraordinarily large profits in unlikely markets. The mis-selling of derivatives to end-users arose out of a lack of suitable information being supplied to the end-user as to the nature and risks of the product. The second context of information shortcomings about derivatives arises in relation to the information that is available to shareholders about the derivatives strategies used and also about the basis on which that business is conducted.

Derivatives are not necessarily dangerous. It is a lack of information and a lack of knowledge that are the dangerous things. Regulation of derivatives needs to be orientated around the user of the product and also around the assets which that

---

[27] *Royal Brunei Airlines v. Tan* [1995] 2 A.C. 378; [1995] 3 W.L.R. 64.
[28] [1995] 1 A.C. 74.
[29] [1996] A.C. 669.

end-user ought to be able to put at risk in entering into those products. Private law remedies ought to reflect the need for informed shareholders and informed management to control the use, and concomitant abuse, of products by their organisations. The litmus test, it is suggested, ought to be a measurement of the suitability of the product for the context in which it is to be used. In relation to claims based on consent, wrongs or unjust enrichment, that is the most consistent benchmark for the availability of a remedy.

Chapter 5

Fair Value Accounting for Credit Derivatives*

by Peter Cossey and Jonathan Davies

5.001 Financial instruments continues to pose problems for institutions in respect of determining their correct value for accounting purposes. The main issue is a general lack of specific accounting guidance on financial instruments issued by Accounting bodies around the world. The primary reason for this is the dynamic nature of the market and products within this. The lack of specific guidance often causes confusion over where "mark to market value" ("MTM"), "current value", "fair value" or other values should be used and how each is defined or determined. This issue is compounded when a specific instrument such as a credit derivative is not included within the scope of guidance that may be relevant. Most issued guidance on financial instruments refers to "fair value" as the appropriate value for accounting purposes and as such is the focus of this chapter. This chapter attempts to assist the reader in determining:

- what is Fair Value?
- the application of Fair Value principles to Credit Derivatives;
- the calulation of Fair Value

Part I: What is Fair Value?

Background

5.002 No definitive finalised guidance has been issued in the United Kingdom, for the calculation of fair value for financial instruments for inclusion in financial statements. However, there are a number of places which include reference to fair value. The formal documentation which has been issued which is applicable, and mandatory for all companies is Financial Reporting Standard 5 "Reporting the substance of transactions". However, this gives only broad definitions, and excludes financial instruments unless linked to an overall transaction. More detailed guidance is given in the British Banker's Association's "Statement of Recommended Acounting Practice ("SORP") on Derivatives" and "SORP on Securities, but these are applicable only for banks, and otherwise represent only best practice. Whilst the SORP on securities does not strictly refer to credit derivatives it's also considered relevant guidance.

---

* This is an extract from the forthcoming publication by PricewaterhouseCoopers on credit deriviatives to be published late 1999.

In addition, the International Accounting Standards Committee ("IASC") issued a standard, International Accounting Standard 39 ("IAS 39") in 1998 on the recognition and measurement of financial instruments, and the United Kingdom's Accounting Standards Board ("ASB") in 1996 issued in discussion paper on accounting for financial instruments. The U.S.'s Financial Accounting Standard Board ("FASB") also has a long-term project to consider these issues, and recently release Financial Accounting Standard 133 "Accounting for Deriviative Instruments and Hedging Activities" on this subject. Note that the implementation date for FASB 133 has recently been deferred and will now be effective for periods beginning after June 15, 2000. All three standard setters are considering if all financial instruments should be measured at fair value and whether specifice rules would apply to financial instrument which serve as a hedge.

The ASB discussion paper currently reflects best practice, due to the absence of formal mandatory statements in this area. This is therefore not mandatory. The IASC standard and the FASB standard are also considered relevant.

A paper has also been released by the Group of Thirty ("G30") on "Derivatives: practices and principles". The recommendations, which the Steering Committee endorsed unanimously, were formulated by the Working Group—a diverse cross-section of end-users, dealers, academics, accountants, and lawyers involved in derivatives. Input also came from a detailed Survey of Industry Practice among 80 dealers and 72 end-users worldwide, involving both questionaaires and in-depth interviews. Appendix I contains a working paper on valuaton including recommendations.

Fair value definitions

United Kingdom

5.003 *U.K. accounting standard—Financial Reporting Standard 5 "Reporting the substance of transactions" (FRS 5)*
The fair value of a financial asset or financial liability is the amount at which it could be exchanged in an arm's length transaction between informed and willing parties, other than in a forced or liquidation sale.

British Banker's Association ("BBA") Statement of Recommended Accounting Practice ("SORP") on Derivatives
"Fair Value" is the amount at which a derivative could be exchanged in an arm's length transaction between informed and willing parties, other than in a forced or liquidation sale.

BBA SORP on securities
This SORP refers to "market price" as the value which could, with reasonable certainty, have been realised in cash. It refers to some appropriate and publicly ascertainable quoted price. The SORP makes further comment that there should not be premature recognition of profit. Particular care is needed in the case of illiquid securities, or where holdings are of a larger than normal market size, or in respect of certain exceptional dealing positions.

Excerpts from the ASB's Discussion paper on Financial Instruments
The ASB's discussion paper refers to current value rather than fair value. It defines
the current value of an instrument as "the amount at which an instrument could be
exchanged in an arm's length transaction between informed and willing parties,
other than in a forced or liquidation sale". This seems to indicate that the terms
"current value" and " fair value" are interchangeable.

The discussion paper expands on "current value" by discussing different methods
of calculating it, such as:

(a) quoted market prices, where the instrument is traded

(b) where quoted market prices are not available, quoted prices for similar
instruments may be used with appropriate adjustments to reflect any
differences

(c) in the absence of a market price, a quote may be obtainable from a broker
or the counterparty. Alternatively, where the entity regularly acquires or
originates similar instruments, current prices for those similar instruments may be used

(d) valuation techniques, including discounted cash flow analysis and option
pricing models (such as the Black-Scholes model and binomial models).
Such models require certain assumptions to be made (*e.g.* the use of the
Black-Scholes option pricing model involves the assumption of a constant
volatility for which a reasonable estimate is required).

5.004   The ASB commented in the paper that it does not believe that it should
prescribe detailed rules on how fair value should be estimated: this is a matter that
is best determined by reporting entities and their auditors. The ASB stated that it
wanted to promulgate the following broad principles:

- ... where a quoted price is available, it should be used ... Where
more than one quoted price is available, the price in the most active
market for transactions of the relevant size should be used.

- otherwise the entity should estimate current value based on either the
quoted price of a similar instrument (adjusted to take account of the
differences) or valuation techniques such as discounted cash flow
analysis and accepted option pricing models. The rate used to
discount future cash flows should be a risk-adjusted rate. Where
practicable the prevailing market rate of interest for an instrument
with substantially the same terms and characteristics (including
remaining term, currency, time for which the interest rate is fixed,
prepayment risk and, for an asset, creditworthiness of the debtor).
Alternatively, an entity may discount at a rate that reflects only some
of these factors and make a separate adjustment to reflect the others
(particularly changes in the creditworthiness of a debtor). Changes in
the entity's own creditworthiness should not be taken into account.

International

5.005 *IAS 39 "Financial Instruments: Recognition and Measurement"*
Fair value is the amount for which an asset could be exchanged, or a liability settled, between knowledgeable, willing parties in an arm's length transaction.

G30 "Derivatives: practices and principles"
Marking to market is the only valuation technique that correctly reflects the current value of derivatives cash flows. Dealers' derivatives portfolios of dealers should be valued based on mid-market levels less specific adjustments, or on appropriate bid or offer levels. Mid-market valuation adjustments should allow for expected future costs such as unearned credit spread, close-out costs, investing and funding costs, and administrative costs.

United States

5.006 *U.S. accounting standards—Financial Accounting Standard 133 (FAS 133)— "Accounting for Derivative Instruments and Hedging Activities"*
The basic definition laid down by the standard is that the amount at which an asset (liability) could be bought (incurred) or sold (settled) in a current transaction between willing parties, that is, other than in a forced or liquidation sale.

The standard also laid down detailed guidance similar to that given by the ASB's discussion paper.

The above summary shows that U.K., U.S. and International GAAP use similar definitions. In particular they refer in the detailed text to the assumption that the business is a going concern and the price that would be agreed by:

- knowledgeable and

- willing counterparties

- who are acting in an arm's length transaction (*i.e.* as if independent of each other).

Part II: Application of the Guidance

5.007 The first step in calculating the fair value of a financial instrument is to establish a MTM value. To calculate the MTM value a number of variables are input into a model. These may include static data for the trade, the applicable discount rate, foreign exchange, credit spreads and volatility measures. Discount rates and credit spreads are commented on below.

Various discount factors are used such as LIBOR, treasury rates cost of funding or some other rate of return. Management should assess the most appropriate rate to use.

Quotes for credit spreads may be obtained from brokers or other market participants. Where there are no or very few quotes available it may be necessary to calculate the credit spread using more data. For example, default and recovery rates would be required as data inputs whereas these inputs are implicit in freely available credit spreads. Sometimes, more sophisticated models are required for this process and this adds further subjectivity and variability into the ultimate MTM value.

Quotes are obtained from the market using bid/offer prices. This in itself can create issues in choosing whether the "bid", "offer" or "mid-market" rate is most appropriate. One key determinant is whether that position is being held within a hedged book or in a book taking proprietary or open positions, *i.e.* taking on outright risk. For open positions they should be marked to the cost of closing out those positions as this reflect the amount which the derivative could be exchanged in an arms length transaction as specified in guidance discussed earlier. This would be the "bid" for long positions (where an asset is held) and the "offer" for short positions (where the asset has been sold and needs to be purchased at a later date to settle the trade).

For example, where a bank holds an equity position this would be marked to the rate applicable to sell the equity, *i.e.* to close out that position. As a third party would need to purchase the equities from the company the "bid" rate would appropriate. This approach reduces any P&L on the trade by the extent of the bid/offer differential. This is because the equity would have been purchased at the offer rate. For example, if the offer rate were $1.05, 1m shares would cost $1.05m to purchase. By marking these equities to a bid of $1, the market value of the position becomes $1m, an immediate unrealised loss of $50,000. This is the bid/offer differential of 5 cents applied to the holding of 1m shares. This approach is very prudent and reduces profit more when bid/offer differentials are large. If in the above example the differential was 20 cents then the immediate unrealised loss would be $200,000. Where a book is hedged and does not retain any material market risk then all positions are usually marked at the same rate, usually mid-market (the average of the bid and other quotes). This reflects the fact that the book will have very low residual risk, as any movement in one position should be largely offset by an opposite movement in the other. The degree of residual risk is that is acceptable for this treatment should be determined and agreed by management.

5.008 Once the MTM is established a number of subsequent considerations are required and where appropriate provisions set up against the MTM in order to obtain an appropriate fair value. These considerations are summarised below:

(a) *A specific instrument liquidity provision ("SILP")*. A SILP arises when an instrument is not sufficiently traded such that the price required to buy or sell may be different to that quoted. Many institutions will argue that liquidity is implicit in bid/offer spreads. Whilst this is generally true there may be situations whereby trades cannot be readily transacted at current bid or offer quotes and a resultant loss may occur. Where mid rates are used, a SILP's will generally be required.

(b) *A position liquidity provision ("PLP")*. This is an adjustment where the size of the position held is of such a size that the price obtained in a transaction may be different to that quoted in the market. To illustrate this, consider a very large position in a bond is held. Even though it may not represent a significant proportion of that bond issue, its sale would still be a much larger volume than is commonly traded. This may mean that the price obtained would likely be different, *i.e.* potentially less (for a sale) or more (for a purchase) than the original quotes, thus resulting in a reduced profit or increased loss.

(c) *A model provision.* This is an adjustment to represent the uncertainty of any model parameters, calibrations or workings assumptions made in designing or using the model. Where a model is used to calculate a mark to market value, then the assumptions underlying the model should be reviewed regularly to consider whether they still reflect the market, and management's understanding of the risks. An example is the cost of funding and investing cashflow mismatches at rates different from the LIBOR rate which models typically assume. Where there are discrepancies or uncertainties then management should quantify then conservatively and reflect this by virtue of a "model provision". This is likely to be higher for more sophisticted models. A reserve may be prudent where the model is new and is not proven in market conditions.

(d) *An administration provision.* This is a provision to allow for costs in relation to administering the book over a period of time in which it would be reasonable to close out all the open positions on a non fire-sale basis. This is only likely to be material for medium to long dated derivative books or books with a significant number of positions.

(e) *A counterparty provision.* This is a provision to allow for the risks that the counterparty may not fulfil its obligations. It is important to distinguish between provisions for current or future losses. Current guidance suggests it is inappropriate to provide for future losses that may occur. In this regard a counterparty provision should endeavour to reflect an "expected" loss at that point in time. This may be based on mathematical probabilities, a detailed review of individual counterparties, etc. The level of correlation between the risk being hedged and the counterparty must be assessed and provided for adequately.

(f) *An "other risks" provision.* This would cover any other risks that are specific to that book. For example, non vanilla products such as credit derivatives, exotic or highly structured trades often have unique risks for which separate provisions may need to be raised, *e.g.* political, foreign exchange, tax, hedging, legal, basis or documentary risks. Each relevant risk should be identified and an assessment made of its significance such that an appropriate provision may be determined.

In quantifying the above points it will be necessary to make estimates and assumptions. It is important to note that the use of reasonable estimates and assumptions does not necessarily undermine the reliability of the fair value calculated so long as a logical process or methodology is applied.

5.009 Often, management will set up a "general" provision against a whole book claiming this will incorporate all the above risks. There are numerous ways of determining this such as a percentage (or number of basis points) applied to the MTM or notional value of the book. Sometimes this figure is chosen on an even more arbitrary basis. A high level or broadbrush provision does not demonstrate a systematic identification and consideration of all of the relevant risks for the transactions involved and accordingly will be difficult to justify. A robust approach is to establish and apply a logical process or methodology as suggested above.

Due to the subjectivity involved, prudence and consistency period on period should be applied when determining assumptions and inputs. In less liquid markets, the use of such estimates and assumptions is often essential in calculating a fair value for financial instruments. It is also important to consider the size, importance, credit rating, relationships and stature of the bank for which fair value is being calculated. A sizeable player may have access to, or the ability to transact at better rates, bigger sizes, etc., whereas a small or lower credit related bank may find the opposite. These are all relevant factors when considering provisioning levels.

Part III: Application of Fair Value Principles to Credit Derivatives

Key characteristics of credit derivatives

5.010   There are certain general characteristics of the credit derivative product range and market of which the reader should be aware:

- Often significant spreads between bid and offer quotes, reflecting limited liquidity in the market.

- Documentation is not standardised. Although ISDA have recently released updated documentation for credit default swaps, this acts more like a template with a requirement to fill in a number of variables. As such, there is continued variability in the terms for credit default swaps and no specific ISDA documentation yet for other credit derivative products.

- Uncertainty over the definition of "Credit Events" and hence effectiveness of the product.

- A lack of accurate data exists for the variable inputs to models such as default rates, recovery rates, volatilities, correlations, etc.

- Prices vary significantly according to the counterparties selling the protection; and

- Due to a number of factors such as demand and supply and the relative inexperience of some market players etc. trades are often transacted at "off-market" prices.

Although the above matters suggest the products are akin to exotic derivatives; these products, mainly credit default swaps and credit spread options, are being traded in a way which is similar to more vanilla products such as currency swaps. As such, they often display attributes both both vanilla (generally liquid markets) and exotic (generally illiquid markets) produts. This should be borne in mind when considering the fair value and accounting treatment. Prudence should be applied whenever accounting estimates or assumptions are made.

Part IV: Calculation of Fair Value

Open positions

5.011 Here, we consider an open credit default swap position. This is where an institution has either bought or sold that credit risk and has no hedge against this position. The institution is fully explosed to market movements in the value of the credit default swap.

Structure I

Credit Default Swap

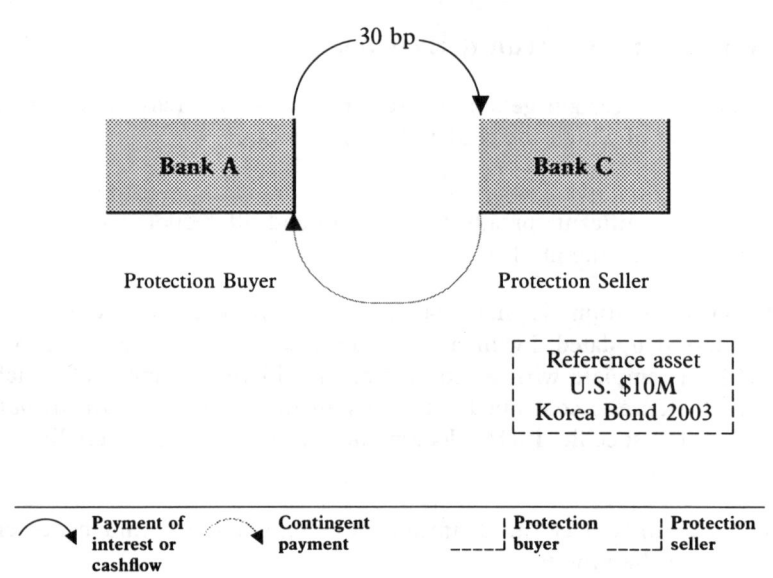

Protection Buyer   Protection Seller

Reference asset
U.S. $10M
Korea Bond 2003

| Payment of interest or cashflow | Contingent payment | Protection buyer | Protection seller |

Fair value of trade

5.012 In calculating fair value the following decision tree can be used.

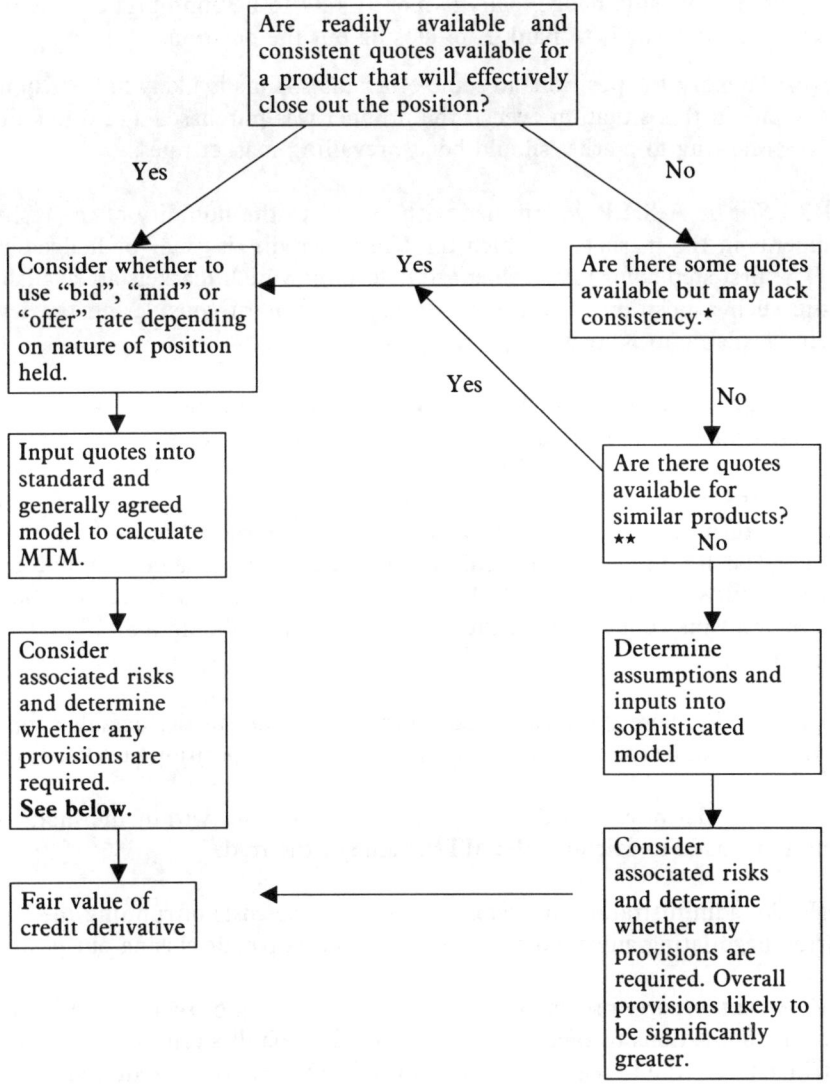

* expect a higher level of provisioning in this situation
** expect a higher level of provisioning again from*

Calculate the MTM value using the applicable credit spreads if available; the consideration of each is included below:

(a) To mark the position to mid market rate. This is more common where the institution is in a hedged position, *e.g.* a market maker.

This approach will not usually be appropriate when Bank A takes an unhedged position because Bank A will need to pay the bid rate to close out this position. This will often be substantially lower than the mid-market price, hence by marking the position at the mid-market rate, Bank

A defers crystallising the loss. It will normally be appropriate to set up higher provisions to reflect the real close out cost.

(b) To mark the position at the value of the bid or offer rate in order to value the applicable hedge. This is more likely to be appropriate, as it reflects the cost/benefit to Bank A of closing out the position.

(c) To mark the positions to some other rates. This is likely to be inappropriate in this situation even if the product was purchased at a different rate. Marking to market should be at prevailing market rates.

5.013   *Step 1:* A SILP determined with regard to the liquidity of the respective instruments in the markets in which the Korean credit risk may be hedged at that time. The first step is for management to determine which markets are available for hedging such a position. These markets are relevant in considering the level of liquidity available in Korean credit risk.

The most effective hedge is likely to be in the credit default swap market as they are similar instruments. It may also be possible to obtain a hedge in the bond, asset swap, loan or other markets. Once the relevant markets have been ascertained management should make assessment of the liquidity of the applicable instruments in each in turn. The applicable instruments are important because, for example, there may be liquidity in the credit default market in general but not for the specific default swaps referenced to Korea. Only where there is no or poor liquidity in the relevant instruments in all the markets identified should a SILP be required in this regard.

Step II: A PLP where the level of exposure of the bank to the default swap is so large that it would experience difficulty in hedging that position at current quotes.

Step III: A model provision due to errors or inaccuracies within the model or in assumptions made to calculate the MTM value of the trade.

Step IV: An administration provision to allow for the costs of running the trade to maturity, negotiating any payout of the credit derivative, or closing out positions.

Step V: A counterparty provision to reflect the possibility of Bank B not being able to meet its obligations to Bank A under the credit default swap. Management must be stringent in their regular assessment of any provision required against a counterparty due to the joint probability risk, and must consider the level of correlation between Bank B and Korea. Correlation can significantly affect the value of the transaction and as such is an essential consideration when determining counterparty provisions. From Bank B's perspective a counterparty provision is required only against the failure of Bank A meet its premium obligations.

Step VI: An "other" provision to cover further specific risks. First, a documentation provision should be considered. This is for a number of reasons, for example trades taking substantial time to be confirmed by both parties, uncertainty as to whether a credit event has actually occurred, and possibly cross-jurisdictional issues if various legal jurisdictions are involved. A basis risk provision should be considered to cover situations where the actual payout may vary from that anticipated. Any foreign exchange exposures, or coupon conversion risk, need to be quantified and appropriate provisions recognised. Political risks should be assessed along with taxation, particularly when the transaction involves more than one jurisdiction, and provided for as required. A hedging cost provision may be required where a transaction or portfolio is difficult to re-balance due to an element of imperfect hedgeability. This may be the case, for example, with digital default swaps.

A flat position

5.014 The second situation is where an institution has both bought and sold a similar credit derivative. This situation gives rise to other considerations which are explained from Bank Y's viewpoint in the example below.

Structure II

Back to Back Credit Default Swap

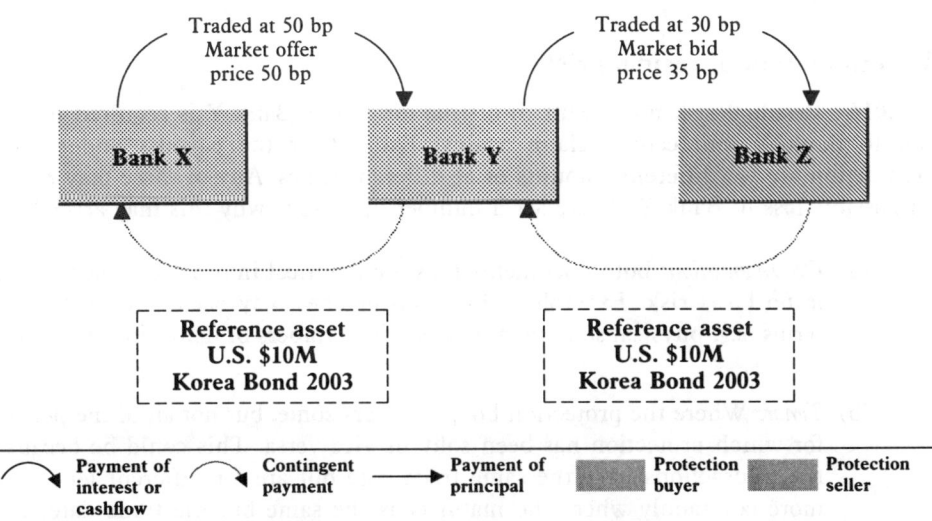

These types of transactions are common in banks which have a trading operation. Their profits or losses are primarily generated by the difference between the cost of purchasing protection and selling protection. This is known as "spread earned". In the above example the spread earned is 20 basis points being the difference between the actual prices attained by the bank, 30 basis points for purchasing and 50 basis points for selling protection.

The "close out" cost

5.015 As discussed previously, an appropriate accounting value for a derivative is the cost to close out that position. Cash instruments such as bonds can be sold and so eliminating any former risks or exposures. However, practically, credit derivative positions are closed out by purchasing or selling an offsetting transaction. This is because a credit derivative is an OTC contract and not a readily transferable asset. The nature of these products is such that it is very difficult to execute an exactly offsetting transaction that reduces all risks or exposures to nil. The institution must therefore endeavour to find a transaction that substantially reduces the risks and exposures. This creates an issue that a position may be closed out yet residual risk is retained.

The main difference in approach from an open position is that the cost to close out is the cost of an instrument or derivative that would be deemed to reduce residual risk to an acceptable, *i.e.* minimal, level. This instrument, once identified, would need to be purchased and the net cost of this purchase would be the relevant close out cost. In essence, this would involve buying an instrument or derivative at the offer rate or selling at bid.

For the transaction above the bank is technically "flat" and as such there is no requirement to purchase or sell a further instrument in order to close out this transaction. It is therefore essential to make an assessment of the residual risk inherent in this transaction to determine whether this has been reduced to an appropriate extent. The degree of residual risk that is acceptable for a position to be deemed closed out is for management to determine. In practice residual risk must be minimal.

Determination of residual risk

5.016   Residual risk may result in a situation where Bank Y is required to pay out to Bank X, but cannot claim against Bank Z or the payouts under each transaction are for different amounts or at different times. Any of these may result in possible loss to Bank Y. There are a number of reasons why this may arise:

(a) *Documentation:* both documents must be identical in order to ensure there is no basis risk. Examples where mismatches may occur are settlement terms (*e.g.* physical settlement or cash) or numbers or definitions of Credit Events.

(b) *Tenor:* Where the protection bought covers some, but not all of the period for which protection has been sold, or vice versa. This could be because the transactions have the same trade date but are for different tenors or more commonly where the maturity is the same but the trade dates are different. This often occurs where a position is taken by buying or selling protection and subsequently closed out. This is often referred to as "warehousing" credit risk.

(c) *Reference asset:* where the reference asset, or seniority of items used, is different under each trade.

(d) *Other factors:* As these are two distinct transactions with different counter-parties, the negotiation and timing of the payouts can very significantly. Often this is a logistical consequence of working out liability (if any), post default value and thus payouts, and determining when these payouts are made. In other words, the documentation may be consistent however the interpretation of the contents may vary, particularly as regards Credit Events.

Management must carefully assess the above and any other relevant basis risk between the two positions. If the degree of residual risk is considered to be unacceptable. *i.e.* greater than minimal, then the two transactions should be considered as two separate open positions and accounted for as discussed in the previous example. If management are of the opinion that there is minimal residual risk then the following approach appears appropriate.

Fair value of trade from Bank Y's viewpoint

5.017 In Structure II we assume that Bank Y has minimal residual risk retained. This is the key difference from Structure I where management attempts to ascertain the cost of transacting the other leg. As both have already been transacted at known rates (*i.e.* 50 basis points receivable and 30 basis points payable) in this situation a different valuation methodology may be appropriate.

As before, the first step is for management to determine whether to use bid/offer, mid or other rates, to apply to the known cashflows of 30 and 50 basis points, for MTM valuation purposes. The most common approaches are:

(a) To mark the position at bid/offer rates. If each position is marked at the worst side of the bid/offer spread Bank Y will report a loss on day one on both trades. This appears overly prudent if the bank has minimal residual risk given it has actually locked into a 20 basis point spread earned.

(b) To mark the position to mid-market rate or in other words use one credit curve to MTM both these positions. Using the mid-market rate, fair value for both positions would be calculated using 42.5 basis points, being the average of the 35 and 50 market bid and offer rates. This will likely record a profit on a day one which appears appropriate as this is in line with the economic substance of the transaction.

As with open positions previously discussed the following framework should be applied to determine any relevant provisions against the MTM calculated above.

Step I: A SILP determined with regard to the liquidity of the markets in which the Korean credit risk may be hedged at that time. In this example there is no requirement to transact a further position and accordingly a SILP becomes irrelevant.

Step II: A PLP where the level of exposure of the bank to the default swap is so large that it would experience difficulty in hedging that position. As per the SILP above, there is no requirement to transact a further position and accordingly a PLP becomes irrelevant.

Step III: A model provision due to errors or inaccuracies within the assumptions made to calculate the MTM value of the trade. Whilst this may remain relevant, any inaccuracies on one transaction should be offset on the other. It is considered likely that only a minor or nil model provision would be required in this situation.

Step IV: An administration provision to allow for the costs of running the trade to maturity, negotiating any payout of the credit derivative, or closing out positions. This would appear applicable to these transactions.

Step V: A counterparty provision to reflect the possibility of Bank Z not being able to meet its obligations to Bank Y under the credit default swap. Management must be stringent in their regular assessment of any provision required against a counterparty due to the joint probability risk, and must consider the level of correlation between Bank Z and Korea. A counterparty provision is required only against the failure of Bank X meets its premium obligations.

Step VI: Other provisions to cover further risks. This may include a provision against basis risks inherent in these two transactions, noting that these must be minimal else each would be treated as an open position. One significant point to consider for Structure II is an early termination provision. This will occur when there is a Credit Event that will terminate both transactions prior to their maturity. This will immediately reduce any profits taken to the P&L account. The initial profit taken represents the present value of the spread earned that was determined by the calculation of the fair value of each transaction. Note that the difference in the two fair values will result in the net profit or loss recorded. The likelihood of early termination is directly related to the risk of default of the underlying reference asset. Accordingly management should consider setting up provisions to reflect the fact that profits may reduce particularly where the reference assets are of poor credit quality.

Other considerations

5.018　The above example shows a default swap hedged with another default swap. Other forms of hedge are often used, *e.g.* a bond or asset swap hedging a default swap. Management needs to make an assessment in each situation of the level of residual risk retained in order to consider the appropriate methodology to apply.

It is worth nothing that a default swap that is hedged by a bond (or asset swap) and have consistent maturities would imply that the bond will be held to term. This suggests that both the bond (or asset swap) and the default swap should be transferred to the banking or investment book. A default swap may be treated similar to a guarantee and thus fair value accounting may not be applicable in this situation particularly where the bond is accounted for on an accruals basis.

Where the maturity of the bond and default swap are materially different then the basis risk would be likely to be greater than minimal and accordingly the two should be considered as separate open positions.

Summary

5.019　As has been noted throughout this Chapter, there is often a high degree of subjectivity involved in calculating the fair value for credit derivative trades. We have attempted to provide a framework for assisting the reader in this process. It is important that management formalise and document a methodology for calculating fair value for credit derivatives for this institution. This should then be confirmed with the external auditors prior to commencing trading.

The following table should assist the reader when determining which risks and the extent to which these are likely to have provisions required against initial MTM valuations.

Table 1	Open	Flat with minimal basis risk	Flat with greater than mininal basis risk	Flat or open with high positive correlation between reference asset and protection seller
MTM— which rates?	Bid or offer	Mid	Bid or offer	As per open or flat
SILP	XX	nil	XX	As per open or flat
PLP	XX	nil	XX	As per open or flat
Model	XX	X or nil	XX	As per open or flat
Administration	X	X	X	X
Counterparty	X	X	X	XXX
Other *e.g.* documentation Tenor reference asset other early termination	XX X or nil X or nil X nil	XX X or nil X or nil X X	XX X or nil X or nil X nil	As per open or flat As per open or flat As per open or flat As per open or flat

Key: X—a small provision is likely
    XX—a higher provision is likely
    XXX—a significant provision is likely.

In interpreting this table it is important to note that each risk takes on greater importance as the credit quality of the reference asset deteriorates because the likelihood of a Credit Event is increased.

Chapter 6

Tax Implications of Credit Derivatives in the United Kingdom

by Richard S. Collier[*]

Introduction

6.001 The U.K. tax issues which are typically encountered in relation to credit derivatives and credit derivative structures can be dealt with according to the following categories of issues:

- status of the vehicle for tax purposes;
- taxation of receipts and deductibility of payments on credit derivatives withholding tax issues;
- potential distribution treatment;
- VAT and transfer taxes.

Background: the status of a vehicle for tax purposes

6.002 For U.K. tax purposes, the status of any company is important. Normally, companies are "trading" companies or "investment companies". Qualification as either a trading company or an investment company is important mainly to ensure that costs and expenses incurred by the company are tax deductible. In isolated cases, a company may fail to qualify as either type of company and be regarded as a "nothing" company in terms of its general tax status. This would often be disastrous.

The above point is particularly relevant to special purpose vehicles (SPVs) used in credit derivative structures. Where these are used for isolated transactions only (for example, issuing a structured note and either lending on the proceeds or entering into a corresponding structured swap contract) then it is doubtful if such SPVs would qualify as trading companies. It is possible that investment company status might be achieved but this would be of little use where a tax deduction was required in relation to payments made under structured swaps and other derivative contracts (see further below, para. 6.008).

The required trading status of such SPVs would normally need to be secured by ensuring sufficient activity in the vehicle to guarantee this status or by specifically agreeing the status with the Revenue. In a worst case situation, it may be necessary to use an offshore vehicle to avoid the difficulties that would arise through failure to secure the required "trading " status of the company.

* Partner in the Banking & Capital Markets Tax Division of PricewaterhouseCoopers.
This Chap. on U.K. tax implications in respect of credit derivatives is an extract from an international tax survey conducted by PricewaterhouseCoopers during 1999 regarding tax implications on credit derivatives in 22 jurisdictions.

Taxation of receipts and deductibility of payments on credit derivatives

6.003 Although the United Kingdom has recently enacted a separate set of tax provisions which deal with derivatives, payments under credit derivatives are normally problematic because they will not fall within this existing legislation. This is because the existing "financial instrument" legislation caters only for "plain vanilla" contracts and options relating to interest rates, currency and debts. The different components which are taken account of in payments under credit derivatives cause such contracts to fall outside such rules, which can apply only where the payments under a derivative fall within certain prescribed (and narrow) categories. Thus, for example, a credit derivative swap will not rank as an interest rate contract for the purposes of these rules (whereas an ordinary interest rate swap would do so) because the rights and obligations to payments under the credit derivative are not calculated wholly or mainly by applying a variable interest rate to a notional principal.

Where the derivatives fall outside the special financial instrument rules, it will be important, for the purposes of securing tax relief, to ensure that any payment is made by a company which qualifies as a trading company and which makes the payment in the course of carrying on that financial trade. If this is not the case, then a tax deduction may well be denied or be at best uncertain. This is an important point for U.K. MNCs which are not financial trading companies as such companies will need to ensure that, should payments be made by them under credit derivative contracts, they will be deductible. There are various possible responses to this difficulty, for example actively using netting arrangements involving receipts and payments and also embedding the credit derivative into a loan (although see further below, para. 6.008).

The uncertainties on this point are exacerbated by the fact that because the credit derivatives market is relatively new, these products have only recently been seen by the Inland Revenue which seems, on some matters, still to be developing its views. Credit derivative structures may also provide for SPVs to make guarantee or "keep well" payments, usually to an affiliate. Such arrangements will often lead to difficulties in relation to determining an appropriate level of charge and also — occasionally — whether thin capitalisation issues are relevant.

Withholding tax issues

6.004 In relation to payments on credit derivatives, withholding tax issues may arise under any of three separate categories, all of which have proved relevant to credit derivative structures in practice. These categories are as follows:

(a) withholding on interest on a loan;

(b) withholding on annual payments;

(c) manufactured payment legislation

Each of these three elements is considered in turn.

Withholding on interest on a loan

6.005 Where structured or simple loans are used in credit derivative structures, any interest paid by a U.K. corporate taxpayer will normally be subject to a 20 per cent withholding tax, although there are various exemptions which may apply, the most relevant of which are that no withholding is due where:

- the interest is paid on a short term (broadly less than 365 day) indebtedness;

- the interest is paid by a U.K. bank in the ordinary course of its business;

- the interest is paid intra group between two U.K. resident group companies (and provided certain formalities have been observed);

- the interest is received by a U.K. bank on an advance it has made;

- the interest is paid on a loan which qualifies as a quoted Eurobond under certain specific legislation;

- there is treaty protection from the withholding (this usually requires certain formalities to be dealt with).

Withholding on annual payments

6.006 Where recurrent payments, other than interest payments are made in respect of a financial product and such payments are received by the recipient representing, in effect, passive investment income, they may be subject to a withholding tax at the rate of 20 per cent. Although this withholding charge may be considered somewhat obscure in relation to credit derivative products, the charge can apply in certain cases depending upon the status of the recipients of the payments.

Manufactured payment legislation

6.007 Where payments under credit derivatives constitute manufactured payments under the U.K. tax legislation they may give rise to a withholding tax at rates that will vary according to the specific circumstances. Payments will fall within the manufactured dividend legislation only if they are made pursuant to a contract or other arrangement for the transfer of securities and the payment is representative of a dividend. In practice, this makes the potential incidence of any withholding on this basis rare. A tax charge may also arise in respect of payments made under a credit derivative if such payments are treated as distributions for U.K. tax purposes. In practice, this is an important area and is therefore dealt with in a separate section below.

Potential distribution treatment

6.008 A number of credit derivative structures involve the use of loans into which the credit derivative is embedded. Given that this will often mean that the loan is accorded special terms to reflect the embedded credit derivative contract, there is a danger that interest paid on the loan could fall within the U.K. "distribution" rules, which deal with dividends and dividend equivalents. If such legislation is applicable then the payment ceases to be tax deductible.

The U.K. distribution legislation can apply in various situations to re-characterise interest as a distribution for U.K. tax purposes. In the context of credit derivative structures, the most likely situations which could arise are as follows.

"More than commercial return"

6.009 The first matter to consider is where the interest paid on the principal represents more than a reasonable commercial return. In this case, the excess amount paid over a reasonable commercial return is re-characterised as a distribution. Where recovery of the principal loaned is contingent upon a credit event (as a result of an embedded credit derivative incorporated in the terms of the loan), there is obviously a risk that some or all of the principal lent will be forfeit on the occurrence of the credit event. In this situation, investors will clearly want to be compensated for this risk and this is normally achieved through an increased level of coupon. The key question is whether the extra coupon return for the assumption of this credit risk can be taken account of in assessing whether the coupon remains a "reasonable commercial return". There is no directly relevant statute or case law on this point and the matter is, in practice, determined by Inland Revenue approach.

Although this issue has in the past been reasonably transparent, there are some signs that this is changing and, accordingly, it is currently difficult to offer generalised comments on the point beyond noting that some account can be taken of such risk but the degree to which this approach can be applied will turn on the facts and circumstances of each case.

"Dependent on the results of the business"

6.010 The other major area where distribution concerns may rise is in relation to the rule that where the return (*i.e.* coupon) on securities (a term which is defined widely to include loans) "is to any extent dependent on the results of the business or any part of it", then that return is wholly re-characterised as a distribution. Again, recent experience of dealing with the Revenue on the point is not entirely comforting. There are certain suggestions that the Revenue view seems to be that this rule can apply in completely hedged situations where, for example, the amount paid out by way of a coupon on a structure is determined by a corresponding receipt (for example, under a separate swap contract or other credit derivative contract).

This is on the basis that the amount of the receipt (which forms part of the income of the company) determines the amount of the coupon payment and thus brings it within the above distribution rule. This seems a highly debatable interpretation which is considered by PricewaterhouseCoopers to be wrong in law. If correct, it would have wide (and adverse) implications for the financial markets in the United Kingdom.

VAT and transfer taxes

6.011 The following section considers the application of various forms of transfer tax and of value-added tax in the context of credit derivatives.

VAT

6.012 Payments under credit derivatives will normally rank as exempt in status for the purposes of U.K. VAT law. Payments under credit derivative contracts are normally treated as payments made under financial instruments. This means that, where a supply is made, it is exempt from VAT where the counterparty is based in the United Kingdom and that no VAT incurred in connection with the transaction is recoverable. Only if the supply is made to a person based outside the E.C. will VAT be recoverable.

In the context of credit default swaps, it is only normally the protection seller who is seen as making a supply for VAT purposes. Alternatively, in the case of total return swaps, it could be argued that both parties are making supplies. However, where payments are netted off, Customs & Excise may argue, as they do for interest rate swaps, that only the person receiving payment is making a supply.

Transfer taxes

6.013   The applicable transfer taxes in the United Kingdom are stamp duty and Stamp Duty Reserve Tax ("SDRT"); each is considered in turn.

SDRT

6.014   The function of SDRT was originally to act as an anti-avoidance mechanism, imposing a charge to duty where a stamp duty was for some reason not applicable. Following the dematerialisation of the U.K. equity market in trading via CREST, however, SDRT has become the primary tax of relevance to securities and financial sector traders.

SDRT is of relatively limited application in that it applies to (broadly) U.K. equities and certain U.K. equity derivatives. Debt securities are normally outside the scope of the SDRT charge, but this exception does not apply to (1) convertibles or loans, the return on which exceeds a reasonable commercial return or (2) is dependent on the results of the business, etc. This point may be of some importance for trading in credit derivative products. Since this charge usually arises only on transfers (which is not on issue in this discussion), dealings in listed options (which are effected by writing contracts rather than by transferring existing rights and obligations) are not subject to the duty.

The charge to SDRT should therefore not apply to credit derivative structures which involve neither U.K. companies nor underlying U.K. reference credits. Where these conditions are not met, the position will need to be checked to ensure that no SDRT charges may arise.

Stamp duty

6.015   Stamp duty has a much broader scope than SDRT but is not well supported by enforcement legislation, making it in certain circumstances a "voluntary" tax. In addition, it is a tax which is based on documents so that the tax may often be avoided by avoiding the creation of a document or avoiding bringing an existing document into the United Kingdom. As such, tax planning in relation to this duty can often be very effective.

Chapter 7

Pricing Credit Risk

by Alan D. Morrison*

Introduction

7.001 This Chapter provides a brief review of some of the approaches which have been adopted within dealing rooms for pricing credit risky securities and in particular for pricing credit derivatives.

Credit risk has traditionally been priced by bankers who use pertinent economic and accounting data in conjunction with specific relationship information to determine the interest rate which a borrower should pay on loans. The primary concern of the originator in traditional relationships of this type is the catastrophic but infrequent event of default. Loan pricing therefore reflects the accumulated wisdom of the bankers in this field.

Credit risk pricing serves a different purpose for credit derivative traders. First, the assets upon which credit derivatives are based are extant loans so that traders can draw upon the expertise of the banker in pricing them: they do not need to perform the same analysis every time they trade. Secondly, traders require mark to market prices every day for reporting and risk management purposes: this is typically not the case for the traditional banker. Finally, an increasing number of credit derivatives provide a payout in response to non-default events such as movements in credit spreads or rating changes so that the models employed in dealing rooms need to capture subtleties not previously considered.

In addressing these points, traders have drawn upon existing expertise in more established products such as interest rate options and swaps so that there is a reliance upon modelling techniques which were developed in those markets in the credit derivatives market. The approaches currently employed therefore have a familiar feeling: models are developed for the underlying processes in the marketplace; they are calibrated against existing instruments to preclude the possibility of arbitrageable price making; finally, they are used for the valuation of new products.

7.002 Notwithstanding the comfort which this familiarity affords, there are significant differences between earlier derivatives and the new credit-risky ones which it is important to understand. Some have arisen to some extent elsewhere and derivatives professionals are therefore comfortable addressing them: for example, the distributions used for traditional option valuation are inappropriate for modelling default and some research has been devoted to the use of others which better fit the data. Others arise from the unique nature of credit risk and in the past have been domain of the banker. We return to this point below, para. 7.016.

For the purposes of this Chapter, we break our discussion of pricing models into the following categories:

(a) *Pricing by comparison to existing trades.* For instruments such as default swaps, a reasonable first cut at the price may be obtained from the asset swap market. This is a natural place to start.

* Oxford Risk Consulting.

(b) *Endogenous[1] models of credit risk.* These models use option theory to provide an explanation of the bankruptcy event. They are widely used in the marketplace and are the basis for the commercial KMV system and for some of the correlation computations employed in CreditMetrics.

(c) *Exogenous models of credit risk.* These models do not attempt to provide an explicit explanation of the default event. Instead, they simply use an exogenously specified model for default which is fitted to market data and used for pricing. This type of model is the basis for both CreditMetrics and Credit Risk+. It allows some familiar techniques to be used when pricing spread options and default options.

(d) *Strategic models.* These attempt to address some of the specific characteristics of debt a contract by explicitly modelling the negotiation process which occurs after a default event. They are not widely employed in the market place, but their importance is increasingly recognised by academics and regulators.

7.003 We will examine the above in turn. Our discussion is not intended to be exhaustive and it certainly does not represent a taxonomy of the models or a full survey of the literature in this field. Similarly, it is not intended to provide a manual for model implementors and model selectors. The aim is to provide a useful discussion of the concepts and methodologies which underlie the various approaches.

Note that there is no attempt in this Chapter to discuss the new portfolio management systems for credit risk — CreditMetrics, Credit Risk+ and Credit View. This is a deliberate attempt to make a clear distinction between credit pricing and credit risk management. For an analogy, consider the equity market. Pricing in that market is largely independent of the Markowitz approach to portfolio management. I contend that the same should be true of the credit markets.

Comparison pricing

7.004 Comparison pricing is conceptually simple. We illustrate it by considering the valuation of a credit default swap, as illustrated in Figure 1. In this trade, the protection buyer makes regular payments to the protection seller. She will receive a contingent payment after a Credit Event which should compensate her from the losses which she has suffered from her position in the reference asset. The mechanics and rationale for this type of trade is discussed in earlier Chapters.

Figure 1: Default swap trade

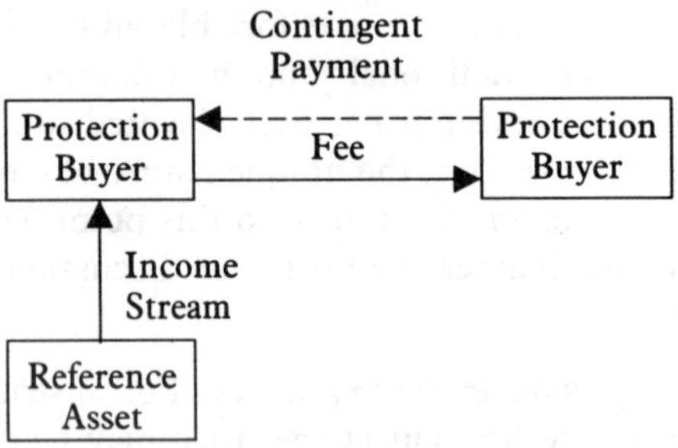

---

[1] As far as I am aware, this term is not commonly used in the context of bankruptcy models. I employ it for convenience.

The protection seller in this trade is effectively assuming the reference asset's default risk in exchange for a regular fee payment. This is effectively what happens in an asset swap trade, as in Figure 2. In the asset swap trade, the protection seller purchases the reference asset and derives a yield F_A from it. The purchase is funded at Libor, as illustrated in the diagram. By performing an interest rate swap at a fixed rate of F_S the protection seller is able to remove the interest rate risk from the trade. He is left with an income of $F_A - F_S$ and the default risk on the asset swap. Of course, we have skimmed over some details: more information may be found in Duffie (1998),[2] where the use of Repo trades in this context is also examined.

Figure 2: Asset swap trade

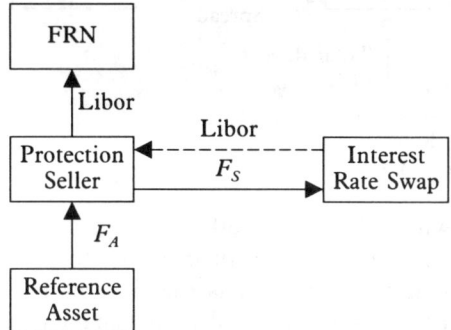

7.005   In view of the close similarity between this trade and the credit default swap, one might expect them to trade at the same price. They are not exactly alike: after default, the asset swapper has to unwind the interest rate swap. If one accepts that interest rates are positively correlated with default rates then this is likely to mitigate some of his losses. If the credit default swap has a different maturity to the reference asset then the asset swapper will experience a mark to market effect at the end of the trade which will not affect the default swapper: it is hard to quantify this. The additional uncertainty associated with these effects may render the asset swap less attractice. There are also regulatory differences between the trades in that the asset swapper has to set aside capital to cover the counterparty risk on two trades instead of one, which will once again tend to render the asset swap less attractive. Notwithstanding these effects, one would expect the asset swap and the default swap to trade at similar prices although at times of severe market turbulence, some decoupling may occur due to the uncertainty over the interest rate swap's price.

A similar effect will obtain when considering the spread at which a total rate of return swap should trade (see Figure 3). In this case, the total return receiver takes the price risk of the reference asset as well as the default risk for the life of the trade and so the asset swap may be a closer approximation to this trade, although one still has to account for the risk associated with closing out the interest rate swap in the event of default.

7.006   A final concern which may arise when pricing credit derivatives with reference to the appropriate asset swap is that of moral hazard. One of the key roles of large lenders such as banks is in monitoring the activities of the borrower to ensure that the money lent is repaid: this was first advanced as a rationale for the existence of banks by Diamond (1984).[3] When the lender transfers his risk to the

[2] D. Duffie, "Credit Swap Valuation, Working Paper", Stanford University (1998).
[3] D. Diamond, "Financial intermediation and delegated monitoring" (1984) 51 *Review of Economic Studies* 393–414.

protection seller in a credit derivative, he has less incentive to perform his duties as a monitor. At the same time, the protection seller has no rights over the borrower and cannot therefore perform the monitoring task herself. The consequence may be an increased likelihood of default. In some cases, this may affect the pricing of the credit derivative.

Figure 3: Total rate of return swap

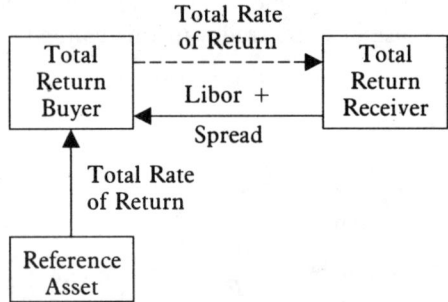

Pricing credit risk with reference to other market instruments is a useful first start and it allows us to relate the new instruments to those which already exist. The primary weakness of this approach is that it does not make any attempt to identify the components of credit risk and their behavioural characteristics. They cannot therefore be extended to cope with more exotic trades such as downgrade options or spread options. To accomplish this, we need to provide a model of the world which can be used to examine the likely behaviour of variables not currently priced. As we saw in the introduction, there are two major types of models: those in which the bankruptcy event is endogenous to the model and those in which it is exogenous.

Endogenous models of credit risk

7.007   The idea which underlies the endogenous models of credit risk is that the shareholders in a company hold a call option upon the real financial assets of the company. Suppose my limited company borrows money from you. When the debt for repayment, I have two alternative courses of action:

(a) I could repay you the money;

(b) I could decide to walk away from the debt and let you take over the management of the company.

The second alternative is the decision to default. I will decide to do so when the company is worth less to me than the money which I owe you. I have effectively bought an option: because I have limited liability, the most I can lose when I buy equity is the amount I pay for it. If the company does well, my profits are theoretically unlimited.

As usual when I buy an option, I prefer the volatility of the underlying to be very high when the option is close to the money. In this case the underlying is the assets of the company and the option will be at the money when the company is on the verge of bankruptcy. The obvious thing for me to do when my firm looks like it might fail is to increase the risks which it takes. Firms who behave like this when they are close to failing are *gambling for resurrection*.

The original Merton model

7.008   The first option model for credit risk was due to the now Nobel laureate Robert Merton (1974).[4] Merton's original model is the foundation for many of the valuation methods currently employed: it is useful to take a quick look at his original assumptions to see why additional complications had to be introduced. Merton assumed that the value of the firm's assets followed a random walk with very similar properties to the Black Scholes one. Merton also assumed that interest rates were constant and that the yield curve was completely flat. He then derived a Black Scholes type differential equation for V and in a simple case, he provided an analytic solution.

In Merton's model, default occurs only when the firm has exhausted all of its assets. In practise, firms tend to default a long time before then and to then enter into protracted negotiations. He also assumes that bankruptcy is costless. Amongst other assumptions, this presupposes:

(a) the cost of bankruptcy negotiations is nil;

(b) the outgoing management will not try to help themselves to the assets of the failing company;

(c) there will be no loss of reputation or of custom as a result of the bankruptcy declaration;

(d) the creditors will be able to generate as much income from the failed company as the outgoing management.

There is an enormous body of evidence which suggests that none of these assumptions is reasonable — certainly, they contradict the experience of most bankers and debt traders. A further assumption inherent in Merton's model is that *absolute priority* is adhered to: in other words, that the holders of the most senior securities are repaid in full before the next most senior receive anything and so on. Typically, this is not the case: in about 80 per cent of bankruptcies the most powerful negotiators tend to do better than they should during the renegotiation phase.

7.009   Merton's assumptions are not realistic. This would not matter if his model gave us realistic prices for traded debt securities: the Black Scholes (1973)[5] model is still used for most option trades, but its distributional assumptions are generally agreed to be false. We could try implementing the model and seeing how well it does in practise. To do so, we need some data for the firm's assets V. For most firms, this is almost impossible to estimate directly: if most of the assets of the firm are static plant and machinery then it is difficult to assign values to them, let alone to determine the volatilities of those values.

We can fall back upon our observation that the stock of the firm is an option on its assets. Some manipulation of the Black Scholes model and a little fiddling about Itô's Lemma then allows us to extract the required data about the asset value from information about the stock price so that we can implement Merton's model. We can then check to see if it correctly prices the debt securities which are trading in

---

[4] R.C. Merton, "On the pricing of corporate debt: the risk structure of interest rates" (1974) 29 *Journal of Finance* 449–70.
[5] F. Black and M. Scholes, "The pricing of options and corporate liabilities" (1973) 81 *Journal of Political Economy* 637–653.

the markets. Unfortunately, it seem dramatically to underestimate credit risk premia, so the model has little value as a trading tool.

Notwithstanding its problems, the Merton model is an attractive approach to credit risk valuation. It tells an economically believable story about the causes of bankruptcy and allows us to apply our intuitions about option pricing to debt. It uses data extracted from stock prices which are forward-looking and which appear to evaluate information efficiently. In this sense, it is more attractive than the exogenous models in which bankruptcy events are surprises. A succession of researchers and practitioners have attempted to refine the Merton model so as to retain these advantages whilst addressing the difficulties it poses.

Extensions to Merton's model

7.010   The first modification to the Merton model was provided by Black & Cox (1977).[6] Rather than assuming that the company will automatically default when the value of its assets hits the par value of the debt, they allow for failure to occur at a lower threshold value *K*. This allows us to incorporate cashflow-based theories of bankruptcy and also to account for gambling behaviour on the part of incumbent management who may conceal the true state of affairs from the asset holders.

The idea which underlies both the Black and Cox model and the Merton model is illustrated in Figure 4. The line shows the random evolution of the company's assets as they trace a geometric random walk, as employed in the Black Scholes model. Bankruptcy is assumed to occur as soon as the assets hit some threshold *K*: this is the par value of the debt for the Merton model and may be selected by the user when the Black and Cox model is employed.

Figure 4: Asset value evolution and bankruptcy in option models of default.

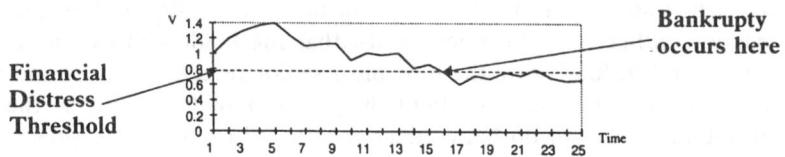

By selecting *K* appropriately, it is possible to generate more realistic prices for debt using the Black and Cox approach. There is an element of curve-fitting here: in selecting *K* we are guided by our knowledge of appropriate debt values and not by any deep intuition or insight. Moreover, the Black and Cox model leaves many of the problems of the Merton model unaddressed. It continues to assume adherence to absolute priority in debt restructuring. It retains the constant interest rate assumption. It still assumes costless bankruptcy.

7.011   Given that the primary purpose of credit valuation models is the valuation of bond type securities, the failure to incorporate interest rate effects appears a significant one, although we now have been dealing with the same assumption for two decades when using the Black Sholes model for option valuation. In theory, we could use the Black and Cox model in the same way, and simply vary the input parameters in order to understand the behaviour of valuations as interest rate varies. This might be enough for general trading

---

[6] F. Black and J.C. Cox, "Valuing corporate securities: Some effects of bond indenture provisions" (1977) 31 *Journal of Finance* 351–368.

purposes, but it would give us no insights into the relative behaviour of asset values and the evolution of the yield curve. To understand this, we need a more complete model which explicitly incorporates both changes in asset values and in the yield curve. The Longstaff and Schwartz (1995)[7] model provides this: it includes explicit models for both interest rates and asset values and it allows for correlation between them. Longstaff and Schwartz also allow the user to select a recovery rate which incorporates her own beliefs about likely recovery rates so that they make some attempt to relax the assumption of strict absolute priority of the other models.

The LS model yields some interesting explanations for familiar market phenomena:

(a) The higher asset values are, the higher the bond's value is. This should be obvious.

(b) If the interest rates rise then the upward drift of asset values will be higher in a risk-neutral world and the value of the discount bond will therefore be increased. As a consequence, the risky bond will have a lower duration than the safe bond.

(c) For very risky bonds, the duration may be negative, as discounting effects will be an irrelevance.

LS performance some empirical research to determine the effectiveness of their model for pricing purposes using Moody's industrial, utility and railroad corporate bond yield averages for a 15-year period starting in 1977. Their empirical results demonstrate the importance of interest rates in corporate debt valuation and are in opposition to the approaches which preceded this model. One remaining difficulty with the model is that bankruptcy costs still have to be placed at a higher level than is commonly observed in order to achieve realistic values. Nevertheless, it is a powerful tool which may be applied in theory to any debt security.

Endogenous models in the marketplace

7.012 The above discussion may appear a little dry and you could be forgiven for wondering whether any of this was of practical import. In fact, the endogenous approach to credit risk modelling has attracted a great deal of interest amongst market players. This is witnessed by the KMV Corporation's success. KMV have combined the Merton approach to debt modelling with empirical analysis of past company behaviour to derive default probability figures for the corporations which they examine. The figure which KMV produce are known as *Expected Default Frequencies* (EDF's).

KMV use the Merton approach to modelling the evolution of company asset values. They assume that bankruptcy will occur in response to cashflow pressures when the size of the company's outstanding current liabilities exceeds its current assets; these figures are estimated using fundamental analysis of the company. The distance between the company's current asset value and the point at which the company will go bankrupt is estimated by the KMV system using this data in standard deviations of the asset value diffusion: this is referred to as the *Distance from Default* (DD). The DD appears to capture most of the factors which are

---

[7] F.A. Longstaff and E.S. Schwartz, "A simple approach to valuing risky fixed and floating rate debt" (1995) 50(3) *Journal of Finance* 789–819.

inherent in default risk and KMV assume that the historical default rate for a given DD will be fairly constant. Under this assumption, the EDF is determined by using KMV's historical database of default statistics for all U.S. publicly quoted companies since 1978. More details of the calculation appear in Vasicek (1997).[8]

7.013 The KMV model has been used by investment bankers to extract company credit quality data from stock prices. The stock market is forward-looking and appears to be efficient: a KMV study of S&P-rated companies suggested that the KMV model anticipates rating changes by six to 18 months. Moreover, the KMV figures appeared to be confirmed in aggregate by actual default frequencies. The KMV approach has also been used by J.P. Morgan for construction of joint probability distributions for rating migrations in the CreditMetrics system, so that they combine the exogenous approach of Jarrow, Lando and Turnbull (1977)[9] for individual credits with the endogenous approach for modelling joint probabilities.

Empirical work by Delianedis and Geske (1998)[10] supports the claim that the KMV system is capable of predicting rating changes several months before they occur. Their work examines risk-neutral default probabilities for between 600 and 1,000 firms between 1987 and 1996. They estimate default probabilities using both Merton's model and also the compound option model for stock option valuation of Geske (1977)[11] and they find that both models are capable of forecasting rating migrations. This suggests that default may be better modelled using the diffusion methods of the endogenous class of models rather than the hazard rate approach of the exogenous class.

Exogenous models of Default

7.014 Exogenous models of credit risk do not attempt to explain the bankruptcy event: they simply assign a probability distribution to bankruptcy occurrences and assume that it will be a surprise. There are many models in this field, so our discussion will highlight only a few so as to give an indication of the ideas employed.

An early and significant contribution in this field was due to Jarrow and Turnbull (1995).[12] They set the tone for this approach by modelling the *arrival rate* of bankruptcy. They observe that companies are either in a state of default or not in a state of default and they assume that the probability that bankruptcy occurs in a short time interval Δt is proportional to Δt. The proportionality term h is assumed to be time-dependent and is usually referred to as the *hazard rate*. We could draw a tree showing how the company's state evolves between non-default N and default D, as in Figure 5. Notice that when a company enters a state of default, it stays there. This is a common assumption in debt models.

As we have already observed, h (t) tells us nothing about the causes of bankruptcy and in this model we have no advanced warning of bankruptcy.

---

[8] O.A. Vasicek, "Credit valuation", *NETEXPOSURE: The Electronic Journal of Financial Risk*, http://www.netexposure.co.uk/1.

[9] R.A. Jarrow, D. Lando and S.M. Turnbull, "A Markov model for the term structure of credit risk spreads" (1977) 10(2) *The Review of Financial Studies* 481–523.

[10] G. Delianedis and Robert Geske "Credit risk and risk neutral default probabilities: Information about rating migrations and defaults", Working paper, University of California, Los Angeles (1998).

[11] R. Geske, "The valuation of corporate liabilities as compound options" (1977) 12 *Journal of Financial and Quantitative Analysis* 541–552.

[12] R. Jarow and S. Turnbull, "Pricing derivatives on financial securities subject to default risk" (1995) 50 *Journal of Finance* 53–86.

Figure 5: Hazard rates $h\ (t)$ and the evolution of default state

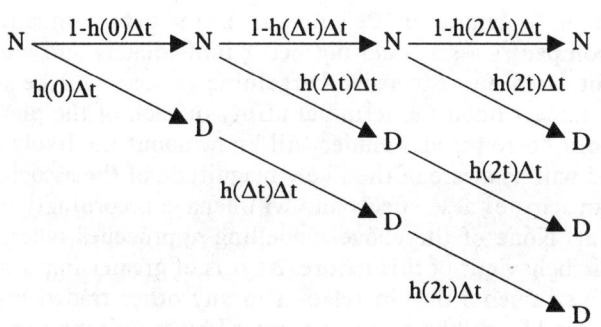

To implement the model, $h\ (t)$ is extracted from bond market prices, so that the JT model will always agree with the quoted market. Its strength is that it gives us an explicit way of thinking about default which may be applied more generally.

7.015 Jarrow and Turnbull use an interesting foreign exchange analogy to explain their recovery rate assumptions. They assume that any company ABC will always meet its debt obligations in ABC dollars. Regrettably, these are of no use and so we need to exchange them for U.S. dollars. When the company is in default, one obtains an exchange rate of 1 between the USD and the ABC; when it is in default, we get a rate of $\delta < 1$. In other words, Jarrow and Turnbull assume a fixed recovery rate, assigned by the model user. They assume that the recovery will occur at the time when the obligation fell due.

The assumption of fixed recovery rates is incorrect: in practice, recovery rates are extremely volatile, particularly for senior debt assets. A hazard rate model which contemplates the effects of stochastic recovery rates is due to Das and Tufano (1996).[13]

One obvious objection to the Jarrow and Turnbull model is that in practice, we have a little more information about an asset's creditworthiness than simply its state of default: the credit rating agencies rate non-defaulting companies according to their likelihood of failure. This information is widely disseminated and employed by investors in making purchase decisions and we should attempt to incorporate this in our modelling. This was accomplished by Jarrow et al. (1977),[14] who employed a rating transition matrix of the type employed in CreditMetrics in conjunction with ideas from the option market to determine derivatives prices which incorporate ratings data. Much of the CreditMetrics system can be understood in these terms.

Finally, the exogenous approach to credit risk can be used to justify our intuitive approach to valuation of credit risky securities. When using this approach, we simply discount all of the payments which the bond makes at a higher interest rate. Duffie and Singleton (1998)[15] used a hazard rate model for default events and assumed a recovery rate $(1 - L)$ which was a fraction of the pre-default bond value. In these circumstances, we can value a bond by discounting its payments as if it were riskless using an interest rate which has been adjusted upwards by the product of the hazard rate and L.

---

[13] S.R. Das and P. Tufano "Pricing credit-sensitive debt when interest rates, credit ratings and credit spreads are stochastic" (1996) 5(2) The Journal of Financial Engineering 161–198.
[14] R.A. Jarrow, D. Lando and S.M. Turnbull, "A Markov model for the term structure of credit risk spreads" (1977) 10(2) *The Review of Financial Studies* 481–523.
[15] D. Duffie and K.J. Singleton, "Modelling term structures of defautable bonds", Working Paper, Stanford University (1998).

Strategic effects

7.016 When an organisation defaults upon its debt obligations transfer of control of the company's assets does not occur immediately and without difficulty. Typically, a protracted and expensive bargaining process will be triggered which will have a real impact upon the terminal utility of each of the players in the debt renegotation. Both borrower and lender will know about the likely impact of these negotiations and will be aware of the likely magnitude of the associated costs. They will rationally anticipate these effects and will behave accordingly in the run-up to the default event. None of the above modelling approaches takes account of the effect of strategic behaviour of this nature. As it is of greater importance in relation to credit-risky instruments that in relation to any other traded product, it seems likely that considerable insight could be achieved by examining these effects. So far, only a few models have done so. These fall into two broad categories. The first use ideas from the theory of real options to determine when default occurs on risky debt. The second employ ideas from game theory.

The real option ideas in this context are explained in a paper by Lambrecht and Perraudin (1996).[16] They observe that when payoffs from investments are stochastic and investment decisions are irreversible, there is some option value associated with waiting to invest; investing now means relinquishing an option to invest in the future. Against this one must weigh the fact that first movers enjoy an advantage in investment. The classic example of this type of decision is that of a large firm considering opening a branch in a small town. The cost of investment may drop if investment is delayed but the town can only support one such outlet and consequently there is value in pre-empting other potential investors.

7.017 These ideas are applied to the financial markets by Mella-Barral and Perraudin (1997).[17] Their paper attempts to explain the high risk premia which corporate debt attracts compared to those predicted by Merton's model by considering the concessions which debt-holders are sometimes forced to make before bankruptcy occurs. As lenders rationally anticipate these concesions, they charge higher spreads than Merton predicts to take compensate themselves. Mella-Barral and Perraudin derive closed form solutions for the value of the debt securities and show that for reasonable parameter values, the proportion of the debt premium which is attributable to strategic behaviour is between 30 and 40 per cent.

A paper by Anderson and Sundaresan (1996)[18] uses game theoretic ideas to examine the effects of non-cooperative negotiation between shareholders and debtholders. In Anderson and Sundaresan's (AS) model, bankruptcy involves a cost which is common knowledge. They model the evolution of company asset values using Merton's model. They observe that when asset values are sufficiently low the lender may be prepared to accept a reduced coupon payment rather than suffer the costs of bankruptcy when winding up the firm. As a consequence, the lender will charge a higher interest rate to companies which are not currently close to default. This model is not currently employed for trading, but it does appear to give considerably better estimates of bankruptcy cost than the Merton model.

Conclusion

7.018 The methods which traders must use for credit risk valuation are materially different from those required in the valuation of more traditional market

---

[16] B. Lambrecht and W. Perraudin, "Real options and pre-emption", Working Paper 26, Institute for Financial Research (1996).

[17] P. Mella-Barral and W. Perraudin, "Strategic debt service" (1997) 52(2) Journal of Finance 531–556.

[18] R.W. Anderson and Suresh Sundaresan, "Design and valuation of debt contracts" (1996) 9(1) *Review of Financial Studies* 37–68.

risk oriented products. Default distributions are very different and there are behavioural complications surrounding the bankruptcy event which do not arise in other markets. Several approaches have arisen to deal with this. The first involves a simple comparison between new trades and existing ones. The second involves the application of contingent claim pricing ideas to debt valuation. The last involves an exogenously imposed probability distribution for credit events. Some modifications to the second type of approach have been made which explicitly recognise the importance of bargaining at default time.

The market has not yet adopted a single approach as it has in the market for options on shares, say, where the Black and Scholes (1973)[19] model has achieved common acceptance. The exogenous models are widely used as the basis for risk management systems but are less effective elsewhere and the importance of the KMV system is evidence of the continuing relevance of the endogenous approach. The most one can hope for at present is an increased level of awareness of the approaches available, their strengths and their weaknesses.

---

[19] F. Black and M. Scholes, "The pricing of options and corporate liabilities" (1973) 81 *Journal of Political Economy* 637–653.

Chapter 8

Restitution of Payments Made under Credit Derivatives

by Dr Alastair Hudson

Introduction

8.001   The aim of this Chapter is to examine the law relating to the termination of credit derivatives transactions where termination is not affected in accordance with the provisions of some existing contractual documentation, or where one or other party makes a claim based on a right to restitution or some general equitable relief. Chapter 4 on *Seller liability* considered the potential forms of liability for the seller of a derivative product concerning the manner in which the credit derivative was created. This Chapter is concerned with credit derivatives which have been performed without to any allegation of wrongdoing involved in their creation and considers claims arising from the nature of the performance of such a transaction or the manner of its termination. The issue of restitution at common law and in equity arises most particularly in the context of credit derivatives with reference to those transactions which are never fully documented, or in the case where the documentation is silent or ineffective.

There are a number of contexts in which the standard market documentation is deficient, in particular in its coverage of issues related to taking proprietary rights, retention of title, and segregation of assets to be delivered. Rather than a criticism of the ISDA and other market formats, this discussion is meant as a recognition of the fact that standard market documentation will not be able to deal with all of the many contexts in which this kind of issue could potentially arise. The message for the lawyer is the need to adapt standard market documentation to cope with the particular context. The following discussion therefore considers the problem of restitution by analysing the commercial context and law surrounding termination of, and recovery of property in relation to, credit derivatives.

Fundamentals of the law of restitution

8.002   Given the lack of decided cases in the area of credit derivatives, compared to other areas of commercial law, the large number of cases arising out of the decision in *Hazell*[1] (that interest rate swaps were beyond the powers of local authorities in the United Kingdom) form a focus for lawyers in this area. It is therefore worthwhile to examine the issues which arose in those cases and their factual background. The view set out in the following analysis is not that the courts reached the wrong decisions on the facts of those cases, but rather that they failed to take into account a number of issues which might have led to those results being reached by more intellectually and commercially satisfactory means.

---

[1] [1992] 2 A.C. 1.

The law of restitution and the core of equitable principle has been changed by the local authority swaps cases. Therefore, the analysis of those swaps cases is centred around a central conviction that the courts were concerned with the development of generally applicable principles at the expense of a detailed analysis of the financial products before them.

The local authority swaps cases revolve around the joined appeals of West-deutsche Landesbank Girozentrale proceeding against the London Borough of Islington (*"Islington"*)[2] and Kleinwort Benson proceeding against Sandwell Borough Council (*"Sandwell"*).[3] There are another important group of appeals which proceeded on a parallel course but raised slightly different points of law as to the availability of defences to restitutionary and equitable claims brought in relation to the avoidance of the interest rate swaps. It was the *Islington* appeal which was pursued to the House of Lords and which forms the core of the following discussion as a consequence. Of the two hundred writs that were served in wake of the judgment of the House of Lords in *Hazell*, two of these appeals were brought by Kleinwort Benson against Birmingham City Council (*"Birmingham"*)[4] and against South Tyneside Metropolitan Borough Council (*"South Tyneside"*)[5] which examine the development of defences to the restitutionary and equitable claims brought. All this is apart from the cases on capacity of local authorities to enter into transactions, *Hazell v. Hammersmith & Fulham*[6] (*"Hazell"*) and the contracts for differences cases, *Morgan Grenfell v. Welwyn Hatfield DC and others*[7] (*"Welwyn"*).

Mapping restitution

8.003   At two levels the title of this section (*the law of restitution*) is a misnomer. First, the focus on restitution would indicate that the intricate debate about the development of restitutionary principles has resolved itself in the promotion of a doctrine of unjust enrichment. In fact, the result of the *Islington*[8] appeal at every stage was that classical principles of equity were employed rather than novel restitutionary techniques,[9] even though the claim was ultimately decided by an order for repayment of money with simple interest, which is evidently an order in respect of money had and received. At first instance, Hobhouse J. employed equity and justice in ordering a proprietary remedy, rather than absence of consideration.[10] Delivering the leading speech in the House of Lords, Lord Browne-Wilkinson expressly dismissed Birks' restitutionary model resulting trust as a suitable remedy, while also advancing a fundamental restatement of the core principles of trusts law. So, in relation to this Chapter, "restitution" is not meant to express a position in the feud between equity and restitution lawyers, rather it is meant to encompass a vague notion of the restoration of value after the failure of a derivatives transaction.

Secondly, the better title for this area of law appears to be "the law of unjust enrichment" as a result of the decisions of the House of Lords in *Lipkin Gorman v.*

---

[2] [1994] 4 All E.R. 890, *per* Hobhouse J., CA; [1996] A.C. 669, HL.
[3] [1994] 4 All E.R. 890, *per* Hobhouse J. The *Sandwell* action did not proceed beyond first instance.
[4] *Kleinwort Benson v. Birmingham City Council* [1996] 4 All E.R. 733, CA, on appeal from Gatehouse J. (unreported).
[5] *Kleinwort Benson v. South Tyneside MBC* [1994] 4 All E.R. 972, *per* Hobhouse J.
[6] [1991] 1 All E.R. 545, HL.
[7] [1995] 1 All E.R. 1, *per* Hobhouse J.
[8] [1996] A.C. 669.
[9] See Birks, "Trusts to be raised to reverse unjust enrichment: the Westdeutsche Case" [1996] R.L.R. 3, 10.
[10] An approach approved by the Court of Appeal.

Karpnale[11] and *Woolwich Equitable Building Society v. IRC.*[12] In those cases the concept of "unjust enrichment" was embraced as forming part of English law as a distinct doctrine.[13] It is a more useful title because it describes more precisely the aim of the doctrine than "restitution". Restitution, in the sense of "restore" or "give back", explains only the anticipated result of the rule rather than its underlying rationale. The term "restitution" leaves at large all of the difficult questions about the types of situation which will give rise to a restitutionary claim. Complexity follows from that. "Unjust enrichment" summarises the purpose of the doctrine, borrowing more freely from Roman law traditions which inform Scots law more than they have ever intruded into modern English jurisprudence.

8.004 The aim of the doctrine of unjust enrichment is to isolate an enrichment, decide whether or not that enrichment was generated in a manner which is considered unjust, and then impose a remedy which restores the value lost by some other person. The scope of the doctrine is nevertheless potentially broad. As indicated at the outset of this section, there is a potential overlap between the operation of equity to regulate unconscionable behaviour and the reversal of unjust enrichment by restitution.

In titling this Chapter *"Restitution"* the aim is to examine the circumstances in which restitution is achieved by reversal of unjust enrichment or by the application of equitable institutions and remedies in the context of termination of a derivatives transaction. Therefore, the remainder of this chapter will set out the variety of claims and remedies appropriate to achieve restitution in the context of credit derivatives, following the *Islington* appeal primarily. First, though, it may be useful to summarise the decision of the courts in *Islington* in the local authority swaps cases.

The basis of unjust enrichment

Introduction to unjust enrichment

8.005 The aim of unjust enrichment is to provide remedies which require a defendant to give up an enrichment received at the plaintiff's expense. Its derivation is often traced to the American *Restatement of Restitution*[14] which states:[15]

> "a person who has been unjustly enriched at the expense of another is required to make restitution to the other".

The appropriate remedy is then one which requires the defendant to give up to another an enrichment received at the other's expense or its value in money. Birks declares his central concern to be with "the second sense of 'restitution' . . . that is, with gains to be given up, not with losses to be made good."[16] The aim is therefore not compensation for loss suffered by rather reparation by return of value. The

---

[11] [1991] 2 A.C. 548; [1991] 3 W.L.R. 10.
[12] [1993] A.C. 70; [1992] 3 W.L.R. 366.
[13] That is in spite of the dicta of Lord Diplock in *Orakpo v. Manson Investment Ltd* [1978] A.C. 95; [1977] 3 W.L.R. 229 which had previously upheld the orthodoxy that there was no such doctrine in English law.
[14] See, for example, Goff and Jones, *The Law of Restitution* (4th ed. Sweet & Maxwell, 1993), p. 13.
[15] Para. 1, American *Restatement of Restitution*.
[16] Birks, *Introduction to the Law of Restitution* (Oxford, 1989), p. 11.

caselaw has seen the law of restitution develop out of "the ties of natural justice and equity".[17] More recently the roots of the unjust enrichment approach has been located in concepts of equity and justice:

> "Any civilised system of law is bound to provide remedies for cases of what has been called unjust enrichment or unjust benefit, that is to prevent a man from retaining the money of or some benefit derived from another which it is against conscience that he should keep."[18]

8.006 The principle of unjust enrichment is not concerned simply with the recognition of rights or the application of institutional rights under constructive or resulting trusts, as is equity.[19] Rather, the aim of unjust enrichment is to create a new right which will achieve restitution. While a restitutionary remedy may arise from the recognition of a pre-existing right, the remedy will be generated by the receipt of the unjust enrichment with the effect of depriving the defendant of the value received at the plaintiff's expense.[20] In Birks' terms: "Restitution is that active or creative response at the moment of enrichment."[21-23] Therefore, restitution on termination of a financial contract is concerned to create a new right for the plaintiff which facilitates the reversal of the unjust enrichment which the defendant has made from the transaction. The importance of restitution in this context is that it is granting a right to the plaintiff which is not necessarily enshrined expressly in a contract. Rather, the focus is on whether or not the defendant has made some gain from its dealings with the plaintiff which the court considers it proper to reverse by ordering that defendant to make some restitution, either by delivery up of property or payment of money, to the plaintiff.

This idea has been considered already in the context of the liability of a seller to the buyer where the buyer acts unconscionably in a way which creates an extra-contractual right in the buyer to receive restitution to the extent of the gain made by the seller from the transaction. This is an important distinction from contractual damages: the buyer is not entitled to a remedy which compensates it for the loss which it has suffered.[24] Rather, the quantum of the remedy is fixed according to the seller's enrichment. This may therefore require the giving up of profit made on a transaction or of the re-transfer of property. This issue could arise from activities before the transaction was formed, activities during the lifetime of the transaction, or actions after termination of the transaction. The local authority swaps cases, which provide much of the decided caselaw in this area, are concerned with the position after termination of the contract.[25]

---

[17] *Moses v. Macferlan* (1760) 2 Burr. 1005, 1012.

[18] *Fibrosa Spolka Akcyjna v. Fairbairn Lawson Combe Barbour Ltd* [1943] A.C. 32 at 61, *per* Lord Wright. Cited with approval in *Woolwich Equitable Building Society v. Inland Revenue Commissioners* [1993] A.C. 70 at 197, 202; and *Westdeutsche Landesbank Girozentrale v. Islington LBC* [1996] A.C. 669, [1996] 2 All E.R. 961 at 1004, *per* Lord Woolf.

[19] As restated most recently by Lord Browne-Wilkinson in *Westdeutsche Landesbank Girozentrale v. Islington LBC* [1996] A.C. 669; [1996] 2 All E.R. 961 at 1004.

[20] The issue which arises in the context of the swaps cases is whether I am deprived of that value if I have already contracted to give it to you?

[21-23] Birks, *Introduction to the Law of Restitution* (Oxford, 1989), p. 14.

[24] Unless the claim is brought against a fiduciary for breach of trust, in which case the property constituting the trust fund must be reconstituted in a manner which must be said properly to be compensatory: *Target Holdings v. Redferns* [1996] 1 A.C. 421.

[25] And therefore, that forms the focus of this Chap.

8.007 The issue which has arisen in the local authority swaps cases in connection with the contracting of credit derivatives is the retention of title and the availability of proprietary remedies. The overlap between property law and restitution is the ability of the latter to create new rights by way of remedy whereas property law codes recognise existing rights.[26] A property law right would be created either by the reservation of title by contract or the segregation of some interest to be held on an express or implied trust. The right arising from unjust enrichment would be the restitutionary response to some unjust enrichment which is not reliant on a pre-existing reservation title but which would be reliant on a pre-existing proprietary base. Most restitutionary remedies are therefore concerned with personal claims in money.[27] However, the difficulty arises in respect of the imposition of trusts which achieve results which are capable of being described as "restitutionary".[28]

The issues which are considered in this Chapter relate to the recovery of money by means of personal claims in restitution and in equity, and then the establishment of rights in property by means of restitution and equity. The common law restitutionary claims in money will focus on money had and received and failure of consideration. The proprietary claims will examine resulting trusts, constructive trusts, subrogation and tracing. The use of rescission and specific performance will also be considered in the context of ensuring that there is no unjust enrichment obtained.

Restitution in *Islington*

8.008 The argument for the development of principle of restitution was commenced by Lord Goff as co-author of *The Law of Restitution* with Professor Jones.[29] The appeal in *Islington* was a battle between the mutual applicability of principles of equity and restitution. The following discussion isolates some of the major categories of restitutionary action and assesses their applicability to the variety of situations which might arise under derivatives contracts.

Restitution by rescission

8.009 The form of restitution which Lord Goff favoured in his speech was one which returned the parties to the positions which they had occupied originally. This rescission approach would appear to achieve two goals. On general restitutionary grounds, it has a superficial attraction in that it terminates the unjust enrichment which the local authorities enjoyed at the expense of the banks. However, as considered below, it would not necessarily restore to the banks the whole of the loss which they have suffered by entering into the transaction, including the cost of hedging arrangements.[30] The second goal achieved by the rescission approach is the avoidance of seeming to enforce the void contract by an award of lost opportunity cost to the parties. In the case of cash-settled derivatives, any award of damages[31] would be equivalent to performance of the contract.

---

[26] Birks, *Introduction to the Law of Restitution* (Oxford, 1989), p. 15.
[27] See Goff and Jones, *The Law of Restitution* (5th ed. Sweet & Maxwell, 1998), Chap. 1.
[28] See below, para. 8.058.
[29] Albeit, it is acknowledged that the latest edition is authored by Prof. Jones.
[30] See on this the discussion of the defence of passing on in *Kleinwort Benson v. Birmingham CC* below, para. 8.059, and Hudson (1999), p. 58.
[31] Providing they are payable in the contract currency.

The central issue is the ability of common law or equitable remedies to restore the parties to the positions which they occupied before they purported to enter into the deep discount swap transaction in *Islington*. Given the nature of the property, all that would be required is a reverse payment of an equal amount of the same currency. As Lord Goff considered the position, ". . . in the present case, there ought to be no difficulty about that at all . . . because the case is concerned solely with money."[32] The restitution-by-rescission approach simply requires that ". . . each party should pay back the money that it has received — or more sensibly strike a balance, and order that the party who has received most should repay the balance . . . with an appropriate order for the payment of interest."[33] The most suitable method of achieving the result would be to affect an equitable set-off in respect of the moneys which remained outstanding.

8.010 The irony is, of course, that the parties had already created a mechanism for the set-off of outstanding claims in the event that the purported contracts were terminated before its due expiry date in the standard form master agreement which was in force between them and also in the pricing and structuring of the deep discount swap at the outset. It is perhaps unfortunate that within Lord Goff's stated intention of "keeping my eyes on the simple outline of the case",[34] this allocation of risks was ignored.

The appropriate remedy of a solvent party in the event of the repudiation by, or insolvency of, the counterparty is to rescind the contract.[35] If the contract represented claims for debts both ways, then unquestionably the solvent party could not cancel its obligation to pay vested debts to the insolvent party and so full, reciprocal rescission would not be possible. In the event that the executory contract analysis[36] is followed, rescission would be possible on the basis that the condition precedent to execution, had not been performed. Rescission plainly requires placing the parties in the position they occupied previously. Where there is only a liability to make payment one way at the date of completion, due to set-off, the availability of reciprocity is altered and it may affect the suitability of rescission. At first blush, rescission is made simpler by a composite executory contract analysis because it makes calculation of the amounts to be repaid more straightforward. However, the incorporation of separate contracts into a single master agreement, makes it equally feasible to achieve rescission across the spread of swaps transactions.

Absence of consideration

8.011 Hobhouse J., at first instance in *Islington*, held that there ought not to be a claim based on "failure of consideration" because the claim, properly understood, depended on their having been a total failure of consideration such that it could be described as an "absence of consideration". In analysing Hobhouse J. framing this novel doctrine of absence of consideration, Lord Goff was concerned that the concerns about the scope of failure of consideration need not be confined as narrowly, as the court at first instance considered, to such a requirement of *total* failure of consideration.[37] Lord Goff referred to the academic commentary which was generated in response to the introduction of absence of consideration,[38] and

---

[32] [1996] 2 All E.R. 961 at 966.
[33] *ibid.*
[34] *ibid.*
[35] *Johnson v. Agnew* [1980] A.C. 367.
[36] As considered in Hudson, *Swaps, Restitution and Trusts* (Sweet & Maxwell, 1999), p. 39.
[37] [1996] 2 All E.R. 961 at 967.
[38] Birks, "No Consideration: Restitution after Void Contracts" (1993) 23 U.W.A.L.R. 195; Swadling [1994] R.L.R. 73; Burrows, "Swaps and Friction between Common Law and Equity" [1995] R.L.R. 15.

held that failure of consideration may be the more appropriate ground.[39] What this does not make clear is the precise attitude which Lord Goff was taking to the utility of a doctrine of absence of consideration replacing failure of consideration.

In the *Islington* appeal the subtle line between a "failure" and a total "absence" of consideration revolved around the partial performance of the swap transaction. If the requirement were for there to have been no consideration at all (absence), then the fact that monies were paid prior to the realisation that the transaction was in fact void *ab initio* under *Hazell* meant that the restitutionary action for absence of consideration would fail. However, if all that was required was a failure of some kind, the finding that the contract was void *ab initio*, despite having been partially performed by five years of swap payments and the deep discount payment, would seem to satisfy the test. It would appear, though, that Hobhouse J. was particularly eager to resolve the case by the use of an equitable remedy rather than restitution.[40] The position is complicated by the finding of Leggatt L.J. that there was no contract at all, on the basis that it was void *ab initio*, such that an argument based on absence of consideration ought to have succeeded — given the total absence of any enforceable contract, on Leggatt L.J.'s terms.

8.012 It is therefore important to see where this doctrine of absence of consideration came from and how it fits into the law of unjust enrichment. The issue of absence of consideration arose in the decision of Lord Thurlow in *Heathcote v. Paignton*[41] in the context of the development of the law on absence of consideration:

> ". . . if the inadequacy of the consideration is so gross that it shows that the plaintiff did not really understand the transaction, or was so oppressed that he was glad to make it, this will amount to fraud. But if that amounts to fraud, it is simply a roundabout way of saying that gross inadequacy of consideration justifies setting aside a contract."[42]

These dicta highlight the problems of the courts of Chancery in considering commercial transactions. The first is that it is often only possible for the courts to interfere with freedom to contract where there has been some unconscionable behaviour which amounts to provable fraud. The other is the difficulty of intruding on freedom of contract by replacing the precise terms of the agreement with some standard arrived at by applying principles according to conscionability — for example, by judges fixing the price of the contract.

Atiyah points out the difficulty of measuring the adequacy of consideration in circumstances concerning speculative transactions, in particular credit derivatives. As he put it[43]:

> "A person who indulges in a foolish speculation is apt to feel, after the speculation has failed, that it was an unfair arrangement. Of course, the same is true of any transaction which necessarily involves some element of risk, though that is not nearly so obvious to the parties involved."

---

[39] He acknowledges, however, that the issue of "absence of consideration" was not, strictly, within the ambit of the appeal which he was required to consider: [1996] 2 All E.R. 961 at 968.
[40] As considered below in, para. 8.058.
[41] (1787) 2 Bro. C. C. 167, 29 E.R. 96.
[42] *The Rise and Fall of Freedom of Contract*, Atiyah (Oxford 1979), p. 174.
[43] *ibid.*

8.013   The buyer of a product which generates a loss is likely to argue that there is little probity in the pattern of dealing which led to the creation of the arrangement in the first place.

The genesis of the doctrine of failure of consideration appears to have been in a decision of Holt C.J. in 1691 where he held that "the money was received without any consideration, and consequently was originally received to the plaintiff's use".[44] Atiyah considered this principle to have emerged from an understanding that contract and quasi-contract grew out of an purposive policy behind contracts existing to confer benefits which were to be recompensed.[45] Therefore, on this approach, there would be some ground for saying that the benefits envisaged by the parties in the creation of a contract are the rights which the court should be seeking to enforce. The context of suitability and risk can be seen as impinging on the manner in which restitution should be carried out in the case of commercial contracts. The parties envisaged a commercial state of affairs — the restitutionary response should mould itself in the image of that mutual expectation. In the light of the comments of Lord Goff, it would appear that the doctrine of *failure* of consideration remains in tact.

Personal restitutionary claims for money at common law

8.014   In considering the appropriate principles affecting restitution at common law, the starting point for Lord Goff was with the speech of Lord Mansfield in *Moses v. Macferlan*,[46] where he held that the "gist of the action for money had and received"[47] is that "the defendant, upon the circumstances of the case, is obliged by the ties of natural justice and equity to refund the money". Thus, in considering whether or not compound interest ought to have been awarded to the bank, Lord Goff felt that it would have been "strange indeed if the courts lacked jurisdiction in such a case to ensure that justice could be fully achieved by means of an award of compound interest".[48]

There was therefore no reason of principle why a personal claim in restitution in favour of the bank should have been refused. In accordance with the prescriptions of the House of Lords in *Sinclair*, permitting such a claim would not have indirectly enforced the *ultra vires* contract "for such an action would be unaffected by any of the contractual terms governing the borrowing,[49] and moreover would be subject (where appropriate) to any restitutionary defences . . ."[50] Further, it achieved Lord Goff's underlying concern that the lender should not be without a remedy.

In *Guinness v. Kensington*[51] it was held that a contract which was ultra vires one of the parties was always devoid of any legal effect. Further, payments made under such a purported contracted were necessarily made for a consideration which had totally failed. Therefore, the money was recoverable under a personal claim in restitution ("money had and received"). A party to such a void swap was entitled to recover an amount equal to the difference between his payments and his receipts over the life of the purported swap. It would make no difference to the analysis that

---

[44] *Martin v. Sitwell* (1691) Holt 25, 25; 90 E.R. 912, 913.
[45] *The Rise and Fall of Freedom of Contract*, Atiyah (Oxford 1979), p. 181.
[46] (1760) 2 Burr 1005 at 1012.
[47] [1996] 2 All E.R. 961 at 980.
[48] *ibid.*
[49] Again, it is important to note that the language of debt is being used.
[50] [1996] 2 All E.R. 961 at 972–3.
[51] *Guinness Mahon & Co. Ltd v. Kensington & Chelsea RLBC* [1998] 2 All E.R. 272.

the swap had been completely performed. There could be no different right to property based on complete performance than had otherwise been the case.

8.015   The question then is: given that there is a right to a personal claim in restitution (formerly known as an action for money had and received) on the basis that the bank has made a payment for which it will receive no reciprocal consideration as was previously understood between the parties, what is the total quantum of the remedy which the bank is entitled to receive? In short, is the bank entitled only to simple interest or is it entitled to a rate of compound interest which it would otherwise have received on its money? To achieve "full restitution"[52] in these terms it is necessary to award compound interest, "having regard to the commercial realities of the case".[53] Lord Goff considered that the bank in *Islington* was entitled to receive what he described as "a complete remedy".[54] What is not clear is what this term means. At one level, a *complete* remedy would seem to require the restoration of Westdeutsche's proprietary rights in the value transferred. On these facts, the suitability of a cash payment by means of settlement would have given Westdeutsche *de facto* the whole of their claim in one judgment order. The *realpolitik* attitude of the courts to this case does appear to have interfered with the form of remedy which was being granted. The understanding that the case is simply about the payment of money avoids the question at law generally of rights in property and the more particular situation of physically-settled contracts. However, we know that there will not be a proprietary remedy on these facts,[55] what is not clear on the restitution lawyer's approach is "why".

The restitutionary approach then seeks to provide a remedy to a claim based on restitution for unjust enrichment on the basis of "justice". While criticising the narrowness of the equitable approach, the implementation of the restitutionary approach by the majority of the House of Lords would have had, it is submitted, an impact identical to the making of a proprietary award. This is despite identifying from the outset, explicitly, that there was no observable reason why a proprietary claim should be awarded to a payer under an *ultra vires* contract. As such, restitution appears to be a remedy lying somewhere between a general intent to do justice by reversing an unjust enrichment in respect of money had and received, and the *de facto* award of a remedy *in rem*. It would only have been in the context of insolvency that there would have been a meaningful distinction between a proprietary and a personal claim. Islington's solvency meant that this question did not apply on the facts. On the facts of the *Islington* appeal, there was no prospect of the judgment order not being performed because the respondent was in funds and the appellant was not seeking money and not specific property. Nor, as a matter of principle, would a proprietary award have been made in any event.

Using equitable institutions to reverse unjust enrichment

8.016   It is clear that it is not possible in English law to impose remedial constructive trusts or remedial resulting trusts.[56] Therefore, the availability of trusts

---

[52] [1996] 2 All E.R. 961 at 975.
[53] *ibid.*
[54] *ibid.*
[55] See the account below, para. 8.019 and the speech of Lord Browne-Wilkinson. It should be remembered that the House of Lords was unanimous in its finding that there ought to be no proprietary right in favour of the bank — it was on the issue of compound interest that their lordships were divided.
[56] See in particular *per* Lord Browne-Wilkinson in *Westdeutsche Landesbank Girozentrale v. Islington LBC* [1996] A.C. 669; [1996] 2 All E.R. 961 at 1004.

implied by law by the courts cannot be imposed at the discretion of the court to achieve a remedial result unless such trust would arise by operation of law.[57] These principles are derived from older authorities such as *Barnes v. Addy*[58] as well as being discernible in more modern ones such as *Scandinavian Trading Tanker Co AB v. Flota Petrolera Ecuatoriana.*[59]

The central contention of this section is that the result of the majority decisions in the House of Lords in the local authority swaps cases is that it impossible for parties to retain a proprietary interest in property transferred under a commercial contract which is found to be void *ab initio*. The restatement of the core rules of equity by Lord Browne-Wilkinson create a test for a proprietary claim in equity which requires that the defendant have knowledge of the factor which is alleged to impose the office of trustee on it. It is submitted that these principles restrict the potential intervention of equity to such a narrow range of cases that the mutual intentions of parties to commercial contracts will frequently not be enforced by either the rules of common law or of equity.

Aside from the important issues of equitable proprietary claims and unjust enrichment claims, are more specific financial issues of the role of market standard contracts, the availability of recovery of property in collateralisation and physically-settled transactions, and the availability of compound interest. For the derivatives lawyer and anyone using the ISDA Master Agreement or the BBAIRS terms for interest rate swaps and other credit derivatives products, the impact of the swaps litigation remains problematic.[60] The core of this argument is that the courts' failure to enforce the credit enhancement and risk allocation provisions of the contracts and standard form agreements between the commercial parties to the swaps contracts, produces inequitable results between those parties, circumscribes the efficacy of English law in the context of financial agreements, and introduces further risk to financial markets by rendering otiose the terms of those standard form agreements.

Concretisation of equitable principles

8.017 Recent development in the rules of equity has seen a drift away from the twelve maxims set out in *Snell's Equity*[61] which have emphasised "its haphazard origin", and a movement towards a "bright line" development of equitable institutions into rigid tests.[62] This change has been illustrated in the decisions of the House of Lords and the Privy Council by means of:

- the solidifying of the appropriate test, and

---

[57] See Underhill and Hayton *Law of Trusts and Trustees* (15th ed., Butterworths, 1995), pp. 298 *et seq.*
[58] (1874) LR 9 Ch. App. 244 at 251, 255.
[59] [1983] 2 A.C. 694 at 703–4.
[60] The use of standard market contracts, particularly in the area of credit derivatives, sought to remove uncertainty and to control systemic risk by standardising the terms of over-the-counter agreements. Among these terms are provisions for the termination of contracts in a manner which reduces systemic risk while also reducing the immediate financial pressure on the parties to a contract on the happening of a termination event. The English courts have chosen to consider these contracts to be unenforceable. As a result, the markets' attempts to introduce effective, consensual, *ad hoc* regulation of the derivatives markets have been rendered ineffective.
[61] *Snell's Equity* (29th ed., Sweet & Maxwell, 1990), p. 27.
[62] See recent decisions such as *Tinsley v. Milligan* [1994] 1 A.C. 340; [1993] 3 W.L.R. 126; *Lloyds Bank v. Rosset* [1991] 1 A.C. 107; [1990] 2 W.L.R. 867; *Westdeutsche Landesbank v. Islington* [1996] A.C. 669; *Target Holdings v. Redferns* [1996] 1 A.C. 421; [1995] 3 W.L.R. 352; *Royal Brunei Airlines v. Tan* [1995] 2 A.C. 378; [1995] 3 W.L.R. 64.

- a restatement of the principles on which equity operates.

Aside from simply developing the understood nature of the equitable principles, there has been a reduced reliance on the general maxims in favour of a greater level of certainty which has been observable more easily in the common law, rather than in equity. In the context of commercial law, this development of principle has focussed on a return to traditional trusts rules. There has been some acceptance of commercial practice in the application of equitable principle to trust investment and in the development of dishonest assistance of the concept of risk.

8.018   One good example of this progression was *Royal Brunei Airlines v. Tan.*[63] The principle of dishonesty required to imposed personal liability to account for assistance in a breach of trust was broadened far beyond any of the more usual tests of whether or not a person is "dishonest" *strictu sensu*. In Lord Nicholls opinion, the test for "acting dishonestly, or with a lack of probity, which is synonymous, means simply not acting as an honest person would in the circumstance. This is an objective standard."[64] Therefore "dishonesty" can be an *active* state of mind or, alternatively, a *passive* "lack of probity". Reckless risk-taking is considered to be a part of this extended notion of "dishonesty" establishing a concept between fraud (necessarily *active deceit*) and negligent failure to appreciate risk (*passive unsuitability*). This form of liability demonstrates the potential liability of one inducing a buyer to enter into a derivative in breach of trust. The same liability would obtain where such dishonest assistance arises in relation to the termination of a transaction arising out of an event of default.

In the context of the credit derivatives markets, the use of equity contains a danger of the application of discretionary remedies by the courts. The refusal of the courts in *Islington* and the other local authority swaps cases to consider the counterparties' attempts to control and allocate risk is therefore to be contrasted with the acceptance in *Tan* and other cases that risk forms a part of the availability of some equitable remedies and institutions.

Equitable institutions in Islington

8.019   The leading speech in the House of Lords in *Islington* was delivered by Lord Browne-Wilkinson, with whom Lord Lloyd[65] and Lord Slynn[66] concurred on all points, with Lord Goff and Lord Woolf dissenting on the availability of compound interest. In short, the majority view was that:

- Compound interest is available only in circumstances where the claimant has an equitable proprietary interest of the property in respect of which compound interest is claimed.

- There was no proprietary resulting trust in favour of the bank because the availability of resulting trust is restricted to two distinct categories.

---

[63] [1995] 2 A.C. 378.
[64] *ibid.* at 386.
[65] Lord Lloyd delivered a judgment which considered, as discussed above, the commercial context of equity rather than focusing, as Lord Browne-Wilkinson did, on the re-drawing of the commonly used equitable remedies and principles.
[66] Lord Slynn did not deliver a substantive judgment, although he did make some reference to awards of compound interest being available generally on where there has been fraud or some breach of fiduciary duty.

- There was no proprietary constructive trust because there was no impact on the conscience of the authority given that it had no knowledge of the invalidity of the contract at the time the money was paid to it.

- *Sinclair v. Brougham*[67] was probably not to be followed in future.

- The controversial decision of Goulding J. in *Chase Manhattan Bank v. Israel-British Bank*[68] can be explained better although the result was probably correct.

Compound interest

8.020 The availability of compound interest in relation to credit derivatives claims was found in *Islington* to represent the rate of return expected by market participants on their money if they were to enter into straightforward lending transactions with it. An award merely of simple interest would be less than the return which the seller would have expected.[69] The award of compound interest is an equitable remedy, however, which was at the only issue strictly at issue before the House of Lords in *Islington*,[70] despite that tribunal deciding it was necessary to consider broader questions. Therefore, in spite of the commercial expectation that compound interest would be available, its award by the courts its only available where the plaintiff can demonstrate a pre-existing equitable proprietary interest in the property in relation to which compound interest is sought. The main shortcoming of equity is that it will not be imposed in many situations in which there has not been evident fraud. As Lord Browne-Wilkinson explained:

> "In the absence of fraud the courts of equity have never awarded compound interest except against a trustee or other person owing fiduciary duties who is accountable for profits made from his position."[71]

In his Lordship's opinion the authorities established that in cases where there was no demonstrable fraud, compound interest would only be awarded against a defendant who is "a trustee or otherwise in a fiduciary position".[72] The appropriate response for a court in such a situation would be "recouping . . . an improper profit made by him": that is, making restitution of that profit.[73] Two points would appear to arise. First, it is possible to identify the restriction, considered above, of equitable remedies such as the provision of compound interest to fairly uncontroversial categories of fraud or breach of fiduciary duty. Secondly, the response advocated by his lordship is one of recouping a profit made outwith such a duty — a response which smacks of restitutionary purpose[74] as much as equitable operation on the conscience of the defendant.

8.021 Lord Goff was prepared to allow an order for the payment of compound interest. The starting point for Lord Goff, as considered above, was with the speech of Lord Mansfield in *Moses v. Macferlan*,[75] where he said that the "gist of the action

---

[67] [1914] A.C. 398.
[68] [1981] Ch. 105.
[69] Rightly, the courts did not attempt an exercise in second-guessing the forms of investment which might have been undertaken other than the vanilla option of a rate of return based on ordinary lending.
[70] [1996] A.C. 669; [1996] 2 All E.R. 961.
[71] *ibid.* at 984.
[72] *ibid.* at 985.
[73] *ibid.*
[74] Birks, *Introduction to the Law of Restitution*, p. 11.
[75] (1760) 2 Burr. 1005 at 1012.

for money had and received"[76] is that "the defendant, upon the circumstances of the case, is obliged by the ties of natural justice and equity to refund the money". Thus, in considering whether or not compound interest ought to have been awarded to the bank, Lord Goff felt that it would have been "strange indeed if the courts lacked jurisdiction in such a case to ensure that justice could be fully achieved by means of an award of compound interest".[77]

The issue, as considered above however, is why it is that the impact of an award of compound interest in relation to cash-settled transactions achieves for the plaintiff precisely the result that an equitable proprietary claim would have achieved in the context of a physically-settled derivative. Westdeutsche would have received a remedy equal in size to a situation where it remained absolute owner of the money which in fact was paid to the authority. What must also be appreciated is that, had there been an order for compound interest, Westdeutsche would have received a remedy equal in *quality* to the situation if it had remained absolute owner of the money which in fact was paid to the authority.[78] In the context of transfers of value held in electronic bank accounts, an award of compound interest is the same as awarding a proprietary claim in respect of the value held in that account.

In Lord Goff's dissenting judgment, an equitable remedy can be used to support a common law claim, particularly where the only common law remedy available was inadequate for the purpose.[79] In Lord Goff's opinion it was satisfaction of a principle of justice that was required from the court to ensure that a personal claim was available for repayment of the balance of the bank's money without any unjust enrichment of the authority by means of its use of the bank's money.[80] Therefore, in Lord Goff's view, an award of compound interest would have been possible to prevent unjust enrichment of the authority in relation to the personal claim for money had and received.[81]

The nature of the trust

8.022 The core of the trust concept is identified as equity operating on the conscience of the person who is the owner of the legal interest: the First Principle. There is a confusing distinction made between an "express or implied trust" on the one hand or a trust imposed "by reason of his unconscionable conduct" which is termed a "constructive trust".[82] Given the importance of conscience, a person "cannot be a trustee of the property if and so long as he is ignorant of the facts alleged to affect his conscience": the Second Principle.[83] It is on this basis that Islington cannot be a trustee because it did not know it was incapable of entering into the swaps contract until after the House of Lords decision in *Hazell*. Where the

---

[76] [1996] 2 All E.R. 961 at 980.
[77] *ibid.*
[78] It was accepted between the parties that Westdeutsche would have received compound interest on the money paid to the authority had it not paid the money to the authority. It is submitted that it would not have been possible to seek to adduce evidence in any event that the money would have been invested in any form other than retaining it in the currency and the amount in which it was paid to the authority.
[79] [1996] 2 All E.R. 961 at 979.
[80] *ibid.* at 977.
[81] It is submitted that it would have been open to Lord Goff to have decided that compound interest is equivalent to a proprietary claim in respect of cash-settled transactions. Therefore, a proprietary claim should have been awarded to do justice between the parties. As it was, Lord Goff would have awarded something equivalent to a proprietary claim — but called it by another name.
[82] [1996] A.C. 669; [1996] 2 All E.R. 961 at 988.
[83] *ibid.*

allegation is that there be a constructive trust imposed, there must be awareness of "the factors which are alleged to affect his conscience".[84]

The further problem which arises is that the property which is transferred under the deep discount payment has ceased to exist when it is transferred from a bank account which is then overdrawn. This offends against the Third Principle that there must be identifiable trust property.[85] As Lord Browne-Wilkinson held, in reliance on *Re Goldcorp Exchange Ltd (in receivership)*[86] "[o]nce there ceased to be an identifiable trust fund, the local authority could not become a trustee".

The Fourth Principle is that a beneficiary acquires an equitable proprietary interest in the trust property from the establishment of the trust.[87] On the facts before him, Lord Browne-Wilkinson held that there was never a coming together of all of these factors before the judgment in *Hazell* was handed down. As his Lordship held:

> "There was therefore never a time at which both (a) there was defined trust property and (b) the conscience of the local authority in relation to such defined trust property was affected. The basic requirements of a trust were never satisfied."[88]

8.023 What is important within the re-definition of the principles of the trust is the assertion that property does not have latent within it a legal and an equitable title. Rather, it is only when the four principles are satisfied that a division between legal and equitable title is created. The legal owner of property simply carries "all rights" until a trust is imposed. It is on this basis that the equity established by Hobhouse J.[89] is to be rejected.[90]

> "... [T]o talk about the bank 'retaining' its equitable interest [after the deep discount payment is made] is meaningless. The only question is whether the circumstances under which the money was paid were such as, in equity, to impose a trust on the local authority. If so, an equitable interest arose for the first time under that trust."[91]

Lord Browne-Wilkinson referred to a number of authorities on this point.[92] As such, equity will not grant any proprietary remedy to the payer under a void

---

[84] *ibid.*

[85] *ibid.* There is an exception to this principle in the case of personal liability imposed under constructive trust on a person who dishonestly assisted in a breach of trust.

[86] [1995] 1 A.C. 74.

[87] [1996] A.C. 669; [1996] 2 All E.R. 961 at 988. There is an exception to this principle in the case of a purchaser for value without notice of the beneficiary's rights.

[88] [1996] A.C. 669; [1996] 2 All E.R. 961 at 988–989.

[89] *I.e.*: that justice required that the local authority be treated as holding the deep discount payment, or its cash equivalent (*infra*) on resulting trust for the bank — thus imposing an equitable proprietary right in favour of the bank in circumstances where there had been no trust or obligation of conscience imposed on the recipient of the payment. The absence of such obligation founded Lord Browne-Wilkinson's rejection of the decision at first instance. Hobhouse J. overlooked the fact that there could be no specific trust fund because the money comprising the deep discount payment had all been spent. Therefore, there was no fund over which a resulting trust could have been imposed. The only possible solution would have been a constructive trust — a solution ruled out by Lord Browne-Wilkinson.

[90] As considered above, para. 8.011.

[91] [1996] 2 All E.R. 961 at 989.

[92] *Re Cook (dec'd), Beck v. Grant* [1948] Ch. 212; *Vandervell v. IRC* [1967] 2 A.C. 291 at 317 *per* Lord Upjohn and Lord Donovan; *Comr of Stamp Duties v. Livingston* [1965] A.C. 694 at 712; Underhill and Hayton *Law of Trusts and Trustees* (15th ed., Butterworths, 1995), p. 866.

contract unless there had been either some effective, express retention of proprietary rights or some unconscionable act on the part of the recipient which would create a constructive trust.

Further, there is the possibility that even where legal and equitable title are separated by the intervention of some other action, that there will not be a personal liability to account as a trustee on the basis of knowing receipt ". . . unless he has the requisite degree of knowledge . . ."[93] This principle is divined from *Re Diplock*[94] and *Re Montagu's Settlement Trusts*.[95] As Lord Browne-Wilkinson expressed it: ". . . innocent receipt of property by X subject to an existing equitable interest does not by itself make X a trustee despite the severance of the legal and equitable titles."[96]

Express proprietary rights

8.024 It is not proposed to consider the whole of the law relating to express trusts because that would be too large an undertaking for this project.[97] All that is important in this context is whether or not there is an express trust formed to retain rights in property and whether or not that accords with the risk management objectives of the parties. Some core points should be raised, however. The property under an express trust must be certain or the trust will be void.[98] There is a question whether the property which is the subject of the constructive trust must be certain in the same way. There are some older authorities which consider that the property must be certain under a constructive trust.[99] It is submitted that this rule can only apply to those trusts where a proprietary remedy is sought because it must be possible to establish which property is to be subjected to a proprietary remedy (see *Tracing* below, para. 8.047). Some of the commentators draw a dividing line between constructive trusts which impose a proprietary remedy (and under which the subject matter of the trust must be certain) and those which impose on a personal liability against some person (and under which there is no need to identify property because only personal liability to account in money is required).

Proprietary rights under void contracts

8.025 Capacity of the counterparty and the enforceability of the subject matter of the agreement are necessary preliminary issues in contracting credit derivatives, given the number of contexts in which their efficacy has yet to be tested by the courts and also given the endless innovation of the markets. Therefore, a void contract creates issues beyond the express termination provisions of the contract itself to do with restitution, and the enforceability of property rights in money or other assets transferred as part of the agreement. The principles of restitution and implied trusts address these commercial concerns in the event of the failure of the contract.

The central question addressed by the House of Lords in *Islington* was:

---

[93] [1996] A.C. 669; [1996] 2 All E.R. 961 at 990.
[94] *Re Diplock's Estate, Diplock v. Wintle* [1948] Ch. 465.
[95] [1987] Ch. 264.
[96] [1996] A.C. 669; [1996] 2 All E.R. 961 at 990.
[97] See perhaps Hudson, *Principles of Equity and the Law of Trusts* (Cavendish, 1999) generally.
[98] *Re Goldcorp* [1995] 1 A.C. 524; [1994] 3 W.L.R. 199.
[99] *Re Barney* [1892] 2 Ch. 265 at 273.

"Does the recipient of money under a contract subsequently found to be void for mistake or as being *ultra vires* hold the moneys received on trust even where he had no knowledge at any relevant time that the contract was void?"[1]

There are two issues arising from this understanding of the question. First, whether an unjust factor will cause the imposition of a trust. Secondly, the establishment of "knowledge" as the appropriate yardstick by which the applicability of the trust would be appropriate. The restatement of the core rules of equity in the speech of Lord Browne-Wilkinson in *Westdeutsche Landesbank v. Islington*[2] created a test that a proprietary claim in equity will only be imposed in circumstances where the defendant has knowledge of the factor which is alleged to impose the office of trustee on him, thus affecting his conscience — which will generally not be the case in respect of transactions entered into in good faith by both parties.

Given that there was no viable express contract between the parties, despite what is said in para. 8.052 about the possible operation of the doctrine of severance, the House of Lords in *Islington*[3] was unanimous in holding that neither the deep discount payment made by the bank nor any of the interest amounts were to be held on resulting or constructive trust and thus liable to attract compound interest. Lord Goff and Lord Woolf dissented on the availability of compound interest: the former asserting that it ought to have been available on the grounds of justice, the latter asserting that commercial people would expect that it would be made available.

Failure of agreement

8.026   One of the difficulties with the imposition of equitable remedies in commercial cases is that the two instances in which equity will usually intervene is where there has been fraud or the breach of a fiduciary responsibility.[4] The issue is then when equity will impose proprietary remedies.[5]

---

[1] [1996] 2 All E.R. 961 at 986.
[2] [1996] A.C. 669, [1996] 2 All E.R. 961.
[3] *ibid.*
[4] For academic commentary on criticisms of requirement for equitable interest before a tracing claim see: Birks, *Introduction to the Law of Restitution, op cit.*, pp. 380–4; Goff and Jones, *The Law of Restitution, op cit.*, pp. 83–6; Oakley, "The Prerequisites of an Equitable Tracing Claim" (1975) 28 *C.L.P.* 64; Pearce, "A Tracing Paper" (1976) 40 Conv. 277; Dewar, "The Development of the Remedial Constructive Trust" (1982) 60 Can. B.R. 265 at 273; McKendrick, "Tracing Misdirected Funds" [1991] L.M.C.L.Q. 378 at 386–387.
[5] For academic commentary on the availability of proprietary remedies arising out of restitution and equity see the following eclectic discussions: Birks, *op cit.*, pp. 375–401; Burrows, *op cit.*, pp. 40–5; Goff and Jones, *op cit.*, Chap. 2; Maddaugh and McCamus, *op cit.*, pp. 78–100; Maudsley, "Proprietary Remedies for the Recovery of Money" (1959) 75 LQR 234; Dewar, "The Development of the Remedial Constructive Trust" (1982) 60 Can. B.R. 265; Goode, "Ownership and Obligation in Commercial Transactions" (1987) 103 L.Q.R. 433 at 436–7; Litman, "The Emergence of Unjust Enrichment as a Cause of Action and the Remedy of Constructive Trust" (1988) 26 Alberta L.R. 407; Hayton, "Constructive Trusts: Is the Remedying of Unjust Enrichment a Satisfactory Approach?" in *Equity, Fiduciaries and Trusts* (Youdan ed., Toronto, 1989), Chap. 9; Paciocco, "The Remedial Constructive Trust: A Principled Basis for Priorities over Creditors' (1989) 68 Can. B.R. 315; Sherwin, "Constructive Trusts in Bankruptcy" [1989] Univ. of Illinois L.R. 297; J. Gummow, "Unjust Enrichment, Restitution and Proprietary Remedies", in *Essays on Restitution* (P.D. Finn, ed., Sydney, 1990, Chap. 3); Elias, *Explaining Constructive Trusts* (Oxford, 1990); Fridman, "The Reach of Restitution" (1991) 11 L.S. 304; Glover, "Bankruptcy and Constructive Trusts" (1991) 19 A.B.L.R. 98; Goode, "Property and Unjust Enrichment", *Essays on Restitution* (Burrows ed., Oxford, 1991, Chap. 9; Annetta, "Priority Rights in Insolvency — The Doctrinal Basis for Equity's Intervention" (1992) 20 A.B.L.R. 311; Rajani, "Equitable Assistance in the Search for Security", in *Insolvency Law: Theory and Practice* (H. Rajak ed., London, 1993, Chap. 2).

The decision in *Islington* can be divided into different categories of liability.[6] First, the core test for the imposition of a constructive established by Lord Browne-Wilkinson that liability is based on knowledge and the impact on the conscience of the legal owner of property. Second, the scope of the "restitution-based personal claim".[7] What is less certain is the impact of the majority view in *Islington* in relation to equitable tracing claims.[8]

The context of the Islington appeal

8.027   It had been conceded in argument by counsel for both sides that there could be no argument on the basis of constructive trust. Rather, the appeal had proceeded on the basis of the restitutionary role of resulting trusts, until their Lordships indicated that they would be amenable to submissions on the correctness of *Sinclair v. Brougham*[9] and the role of the constructive trust. In the opinion of Lord Browne-Wilkinson, the imposition of a trust on the authority would have been the retrospective duties of a trustee imposed on it and that the proprietary rights thus created[10] would have bound any subsequent owner of the property retrospectively also.[11] The House of Lords were unanimous, however, in holding that, in relation to the proprietary claim sought by the bank, there was no apparent, common sense reason why they should be entitled to a proprietary claim.[12] The decision that there was no efficacy in the terms of the contractual agreements meant that the judicial committee did not consider whether or not the standard form contracts would have generated such a common sense need for a proprietary remedy. As Lord Browne-Wilkinson held:

> "[i]f the contract had been valid, [Westdeutsche] would have had purely personal rights against [the authority]. Why should [Westdeutsche] be better off because the contract was void?"[13]

This is the primary failing of the contracts in force between the parties, they had made no effort to reserve themselves any rights to specific property. The mechanisms for taking proprietary rights are important to establish to put assets beyond the risks of the main contract being held void or otherwise unenforceable.

The impact on third parties and on the certainty of the enforcement of commercial contracts of these agreements as to credit support is dealt with in the following passage which explains why a proprietary right for the banks would be unsuitable on principle:

> ". . . a businessman who has entered into transactions relating to or dependent upon property rights could find that assets which apparently belong to one person in fact belong to another; that there are off balance sheet liabilities of which he cannot be aware; that these property rights and liabilities arise from circumstances unknown not only to himself but also to anyone else who has been involved in the transactions."[14]

---

[6] Oliver, K.C.L.J. 8 (1997/98) 147.
[7] Which Lord Goff established as standing for the common law category of money had and received.
[8] Considered below, para. 8.047.
[9] [1914] A.C. 398; [1914–15] All E.R. Rep. 622.
[10] This would appear to include the receipt or mixing of the moneys by the "trustee".
[11] [1996] A.C. 669, [1996] 2 All E.R. 961 at 986.
[12] *ibid.* at 987.
[13] *ibid.*
[14] *ibid.*

8.028 The problems which arise here are numerous. It is true to say that interest rate swaps were always held off-balance sheet. As had been recognised, there are general problems of systemic certainty with allowing these products to be undeclared in published accounts. Secondly, in relation to specific property, there would be problems with causing property to be pledged to more than one secured interest. However, these contentions did not necessarily apply on the facts of the *Islington* litigation. First, given that the deep discount payment was held off-balance sheet, no third party could have relied on its existence for security purposes. Secondly, Islington was in funds to meet the proprietary obligation in any event although reaching a principled position for all cases appears to be a preferable approach rather than restricting the application of the principles solely to the facts. Thirdly, it is not clear that any third party would have had secured rights over the general purpose bank accounts into which this money was paid.

In Lord Browne-Wilkinson's view, the upshot of granting a proprietary claim would be that "[a] new area of unmanageable risk will be introduced into commercial dealings."[15] However, the real impact of their Lordship's approach remains the difficulty of asserting a proprietary claim in void commercial contracts at all. The commercial risk could be said to have been created by failing to implement the termination provisions of agreements entered into in good faith and at arm's length.

Duties of trustees, current portfolio theory and risk

8.029 The most interesting recent development in the area of risk and equity is the decision of the Privy Council in *Royal Brunei Airlines v. Tan,*[16] in the leading speech of Lord Nicholls, which held that liability for dishonest assistance in a misapplication of trust property does not require a dishonest act on the part of the trustee. Rather, it is sufficient to attach liability to the dishonest assistant that the assistant acted dishonestly to be fixed with liability for the breach of trust. The correct approach to this issue set out by Lord Nicholls creates a test of "dishonesty" which extends beyond actual fraud to taking risks recklessly with trust property. With this broad understanding of the forms of risk which are capable of founding liability on grounds of "dishonesty", it is important to consider liability which will found general equitable liability in contexts where the defendant is involved in the performance of credit derivatives contracts founded on the notion of risk-taking.

The courts have begun to accept the need to adapt to the manner in which financial markets and finance professionals operate in the modern context. In this way, principles of equity relating to the investment powers and obligations of trustees have altered. Hoffmann J., in delivering judgment in *Nestlé v. National Westminster Bank plc,*[17] held that:

> "Modern trustees acting within their investment powers are entitled to be judged by the standards of current portfolio theory, which emphasises the risk level of the entire portfolio rather than the risk attaching to each investment taken in isolation."

---

[15] *ibid.*
[16] [1995] 2 A.C. 378.
[17] [1993] 1 W.L.R. 1260; see also Underhill and Hayton, *The Law of Trusts and Trustees* (15th ed., Butterworths, 1995), pp. 598 *et seq.*

8.030   In developing this point, his Lordship held that a trustee is required to act fairly between all the beneficiaries of the trust fund which he was empowered to invest. However, the reference back to the behaviour of trustees acting in the context of the modern financial markets indicates the appropriateness of trustees balancing their investments between different types of product to even out risk, as well as taking into account the necessary risk required to make the maximum return for the trust.

The position which the trustee is placed in by equity appears to be a deeply invidious one, without some reference to common market practice. The duty to act evenly between different categories of beneficiaries requires a difficult balancing act between generating short-term return and protecting the integrity of the long-term fund. High-risk short-term investments are necessary to satisfy the requirements of the rule to make the maximum possible return for the trust.[18] However, within that doctrine of maximum gain there is a requirement to act as a prudent person of business would act[19] specifically with reference to someone for whom he felt morally bound to provide (over and above dealings in that person's own affairs). The types of transaction available for the trustee's investment without stricture are similarly limited by statute[20] and by common law.[21]

The trustee is similarly required to supervise professionals to whom delegation of the investment function is made. The principle in *Learoyd v. Whiteley*[22] indicates that the trustee when investing trust property must not only act as a businessperson of ordinary prudence, but must also avoid all investments of a hazardous nature. Whereas in *Bartlett v. Barclays Bank*,[23] a distinction was drawn between a prudent degree of risk and unacceptable hazard; the former would be acceptable whereas the latter would not.[24] The trust and the duties of the fiduciary are comprised partly of rules of property and rules of personal obligation.[25] Whereas equity operates on the property that is held as the trust fund by means of proprietary principles, there are also a range of personal claims against the trustee in connection with the manner in which the function of minding the trust fund is carried out.[26] There are obligations for making too little profit,[27] making profits for himself which were not open to the trust,[28] and taking risks to make greater profit which then caused loss to the trust.[29]

8.031   The trustee's duty of investment can be summarised as being threefold: to act prudently and safely, to act fairly between beneficiaries, to do the best for the beneficiaries financially. As Megarry V-C held in *Cowan v. Scargill*:[30]

---

[18] *Cowan v. Scargill* [1985] Ch. 270.
[19] *Bartlett v. Barclays Bank Trust Co. Ltd* [1980] Ch. 515.
[20] Trustee Investment Act 1961.
[21] Aside from the requirement of prudence, there are prohibitions on lending on personal security: *Holmes v. Dring* (1788) Cox Eq. Cas. 1; *Khoo Tek Keong v. Ch'ng Joo Tuan Neoh* [1934] A.C. 529.
[22] (1887) 12 App. Cas. 727.
[23] [1980] Ch. 515.
[24] Under s.6 of the Trustee Investments Act 1961, there is a statutory duty to consider the suitability of particular investments, especially in the light of the need for diversification.
[25] See Birks [1996] R.L.R. 3.
[26] As to the nature of trusteeship in this context, see Hayton, "The Irreducible Core Content of Trusteeship" in *Trends in Contemporary Trusts Law* (Oakley ed., Oxford 1996), p. 47, emphasising the core of the nature of the trust being the ability of the beneficiary to enforce the trust by personal obligations enforceable against the trustee.
[27] *Cowan v. Scargill* [1985] Ch. 270.
[28] *Boardman v. Phipps* [1967] 2 A.C. 46.
[29] *Bartlett v. Barclays Bank* [1980] Ch. 515.
[30] [1985] Ch. 270.

"When the purpose of the trust is to provide financial benefits for the beneficiaries, the best interests of the beneficiaries are their best financial interests ... Trustees may even have to act dishonourably (though not illegally) if the interests of their beneficiaries require it."

There is an obligation on the fiduciary to take a level of risk which will generate the best return for the beneficiary, regardless of extraneous factors.

The liability of third parties to the trust (that is, persons who are neither trustees nor beneficiaries) arise principally in circumstances in which the trustee delegates its authority to invest. The trustee's obligation can be described as follows:

"It seems to me that on general trust principles a trustee ought to conduct the business of the trust in the same manner that an ordinary prudent man of business would conduct his own, and that beyond that there is no liability or obligation on the trustee."[31]

Exceptionally in *Re Vickery*,[32] where a trustee had given money to solicitor who absconded with it, Maugham J. considered the central issue to be whether the trustee was negligent in employing the solicitor or permitting money to remain in his hands. It was held that there was no liability on the trustee unless there had been some "wilful default" by him, being something more than a lack of care. This test has come in for much academic criticism,[33] being based on *Re City Equitable Fire Insurance*,[34] a company law case looking at the obligations of fiduciaries in the context of specific articles of association. Jones contends that the better test is one based on "want of reasonable care" rather than "wilful default".

8.032   The core issue appears to be whether or not the law should recognise that you have to trust market professionals to do things which trustees cannot do. As such, the role of equity ought to be to impose liability in contexts of the reasonable allocation of risks under the trust structure. The requirement of equity that beneficiaries under trusts should be insulated from risk of market movement and personnel default (whether by trustees or market professionals) in making investment decisions, does not accord with the basis upon which financial professionals are prepared to enter into terms of business. The client is required to accept the risk of loss as well as the possibility of gain. In this context equity must also consider how to balance the need to make best profit against requirement not to lose trust money.[35] Therefore, there is a direct conflict between established principles governing the liability of trustees and the manner in which the sellers of products in the financial markets are prepared to enter into agreements.

The context of risk therefore remains problematic in equity in circumstances where the courts have imposed near strict liability in the context of fiduciaries.[36] The decision of the Privy Council in *Tan* indicated a growing acceptance of reckless risk-taking as part of the unconscionable behaviour against which equity will act. However, *Islington* fails to accept the commercial context of risk management as

---

[31] *Speight v. Gaunt* (1883) 9 App. Cas. 1, *per* Lord Jessel M.R.
[32] [1931] 1 Ch. 572.
[33] Jones (1968) 84 L.Q.R. 474; Hayton "Investment Management Problems" (1990) L.Q.R. 89–93.
[34] [1925] Ch. 407.
[35] One solution might be to grant an automatic trustee indemnity where the trustee is able to obtain an indemnity from the market professional, thus freeing trustees from the need to control that which they cannot control in standard terms of terms of business letters.
[36] See *Bartlett*, *Nestle*, etc., *op cit.*

something which ought similarly to be encompassed in granting remedies on a restitutionary or equitable basis. The context of equitable proprietary remedies remains outwith the ambit of these developing principles, except for the protection of beneficiaries.

Resulting trusts

8.033   Lord Browne-Wilkinson in *Westdeutsche Landesbank v. Islington LBC*[37] set out the two situations in which he considered that a resulting trust would arise. It is contended, however, that resulting trusts do arise in more circumstances than those two identified by Lord Browne-Wilkinson.

> "Under existing law a resulting trust arises in two sets of circumstances:
>
> (A) where A makes a voluntary payment to B or pays (wholly or in part) for the purchase of property which is vested either in B alone or in the joint names of A and B, there is a presumption that A did not intend to make a gift to B: the money or property is held on trust for A (if he is the sole provider of the money) or in the case of a joint purchase by A and B in shares proportionate to their contributions. It is important to stress that this is only a *presumption*, which presumption is easily rebutted either by the counter-presumption of advancement or by direct evidence of A's intention to make an outright transfer.[38]
>
> (B) Where A transfers property to B *on express trusts*, but the trusts declared do not exhaust the whole beneficial interest.[39] Both types of resulting trust are traditionally regarded as examples of trusts giving effect to the common intention of the parties. A resulting trust is not imposed by law against the intentions of the trustee (as is a constructive trust) but gives effect to his presumed intention."[40]

The classical statement of the divisions of resulting trust are typically identified in the judgment of Megarry J. in *Vandervell (No. 2)*.[41] His Lordship divided resulting trusts between 'automatic resulting trusts' and 'presumed resulting trusts'. However, Lord Browne-Wilkinson in *Westdeutsche Landesbank v. Islington* doubted that this division could be said to be correct in all circumstances:

> "Megarry J. in *Re Vandervell's Trusts (No. 2)*[42] suggests that a resulting trust of type (B) does not depend on intention but operates automatically. I am not convinced that this is right. If the settlor has expressly, or by necessary implication, abandoned any beneficial interest in the trust property, there is in my view no resulting trust: the undisposed-of equitable interest vests in the Crown as *bona vacantia*.[43]"[44]

---

[37] [1996] 2 All E.R. 961; [1996] A.C. 669
[38] See Underhill and Hayton, *Law of Trusts and Trustees* (15th ed., Butterworths, 1995), pp. 317 *et seq.*, *White v. Vandervell Trustees Ltd* [1974] Ch. 269 at 288 *et seq.*
[39] See Underhill and Hayton, *Law of Trusts and Trustees* (15th ed., Butterworths, 1995), pp. 317 *et seq.*, *White v. Vandervell Trustees Ltd* [1974] Ch. 269, 288 *et seq.*; *Barclays Bank Ltd v. Quistclose Investments Ltd* [1970] A.C. 567.
[40] [1996] 2 All E.R. 961 at 990–991.
[41] [1974] Ch. 269 at 294; [1974] 1 All E.R. 47 at 64.
[42] *ibid.*
[43] See *Re West Sussex Constabulary's Widows, Children and Benevolent (1930) Fund Trusts* [1971] Ch. 1.
[44] [1996] 2 All E.R. 961 at 990–991.

8.034   Lord Browne-Wilkinson is therefore taking issue with the categorisation of some resulting trusts as being "automatic". His lordship considered that where the settlor had sought to divest himself absolutely of his right, there should not be a resulting trust in favour of the settlor. There are two issues which arise here. The first is that English property law has never expressly recognised that it is possible to "abandon" rights in property. English law has taken the view that one cannot dispose of property other than by transferring or terminating rights in it. What is not possible is simply to say that those rights of ownership which continue to exist simply belong to no-one.

Further, a resulting trust will not arise where contract for payment of interest was subsequently found to have been void *ab initio*. It is incorrect to say that there is a division in the legal and equitable title to money paid such that the equitable interest remains with the payer.[45] There is no division between legal and equitable title until a trust is declared or some event happens to divide those titles. The only claim that arises in favour of the payer is a personal claim for restitution ("money had and received"). Rather, Lord Browne-Wilkinson restricts the resulting trust to two categories and denies that there should be extension of those categories. First, a resulting trust arises where there has been a failure to dispose of the entire equitable interest; and, secondly, where the beneficiary has contributed to the purchase price of the property.[46]

8.035   The point raised by Chambers is whether or the resulting trust "properly understood, might not be equity's principal contribution to reversing unjust enrichment".[47] Elsewhere Professor Martin has described the resulting trust as "a situation in which a transferee is required by equity to hold property on trust for the transferor; or for the person who provided the purchase money for the transfer."[48] Waters describes the resulting trust as arising whenever legal or equitable title to property is in one party's name, but that party, because he is a fiduciary or gave no value for the property, is under an obligation to return it to the original title owner, or to the person who *did* give value for it.[49] Chambers cites a Canadian interpretation of the resulting trust as containing the essential characteristic[50] that "the person in whose favour the trust arises is the person who provided the property or equitable interest vested in the person bound by the trust."[51]

The difficulty with the use of resulting trust, is that the obligation is placed on the trustee from the time of receipt of the property impressed with a trust, at a time when that person could not have known of that obligation. The distinction between the trustee under a resulting trust and a constructive trust could be summed up in the following way:

> "The term 'constructive trustee' is sometimes used to describe someone who holds no property in trust, but has assisted a breach of trust and is under a personal liability to compensate the beneficiary for losses caused thereby. 'Resulting trustee' is never used in this fashion. There must be identifiable assets vested in the resulting trustee capable of being the subject matter of a trust."[52]

---

[45] *Westdeutsche Landesbank v. Islington LBC* [1996] 2 All E.R. 961; [1996] A.C. 669.
[46] *ibid.*
[47] Chambers, *Resulting Trusts* (Oxford, 1997), p. 1.
[48] Hanbury and Martin, *Modern Equity* (13th ed., Sweet & Maxwell, 1993), p. 233.
[49] Waters (1984), p. 300.
[50] Chambers (1997), p. 1.
[51] *Baird v. Columbia Trust Co.* (1915) 22 D.L.R. 150 at 151, B.C.S.C., *per* Morrison J.
[52] Chambers (1997), p. 2.

Establishing proprietary claims

8.036 There is a division in restitution between two different measures in which the plaintiff may recover. The first measure is "value received"; the second measure is "value surviving".[53] As Chambers delineates the subject:[54]

> "First measure claims to the value received are necessarily personal, whereas second-measure claims to the value surviving are usually, but not necessarily, proprietary[55] . . . The resulting trust itself always effects restitution in the second measure (of the value surviving), because it can arise 'only in respect of something identified as existing in the defendant's hands'.[56] Like all trusts, it cannot exist unless it is 'possible to identify clearly the property which is subject to the trust.' "[57]

Thus the proprietary claim based on the restitutionary resulting trust is necessarily bound by the established rules of equity as to the identity of property. The issue of founding equitable proprietary claims therefore remains central, in the light of a need for a proprietary base for such a claim. This discussion returns to the foregoing analysis of the availability of proprietary remedies as delineated by Lord Browne-Wilkinson in *Islington*.

Chambers' assumption is that the resulting trust is motivated by the removal of some unjust enrichment from the recipient of property.[58] While it is possible that the prevention of unjust enrichment could be identified as an unspoken common principle which motivates the manner in which resulting trusts have been imposed in past cases, there is little evidence that unjust enrichment was *the* ratio for any of those decisions. The restitutionary role of the resulting trust is potentially a large one. As discussed above, the resulting trust has many features which make it an appropriate vehicle for achieving restitutionary goals. However, the import of Lord Browne-Wilkinson's decision in *Islington*, as considered above, must be that the operation of the resulting trust is to be considered as greatly limited. Rather, the remedial constructive trust would appear to have acquired the pre-eminent position as the most likely tool of providing restitution in future cases.

Constructive trusts

8.037 The English law attitude to the constructive trust is controversial and intellectually problematic. In family home cases, the constructive trust is used more usually to fulfil some expectation rather than to prevent unjust enrichment.[59] Thus, in the United States, the constructive trust is used primarily to provide interests in homes. The resulting trust has been removed from the jurisprudence as a consequence. There is a dividing line between the U.S. remedial constructive trust in this circumstance and the English common intention constructive trust. The role of the resulting trust is thus withdrawn in both jurisdictions and the concept progressively elided with the common intention than founds a constructive trust in that context. The question also arises whether or not these trusts are really a kind of

---

[53] Birks (1989), p. 6.
[54] Chambers (1997), p. 105.
[55] See Birks (1989), p. 85.
[56] Birks (1989), p. 85.
[57] Waters (1984), 117; *Cowcher v. Cowcher* [1972] 1 W.L.R. 425 at 430.
[58] Chambers (1997), p. 222.
[59] Chambers (1997), p. 226.

informal express trust. In considering borderlines between different concepts, many theorists have propounded the view that constructive trusts have closer links to contracts than do resulting trusts.[60] This is based on the constructive trust's response to an intention to dispose of property in favour of another and an inducement in that other to behave in a certain manner. This coming together of inducement, reliance and detriment is also true of proprietary estoppel. In some sense the element of consideration is provided by this detriment in the constructive beneficiary. The unjust factors of inducement and detriment is restitution's equivalent to consideration in the law of contract.

In considering the lay-out of constructive trusts, Elias' *Explaining Constructive Trusts*[61] attempts the seemingly impossible task of identifying the principles on which the constructive trust can *be said* to exist and the principles on which it *ought to be* said to exist. The aim of Elias' book is said to be "rationalisation",[62] whereas no general definition of the constructive trust is possible.[63] Elias sets out five representative rules on constructive trusts.[64] Among the rules which Elias identified is the 'fourth rule' which is said to compel one who receives money under mistake of fact to hold the money on trust for the payer.[65] In the light of the decision in *Islington*, this rule cannot be asserted as a rule where there is no knowledge in the recipient that the payment has been made on the basis of a mistake.[66]

The creation of proprietary rights under constructive trust

8.038 The need to demonstrate a proprietary right arises in three kinds of situation: the first is where the contract has sought to retain rights in particular property; the second is where the parties are attempting to establish rights in specific property after an event of default or the insolvency of their counterparty; the third is where the plaintiff is claiming compound interest. The issues considered in that chapter deal with the former issue of establishing rights in specific property as part of the creation of the credit derivatives contract, particularly in relation to collateral agreements and retention of title language in the master agreement. The latter category is the subject of this section. Of particular interest is the impact of the swaps cases *Westdeutsche Landesbank v. Islington*[67] and *Kleinwort Benson v. Glasgow City Council*[68] on the contractual and restitutionary effect of void contracts.[69]

The most important recent statement of the core principles of the areas of implied trusts law was made by Lord Browne-Wilkinson in *Westdeutsche Landesbank*

---

[60] Elias, *Explaining Constructive Trusts* (Oxford, 1990), pp. 56–66; Gardner (1990), pp. 225–8, 231–2; Chambers (1997), p. 224.

[61] Elias, *Explaining Constructive Trusts* (Oxford, 1990).

[62] *ibid.* p. 2.

[63] *ibid.* p. 3.

[64] *ibid.* p. 1.

[65] *Selangor v. Cradock* [1968] 1 W.L.R. 1555.

[66] There is also the third rule which identifies the old rule imposing a constructive trust relating to dishonest assistants to a breach of trust as compelling a stranger who negligently assists in a breach of trust. As discussed above, the decision of the Privy Council in *Tan* now establishes the law in that area.

[67] [1996] A.C. 669.

[68] [1997] 4 All E.R. 641.

[69] Similarly, the decisions in *Morris v. Rayner Entreprises Inc* and *Re Bank of Credit and Commerce International SA (No. 8)* are important on the availability of set-off in case of insolvency.

v. Islington where his Lordship went back to basics. the first of his "Relevant Principles of Trust Law" was identified as being that that:

> "Equity operates on the conscience of the owner of the legal interest. In the case of a trust, the conscience of the legal owner requires him to carry out the purposes for which the property was vested in him (express or implied trust) or which the law imposes on him by reason of his unconscionable conduct (constructive trust)."[70]

8.039   One important issue arises: does the constructive trust take effect by granting proprietary rights over specific property, or does it simply impose a personal obligation on a person who has dealt with property? It is the distinction between a right *in rem* to the property and any increase in value associated with the property, and a right *in personam* being a personal claim against a person for money. There are situations, considered below, which fit into both categories. The third fundamental principles identified by Lord Browne-Wilkinson operates as follows:

> "(iii) In order to establish a trust there must be identifiable trust property. The only apparent exception to this rule is a constructive trust imposed on a person who dishonestly assists in a breach of trust who may come under fiduciary duties even if he does not receive identifiable trust property."

The constructive trust comes into effect at the date this knowledge is acquired and "as from the date of its establishment the beneficiary has, in equity, a proprietary interest in the trust property". The proprietary interest is then "enforceable in equity against any subsequent holder of the property (whether the original property or substituted property into which it can be traced) other than a purchaser for value of the legal interest without notice".[71]

> "(iv) Once a trust is established, as from the date of its establishment the beneficiary has, in equity, a proprietary interest in the trust property, which proprietary interest will be enforceable in equity against any subsequent holder of the property (whether the original property or substituted property into which it can be traced) other than a purchaser for value of the legal interest without notice."

In commercial situations, for example that in *Westdeutsche*, it is important for the parties to know who has which rights in property dealt with as part of a contract. A proprietary constructive trust will give a right *in rem* to the beneficiary. That is, a right in the property itself which is enforceable against any other person. The *in rem* right comes into operation from the moment that the proprietary right is validly created, under an express trust[72] or other security structure, or at the moment when the defendant has knowledge of the factor which fixes it with liability under a constructive trust.[73] The alternative is a mere *in personam* right entitling the

---

[70] [1996] 2 All E.R. 961 at 988.

[71] *ibid.*

[72] An express trust is validly created either on a valid declaration of trust by the settlor (*Richards v. Delbridge* (1874) L.R. 18 Eq. 11) or at the time when legal title in the trust property is transferred to the trustee (*Milroy v. Lord* (1862) 4 De. G.F. & J. 264).

[73] *Westdeutsche Landesbank v. Islington* [1996] A.C. 669; [1996] 2 All E.R. 961 at 988.

successful plaintiff to a claim in money only and not to any specific property. In cases of insolvency this would mean that the plaintiff would have no secured rights but only a *pari passu* debt claim with other unsecured creditors. The further shortcoming of the personal claim is that it grants only an entitlement to simple interest on the money claim and not compound interest.[74]

The law relating to compound interest and the nature of the constructive trust is now the subject of a more concrete test than had been the case hitherto. However, the operation of the constructive trust, first, as an institution created by operation of law, and, secondly, as a retrospective device which imposes trusteeship on a person after the occurrence of the event alleged to have affected its conscience, make the constructive trust a device that is conceptually difficult in commercial contexts given its uncertainty until the court order is made.

Subrogation

8.040   A particular form of subrogation claim is considered in this section. The remedy of subrogation in the event of property being used to satisfy a pre-existing obligation, is a conceptually difficult remedy. Mitchell expresses his view to be that:

". . . subrogation is best understood as a restitutionary remedy: the cases in which subrogation has been awarded to date can all be explained in restitutionary terms, and the award of subrogation in the future should be guided by reference to the principle of unjust enrichment".[75]

There are two forms of subrogation in Mitchell's analysis: simple subrogation and reviving subrogation. Simple subrogation operates to transfer "subsisting rights of action from one party to another".[76] The most straightforward example of this form of action is in an indemnity insurance contract where the insurer is subrogated to the rights of the insured against the tortfeasor who has caused the insured loss.[77] Reviving subrogation is the second order of subrogation referred to above. It is said that it "works to revive extinguished rights of action and then to transfer them from one party to another".[78] Burrows[79] has observed that simple subrogation must be outwith the law of restitution because it is a preventative remedy rather than a response imposed after the event to restore property or value to the plaintiff. The concentration of restitution must therefore be on reviving subrogation as a restitutionary response to unjust enrichment arising from the use of property.[80]

Reviving subrogation is therefore the more complicated of the forms of subrogation in that it takes rights which have expired and resuscitates them in favour of a party other than the original right holder. Mitchell categorises the parties as the original right holder (RH), the person who is "primarily liable" to the RH (PL), and the person who is to be subrogated to RH's rights (S). The example Mitchell uses is that of a surety arrangement. When a surety (S) pays a creditor (RH), that creditor's right of action is extinguished as against the debtor (PL). However, section 5 of the Mercantile Law Amendment Act 1856 entitles S to recover the

---

[74] *ibid.*
[75] Mitchell, *The Law of Subrogation* (Oxford, 1994), p. 4.
[76] *ibid.* p. 5.
[77] *ibid.* p. 6.
[78] *ibid.* p. 5.
[79] Burrows, *The Law of Restitution* (Butterworths, 1994), pp. 81, 92.
[80] Mitchell, *op cit.*, p. 10.

payment to RH from PL, despite the extinction of the rights originally held by RH.[81]

When can a claimant acquire secured rights via subrogation?

8.041   The question when a claimant should be entitled to acquire secured rights via subrogation is related to the restitutionary issue as to the circumstances in which a plaintiff ought to be able to assert any kind of proprietary claim.[82] In Birks' view: ". . . a claimant should be permitted to assert a proprietary claim only where he can show that he began by owning, and that he thereafter retained some legal or equitable proprietary interest in, the property which he seeks to recover. . .".[83] The view taken by Goff and Jones' is that ". . . the courts can in appropriate circumstances retrospectively deem a claimant to have an equitable proprietary interest sufficient to allow him to assert a proprietary claim" including within that the issue "whether the plaintiff has voluntarily assumed the risk of the defendant's insolvency" should be a key factor in the decision of whether the plaintiff should be given priority over the defendant's other creditors.[84]

These disparate approaches have been summarised as follows:

"In some [instances of awards of proprietary remedies] the dominant factor appears to have been that an equitable interest in moneys was regarded as not having been relinquished and in others it appears to have been unconscionability in retaining moneys against claimants"[85]

In Mitchell's view:

". . . Birks' approach provides the most cogent explanation of many of the cases in which the claimants have been allowed to acquire secured rights via subrogation. However, it must be concluded that his analysis cannot explain all the cases of this kind."[86]

8.042   Therefore, the plaintiff should only be entitled to a proprietary remedy where he can demonstrate that he has a "proprietary base" to the claim. Birks has also pointed out that the effect of reviving subrogation is the same as allowing S to trace property into a "negative asset" [the obligations formerly owned by RH] in PL's hands.[87] "[reviving subrogation] is only semantically different from the imposition of direct restitutionary obligations".[88] In that instance it is said that there is a different kind of asset involved, but not a different mode of effecting restitution.[89] Birks' analysis does not apply cleanly in the context of the failure of consideration cases where ". . . claimants have been allowed to acquire extinguished secured rights via reviving subrogation, even though property in their hands must

---

[81] The other principle difference in the types of subrogation is that in simple subrogation S cannot pursue those rights in his own name, whereas in the context of reviving subrogation S in entitled to bring the action in his own name.

[82] Mitchell, *op cit.*, p. 27.

[83] Birks, *Introduction to the Law of Restitution* (Oxford, 1989), p. 93.

[84] Goff and Jones, *The Law of Restitution*, (4th ed., Sweet & Maxwell, 1993), p. 601.

[85] *Liggett v. Kensington* [1993] 1 N.Z.L.R. 257 at 281, *per* Gault J.

[86] Mitchell, *The Law of Subrogation* (Oxford, 1994), p. 28.

[87] Birks, *Introduction to the Law of Restitution* (Oxford, 1989), pp. 94–7; see also Mitchell, *op cit.*, p. 29.

[88] Birks, *Introduction to the Law of Restitution* (Oxford, 1989), p. 191.

[89] *ibid.* p. 96.

unequivocally have passed away from them at the time when they made their payments, with the result that they cannot be said to have had a proprietary base to their claim."[90] This instance, it would appear, cannot be explained by simple reference to Birks' model.

For example, Beatson disagrees with Birks in that ". . . subrogation . . . puts the intervener in the creditor's shoes for the purpose of taking over claims previously maintainable by the creditor. This means that, like the assignee, the intervener will be in no better position than the creditor . . . It is for this reason that it is not possible to regard restitutionary subrogation as only semantically different from the imposition of direct restitutionary obligations."[91]

Reviving extinguished rights

8.043 One analysis of the Court of Appeal's decision in *Re Diplock*[92] is that it was founded on the assumption that:

> "no mechanism exists in English law to revive extinguished rights of action for the benefit of claimants whose money has been paid to the former right-holders . . . the next of kin in *Re Diplock*[93] should have been allowed to acquire the securities formerly held by the charities' former creditors by means of reviving subrogation."[94]

Support for this approach comes from *Re Byfield*[95] and also from Birks[96] and Martin[97] especially in connection with the decision in *Boscawen v. Bajwa*.[98] In this context it would be argued that *Boscawen v. Bajwa* and *Roscoe v. Winder*[99] lead to the conclusion that, while there is no right to trace into an overdrawn account, there could be a claim based on reviving subrogation in respect of the contract with the bank.

However, a different approach is taken by Hayton[1] where it is argued that no reviving subrogation ought to be available because it would be inequitable to have ordered a sale of the charities' property in *Re Diplock*. For example, in *McCullough v. Marsden*,[2] where beneficiaries subrogated to the rights of a mortgagee where trustee misappropriated trust property to pay off a mortgage.

8.044 The latest edition of *The Law of Restitution* by Goff and Jones has altered their view that as to the courts' discretion to award proprietary remedies. It is now their view that such remedies should be awarded where this seems just and equitable.[3] Their fundamental concerns with regard to the award of restitutionary remedies are the basis of the plaintiff's claim, the defendant's knowledge of the

---

[90] Mitchell, *The Law of Subrogation* (Oxford, 1994), p. 31.
[91] Beatson, *The Use and Abuse of Unjust Enrichment* (Oxford, 1991), p. 204.
[92] [1948] Ch. 465.
[93] *ibid.*
[94] Mitchell, *The Law of Subrogation* (Oxford, 1994), p. 31.
[95] [1982] 1 Ch. 267 at 272, *per* Goulding J.
[96] Birks, *Introduction to the Law of Restitution* (Oxford, 1989), pp. 372–375.
[97] Martin, *Hanbury and Martin: Modern Equity* (15th ed., London), p. 675.
[98] [1996] 1 W.L.R. 328.
[99] [1915] 1 Ch. 62.
[1] "Constructive Trusts: Is the Remedying of Unjust Enrichment a Satisfactory Approach?" in *Equity, Fiduciaries and Trusts* (Youdan ed., Toronto, 1989), Chap. 9.
[2] (1919) 45 D.L.R. 645.
[3] Goff and Jones, *The Law of Restitution* (5th ed., Sweet & Maxwell, 1998), p. 29.

supporting facts, and the question whether or not the defendant is solvent. Their view of subrogation is that it is an equitable remedy created and imposed by the courts in the same manner as constructive trusts and equitable liens.[4]

In seeking to establish the role of subrogation claims as a restitutionary response, Mitchell argues that:

> "[a] person who confers a benefit, normally a money payment, under mistake, compulsion, necessity, or in consequence of another's wrongful act or unconscionable conduct will be *deemed* to have retained the equitable title in the money paid."[5]

This is clearly not the case after *Islington* in the House of Lords — is it even Lord Goff's dissenting argument on that appeal? Goff and Jones are content that subrogation advances the S's rights over the creditors of the PL:

> ". . . where it can be shown that the defendant's creditors have, and the claimant has not, voluntarily undertaken the risk of the defendant's solvency."[6]

8.045 Mitchell's criticism of the risk approach (drawing on Burrows[7]) is that it cannot be said that the defendant's other creditors will have consciously taken the risk of his insolvency.[8] Rather, there is a need to weigh up the respective claims of a defendant's creditors.[9] In the swaps cases, no such concern about the other creditors of the local authorities arises because the transactions were held off balance sheet in any event. Burrows is of the view that where a claimant has advanced money on the basis that his advance should be secured, and the borrower fails to execute the security as agreed, the lender should be entitled to acquire secured rights via subrogation where this serves to give effect to the parties' thwarted common intention that the loan should be secured.[10]

In the case of swaps agreements which provide for termination provisions in the case of a misrepresentation as to status and the availability of credit support. One argument might be a claimant in this position has never voluntarily agreed to expose himself to the risk by virtue of having contracted out of it. Alternatively, it could be said that one party to the derivative has induced the counterparty to enter into the transaction on the basis that his participation will be secured. As a result, it is submitted, the courts should give effect to this promise in whatever way they can, in the event that the promised security fails to materialise because the agreement between the parties has turned out to be invalid.[11] Therefore, following Burrows' core view, a claimant should have his security or credit enhancement supported by the court where that gives effect to the mutual contractual intention of the parties.[12]

---

[4] *ibid.* p. 91; and Mitchell, *op cit.*, p. 32.

[5] *ibid.* p. 94.

[6] Mitchell, *op cit.*, p. 33; see also *per* Lord Templeman in *Space Investments Ltd v. Canadian Imperial Bank of Commerce Trust Co (Bahamas) Ltd* [1986] 1 W.L.R. 1072 at 1074; and *Lord Napier and Ettrick v. Hunter* [1993] 1 A.C. 713 at 737.

[7] Burrows, *The Law of Restitution* (Butterworths, 1993), p. 42; also Tettenborn, [1980] C.L.J. 272 at 324–325.

[8] See also Paciocco, "The Remedial Constructive Trust: A Principled Basis for Priorities over Creditors" (1989) 68 *Can. B.R.* 315.

[9] Mitchell, *The Law of Subrogation* (Oxford, 1994), p. 33.

[10] *ibid.* p. 28.

[11] *ibid.* p. 34.

[12] Burrows, *The Law of Restitution* (Butterworths, 1994), pp. 85–87 and 89–90.

The importance of subrogation in the derivatives context could be threefold:

(a) there is a perfecting of security by subrogation where there was no effective security in fact;

(b) it is one analysis of the rights owned by the floating rate payer in an interest rate swap contract; and

(c) it provides a possible means of effecting restitution where there is no payment (or where there is some failure of consideration possibly).

The subrogation remedy might enable the payer under a void swaps contract to seek to be subrogated to the rights of the creditors whose debts were discharged by the used of the payment. As considered above, the primary obstruction to this remedy would be whether or not it would be possible to identify the debt which had been discharged. Alternatively, the remedy would be equivalent to a charge over the general current account of the payee.

Tracing

8.046 From the point of view of the commercial or financial lawyer, it is a problematic notion that it is necessary to start an analysis of the availability of proprietary rights to electronically transferred funds with the example of physical possession of tangible chattels. "The stolen bag of coins" is the title which the speech of Lord Browne-Wilkinson gives to the opening of this segment of the analysis in the *Islington* appeal. The phrase reveals a lot about the attitude of English law to tracing claims for money in banking cases. Rather than recognising money in modern banking as being, in truth, a series of choses in action registered in electronically-held bank accounts, English law still sees electronically-held money as being tangible chattels. Thus, there is a theme running through the law of tracing and following which has to do with the conceptualisation of the property involved.

Common law tracing

8.047 Common law tracing is perhaps more accurately rendered as "following"[13] in that it has generally only permitted a claim based on tracing where the plaintiff has been able to identify either the exact property misappropriated or a clean substitute (in that the property has not been inextricably mixed with other property) of that exact property. Thus, in *Lipkin Gorman v. Karpnale*[14] it was held that the plaintiff can trace at common law into bank accounts where the very money misappropriated remains identifiable. Similarly, in *Agip Africa v. Jackson*[15] it was held that common law tracing only possible in clean, physical substitutions.[16]

The decision of the Court of Appeal in *F.C. Jones & Sons v. Jones*[17] has suggested a broader role for common law tracing by holding that it does operate to provide

---

[13] See Smith, *The Law of Tracing* (Oxford, 1997), pp. 1 *et seq.*
[14] [1991] 3 W.L.R. 10; [1992] 4 All E.R. 512; [1991] 2 A.C. 548.
[15] [1991] Ch. 547; [1991] 3 W.L.R. 116; [1992] 4 All E.R. 451.
[16] This approach was supported by Sir Peter Millett writing extra-judicially: Millett, "Tracing the Proceeds of Fraud" (1991) 107 L.Q.R. 71 — where his Lordship argued that the proper approach for English law would be to do away with common law tracing completely on the basis that it is of restricted potential use, and of no use where property is mixed or no longer separately identifiable.
[17] [1996] 3 W.L.R. 703; [1996] 4 All E.R. 721.

rights not only to identifiable property but also to profits made from such property.[18] In that case a sum of £11,700 was paid from a partnership bank account to Mrs Jones, wife of one of the partners. She invested the money in potato futures and made a large profit. Ultimately, she held a balance of £49,860. It transpired that the partnership had committed an act of bankruptcy under the 1914 Bankruptcy Act and therefore all of the partnership property was deemed to have passed retrospectively to the Official Receiver. Therefore, it was claimed that Mrs Jones had had no title to the original £11,700.

8.048   It was held that all the money be paid to the Official Receiver. However, in the judgment of Millett L.J., the plaintiff was allowed a proprietary common law claim on the basis that the money at issue was perfectly identifiable. It was held that there could be no claim in equity against Mrs Jones because she had never stood as a fiduciary in relation to the partnership. It was held that the right was a proprietary right to claim whatever was in the bank account held, whether more or less than the original amount deposited and it was immaterial whether or not those amounts constituted profits on the original money.

It is therefore at issue whether or not common law tracing could operate to grant a plaintiff the right to claim a right against a market counterparty to the restitution of property and of profits made on that property, even where no fiduciary relationship exists between those parties. It is contended that this constitutes an important potential claim for derivatives counterparties even where they are entities of equal bargaining strength, to recover profits on grounds of unjust enrichment, from the counterparty which has made profit from the transaction.

Equitable tracing

8.049   Equitable tracing operates, in contradistinction to common law tracing, by permitting the claimant to trace into mixed property which is alleged to be comprised in part by property in which the claimant has an equitable interest (or the traceable substitute of such property). Typically all property which is not land, is considered to be a tangible chattel. The rules on tracing, and the deemed disappearance of money when the account in which it is held goes overdrawn,[19] embody the underlying principle that money is not value in an electronic bank account, but rather that it is to be considered in the same way as ordinary, tangible chattels. Thus, in analysing the possibility of tracing the stolen bag of coins, Lord Browne-Wilkinson agrees that they are traceable in equity. The nature of the proprietary interest recognised by equity "arises under a constructive, not a resulting, trust."[20]

In *Chase Manhattan*,[21] Goulding J. saw the issue as one of tracing payments made under a mistake into the assets of the recipient bank. In his judgment the receipt of the money under a mistake, without more, constituted the recipient a trustee of that money. Lord Browne-Wilkinson reacted as follows:[22]

"First, [the decision of Goulding J.] is based on a concept of retaining an equitable property in money where, prior to the payment to the recipient bank,

---

[18] Ironically, Millett L.J. gave the leading judgment in that Court of Appeal.
[19] *Roscoe v. Winder* [1915] 1 Ch. 62; *Bishopsgate Investment Management v. Homan* [1995] Ch. 211, [1995] 1 All E.R. 347, [1994] 3 W.L.R. 1270 — no possibility of claiming into an overdrawn account because the fund no longer exists.
[20] [1996] 2 All E.R. 961 at 998.
[21] [1987] Ch. 264.
[22] [1996] 2 All E.R. 961 at 997.

there was no existing equitable interest . . . Chase Manhattan may well have
been rightly decided. The defendant bank knew of the mistake made by the
paying bank within two days of the receipt of the moneys . . . Although the
mere receipt of the moneys, in ignorance of the mistake, gives rise to no trust,
the retention of the moneys after the recipient bank learned of the mistake may
well have given rise to a constructive trust . . ."

8.050   As held in general, lack of knowledge of the unconscionable receipt of
property negates any possible imposition of a constructive trust on equitable
principles. Therefore, the equity approach sees the constructive trust as an
institutional construct which is imposed in response to the defendant's knowledge
of its own unconscionable receipt of property. The imposition of a proprietary
remedy based on equitable tracing will be available only where there was some pre-
existing fiduciary duty owed by the defendant recipient of the property in question.

Birks suggests that, in the light of the speech of Lord Browne-Wilkinson in
Westdeutsche Landesbank,[23] there is no need to prove a prior equitable interest in
the property.[24] In Birks' terms, there is no need to establish a proprietary base to
found an equitable tracing claim. The effect of this apparent change in the law would
be to enable the purchaser of a physically-settled option to establish a tracing claim
via the assets which are to be physically-settled at some time in the future, even
though they have not been allocated to the recipient in advance. This would be in
contradistinction to the well-established understanding that such a fiduciary relationship, or an equitable proprietary interest, is a pre-requisite to any claim based on
equitable tracing.[25] In the light of Lord Browne-Wilkinson's decision in support of
the principle in *Re Goldcorp*[26] that property must be segregated before it can be the
subject matter of a trust, there must be some restriction on the ability to found an
equitable tracing claim. The question is not addressed by Lord Browne-Wilkinson.

Presuming this conflict with *Goldcorp* to be more apparent than intended, at what
point does this right crystallise? Does the right to the equitable tracing claim arise
at the date of the unconscionable or fraudulent action, or does it not crystallise on
maturity of the option, given that there would not have been any right to the
property before maturity if there had not been such unconscionable act? The
further question is with reference to a cash-settled derivative, as to whether an
equitable proprietary claim will obtain even where there is only a right to receive
cash. Finally, it is not clear where an equitable proprietary claim will arise where
there is an option which can be physically — or cash — settled at the buyer's
election. By contra-distinction, it now appears possible that a common law right to
trace arises to protect a legal right. As considered above, *Jones v. Jones*[27] appears to
allow tracing at common law into an exchange product, rather than being restricted
simply to identification or following of the original property which is the object of
that tracing claim.[28]

---

[23] [1996] 2 W.L.R. 802, 838–839 ("The stolen bag of coins").
[24] Birks, "Trusts to be raised to reverse unjust enrichment: the Westdeutsche Case" [1996] R.L.R. 3 at
10.
[25] *Re Diplock* [1948] Ch. 465; *Chase Manhattan Bank NA v. Israel-British Bank (London) Ltd* [1981] Ch.
105; [1980] 2 W.L.R. 202; [1979] 3 All E.R. 1025 — mistake grounds a "proprietary tracing claim"; *Agip
Africa v. Jackson* [1991] Ch. 547, [1991] 3 W.L.R. 116; [1992] 4 All E.R. 451; *Boscawen v. Bajwa* [1995] 4
All E.R. 769.
[26] [1995] 1 A.C. 74.
[27] [1996] 3 W.L.R. 703.
[28] Hanbury and Martin, *Modern Equity* (13th ed., Sweet & Maxwell, 1993), p. 660.

Miscellaneous principles

8.051   The following sections consider aspects of the laws of restitution, contract and principles of equity which were not considered in the swaps cases but which, it is submitted, would be of potential importance in credit derivatives litigation in future.

Severance

8.052   The doctrine of severance provides that, where a contract is held to void on grounds that it offends public policy or is illegal, the offending part of the agreement can be severed from those elements which do not offend against lawfulness or public policy. This severance has the effect of ensuring the validity of those parts of the contract which are maintained.

The issue arises then whether any part of the agreements entered into in the swaps cases would have been capable of severance in the manner considered by Dillon L.J. The offensive parts of the swap agreements, as considered by Lord Templeman in *Hazell*, were the elements relating to the *ultra vires* borrowing. The issue remains whether *Hazell* constitutes a case motivated by the desire to rectify the potentially enormous obligations which would have been visited on the ratepayers of Hammersmith and Fulham. Debt management with speculative financial products is the objection identified by the House of Lords.

The classic statement of the doctrine of severance is that: "where you cannot sever the illegal from the legal part of a covenant, the contract is altogether void; but, where you can sever them, whether the illegality can be created by statute or by common law, you may reject the bad part and retain the good."[29]

The decision of Megarry J. in *Spector v. Ageda*[30] held that the whole of the contract must be considered to be void even where a part only of the agreement had been found to be illegal by operation of statute. The policy identified in this decision was to prevent parties to illegal contracts from putting themselves into further harm by enforcing other contracts. Similarly, in *Esso Petroleum v. Harper's Garage (Stourport) Ltd*[31] it was held that where covenants in a contract are so closely connected that they can be deemed to stand or fall together, the whole contract will fail even though some sections may appear to be severable.

8.053   It is submitted, however, that the risk management features of standard market financial documents introduce greater certainty and lessen the cash amounts required to be paid between market participants. Therefore, the identified policy of precluding the parties from entering into further damaging transactions does not apply in the context of a provision, such as a netting clause on termination, which reduces the net amount of the parties' exposure to one another. The validity of an instrument need not be compromised because some element of it is held to unenforceable.[32]

The purpose of the interest rate swap is the creation of two streams of cash flows related to a notional amount of money, with the underlying purpose of acquiring some speculative return or hedging a financial risk. The conservative argument

---

[29] *Pickering v. Ilfracombe Railway* (1868) L.R. 3 C.P. 235 at 250; *Payne v, Brecon Corporation* (1858) 3 H. & N. 572; Royal Exchange Assurance Corporation v. Siforsakrings Aktiebolaget Vega [1901] 2 K.B. 567 at 573; *Chitty on Contracts* (27th ed., Sweet & Maxwell, 1994), para. 16–165.
[30] [1973] Ch. 30.
[31] [1968] A.C. 269 at 314, 321.
[32] *Gaskell v. King* (1809) 11 East. 165; *Gibbons v. Harper* (1831) 2 B. & Ad. 734.

would provide that, where those functions are held to be *ultra vires ab initio*, there is no possibility of upholding any part of the agreement. However, those elements of the agreements which relate to the termination of those agreements and the calculation of termination amounts to settle all outstanding obligations and to deal with the re-allocation of property, do not appear to fall into the same category as the active provisions of the swap agreements which provide for the economic terms of the contracts. Therefore, it is submitted, that as part of the Suitability Approach, it would have been possible for the courts to have segregated the economic provisions that created the interest rate swaps, from those risk management provisions which seek to provide for termination and risk allocation.

It is settled law that the court will not re-write the contract as part of severance.[33] The court will not, therefore, blue-pencil any part of the agreement such that there is an effect which is materially different from that which the parties had agreed to originally. However, it is not clear that the effect of enforcing the termination provisions of a financial agreement, where they regulate the manner in which termination takes effect and the rights of the parties to property, would effect a materially different agreement.

The problem with the application of this principle is the basic assertion by the courts that the entire contract is void *ab initio*, even though the courts did not consider the range of terms contained in the master agreements.[34] It is this ground of public policy which would appear to militate most strongly against application of the credit support or termination provisions.[35] The central question is, therefore, as to the appropriate basis for public policy in this area. It is submitted that the most appropriate policy is to respect the market practice of controlling risks through standard contracts and to recognise the impact these provisions have on lowering systemic risk in relation to credit derivatives contracts.

8.054 The doctrine of severance might also apply with reference to the distinction between executed and non-executed transactions. It could be submitted that, where the parties have acted consensually, and without any other unjust factor such as fraud or undue influence, there is no injustice in requiring the parties to observe their agreement.

A further issue arises where one type of derivative only is found to be inefficacious or void. The question would arise whether a credit support document, such as an agreement to provide collateral, in support of a range of derivative transactions, would be held to be partly valid to the extent that it covered the valid transaction. The all-or-nothing approach of the courts in the swaps cases does little to appreciate the habitual commercial usage of the credit support structure across a range of transactions potentially in different jurisdictions.

The correct approach would appear to be that the credit support document would continue in full force and effect in relation to those transactions which have not been declared to be void. That does not answer the question whether or not it should be applicable even though the agreement to which it is collateral has been held to be void. It is submitted that the credit support document should be upheld on the grounds that it lowers the financial risk at large between the parties without

---

[33] *Goldsoll v. Goldman* [1914] 2 Ch. 603, [1915] 1 Ch. 192; *Ronbar v. Green* [1954] 1 W.L.R. 815; *Scorer v. Seymour Jones* [1966] 1 W.L.R. 1419.
[34] Alternatively, the issue arises whether any credit support documentation, being collateral to the void contract, could be effective against the defaulting party. The doctrine of severance would suggest that any collateral credit support documentation could be made effective against the counterparty.
[35] *Kuenigl v. Donnersmarck* [1955] 1 Q.B. 515; *Hyland v. Barker* [1985] I.C.R. 861 at 863.

impacting on third party creditors who must have proceeded on the basis that such agreements were valid until they were declared to be void by a court.

Specific performance

8.055 The importance of the equitable remedy of specific performance in this context is its availability only in respect of circumstances in which damages are not an appropriate remedy.[36] Therefore, specific performance will not usually be available for an executory contract, where that is the appropriate analysis of the derivatives contract, because damages are invariably an adequate remedy for a cash-settled contract that has been part-performed. The authorities with reference to a contract to pay a loan, satisfy the proposition that courts will not exercise their discretion to grant specific performance where damages could satisfy the remedy. Therefore, specific performance will not be appropriate for cash settled deals under the executory contract analysis. However, in respect of a transaction in which physical delivery is required, specific performance will be available where damages would not be a sufficient remedy.[37]

The issue may then turn on whether or not it is possible to receive damages and obtain substitute securities or assets in the market without too much difficulty. Thus, where it is relatively easy to acquire replacement government bonds in the market, specific performance will not be ordered,[38] whereas the unavailability of securities will make specific performance appropriate.[39] Physical delivery may be appropriate in foreign exchange transactions where the notional amounts *are* occasionally paid or in some equities transactions where physical settlement of shares are required. This, it is submitted, is a ground upon which one could distinguish the loan cases and look to specific performance even on an executory contract basis.[40] However, the mutual debts analysis permits of specific performance of each of the debts. The ideal restitutionary solution might therefore be for rescission or specific performance to be coupled with damages; which would only be possible under a mutual debts analysis.

Rectification of contracts

8.056 The Court of Appeal decision in *Britoil v. Hunt Oil*[41] considered the ability of contracting parties to rectify an agreement on the basis that it did not correctly reflect their common intention. Hunt Oil argued that a provision of the signed agreement failed to reflect the true intention of the parties and that this true intention could be found in an earlier and non-bonding Heads of Agreement letter (which was found to be equivalent to a draft of the final form of the contract) exchanged between the parties. Accordingly, they requested rectification of the signed agreement. The Court of Appeal made several comments about the availability of rectification in denying Hunt Oil's application. First, all complex commercial transactions are preceded by draft versions which gradually isolate ambiguities and disagreements between the parties, a court would generally be

---

[36] *Hutton v. Watling* [1948] Ch. 26; [1948] Ch. 398.
[37] *Cohen v. Roche* [1927] 1 K.B. 169; *Snell's Equity* (29th ed., Sweet & Maxwell, 1990), p. 586.
[38] *Cuddee v. Rutter* (1720) 5 Vin.Abr. 538.
[39] *Duncruft v. Albrecht* (1841) 12 Sim. 189; *Kenney v. Wexham* (1822) 6 Madd. 355; *Sullivan v. Henderson* [1973] 1 W.L.R. 333.
[40] *South African Territories v. Wellington* [1898] A.C. 309; *Astor Properties v. Tunbridge Wells* [1936] 1 All E.R. 531.
[41] May 24, 1994, unreported.

reluctant — as a matter of policy — to conclude that an informal document should be treated as a superior statement of the parties' agreement than the final and executed document. Any other policy would undermine the certainty that parties expect when they sign final agreements — if "the relevant document is a legally binding document, it is appropriate to hold the parties to the objectively ascertained meaning of the words used".

Secondly, the only way to obtain rectification is to show that, as a matter of fact, there was a common mistake which resulted in there being no legally binding force to the signed agreement.[42] The claimant bears the burden of proving that there has been a mistake which is common between the parties. The Court of Appeal refused to accept that there was a mistake simply on the basis of a disparity between the wording of the draft letter and the wording of the executed document. It was not enough that there was ambiguity between the wording in the two different documents. The Court of Appeal held that it would be necessary to show something with "the objective status of a prior agreement", either written or oral, which provides the evidence of a continuing intention clearly different to that of the executed agreement, thereby proving the common mistake.

This decision has ramifications for financial institutions which act as managers of derivatives transactions. In documentation where the manager distributes selling information to investors, stating that the advertising material is not an offering document for the underlying financial product, these will be the only legally binding terms dealing with the constitution of the product, between the parties when the transaction is confirmed by telephone and telex/fax. In the case of warrant transactions, a final offering circular is distributed before the products are sold. There are difficulties in arguing that the initial documentation has the "objective status of a prior agreement", given that it is stated not to be a binding document at all. However, this document might constitute a material part of the terms of that agreement. A common mistake must be made by the contracting parties. However, a mistake that involves the manager will not be a common mistake because the manager is not a party to the contract. In the case of warrants, the commercial paper is generally issued through a third party in any event — therefore the manager is kept very much at arm's length. None of the defences[43] open to manager will be open to the issuer because it is not party to all of the relevant discussions, between it and the investor.

The conflict between equity and restitution

8.057 At the outset of this section, we considered the development of the doctrine of unjust enrichment and the role of the established principles of equity. It is worth examining the attitude of the courts in *Islington* to this debate. Given the acceptance by the House of Lords that there is such a doctrine of unjust enrichment, it remains to be seen how it will develop and whether it will offer a flexible general principle on the model set out partially in the preceding discussion in this chapter. The categories of equitable remedy and institutional trusts do not appear to have reacted to the commercial challenge of credit derivatives. As Lord Browne-Wilkinson held in *Target Holdings*:

---

[42] It should be remembered that meeting the standard of proof for this equitable remedy is difficult.
[43] For example, estoppel, which is probably open to the manager during negotiations.

". . . in my judgment it is important, if the trust is not to be rendered commercially useless, to distinguish between the basic principles of trust law and those specialist rules developed in relation to traditional trusts which are applicable only to such trusts and the rationale of which has no application to trust of quite a different kind."

Given the scope for the development of a commercially useful principle to replace the traditional trusts institution, the competition which appears to have developed between equity and unjust enrichment remains latent — subject to the judgments in *Islington*.

Hobhouse J. found that there ought to be a division between legal and equitable ownership. In the words quoted immediately above he considers that the arrangement consists of:

". . . payments in which the legal property in the money passes to the recipient, but in equity the property in the money remains with the payer . . ."

8.058   On the basis that there was no express trust structure created in *Islington*, Hobhouse J., is clearly employing the equitable analysis on the basis of some "unconscionability" of enabling the payee to retain the benefit of absolute ownership of the deep discount payment despite the avoidance of their contract. It is this analysis which Lord Browne-Wilkinson criticises in his speech in the House of Lords. There is, in his analysis, to be no deemed division of title *ex post facto* as Hobhouse J. suggests, without the occurrence of some factor (such as knowledge of an unconscionable action) which, on principle, would require that equity grant a right in property.[44]

Hobhouse J. dismissed the argument based on restitution, aside from his conviction that the absence of consideration claim was inappropriate, with the following sentence above:

"Neither mistake nor the contractual principle of total failure of consideration are the basis for the right of recovery."[45]

However, as considered below, it is not necessarily an easy matter to decide whether Hobhouse J. himself did intend his decision to be purely equitable or partly restitutionary. The former seems to have a stronger claim in the context of the judgment but there are clear acknowledgements of the role of restitutionary thinking in his Lordship's decision.

The reservations expressed by trusts lawyers with respect to the doctrine of unjust enrichment are summed up by Lord Goff himself, ironically in the light of his own role in the development of the principles of restitution[46]

"Equity lawyers . . . have displayed anxiety that the equitable principles underlying these institutions may become illegitimately distorted . . . they

---

[44] It is here that the Equity lawyer would look to knowledge, while the Restitution lawyer would look for some unjust factor.

[45] [1994] 4 All E.R. 890 at 929.

[46] With the publication of the first edition of *The Law of Restitution* with Prof. Jones in 1966.

remain concerned that the trust concept should not be distorted, and also that the practical consequences of its imposition should be fully appreciated."[47]

The anxiety concerns the shaping of trusts concepts to achieve conceptually novel, restitutionary goals. The core aim of restitution is restated by Lord Goff as being founded ". . . upon a principle of justice, being designed to prevent the unjust enrichment of the defendant . . ." in which context his Lordship cross-referred with the seminal decision of the House of Lords in *Lipkin Gorman*.[48] Lord Goff's dissenting judgment on the issue of the availability of compound interest is founded on a principle of justice and therefore it is clear that Lord Goff is applying principles akin to those which underpin restitution even though he is not expressly reaching any opinion on the turf war between restitution and equity.

8.059   The preference for a restitutionary approach appears from the assertion of the scope of the equitable jurisdiction to award compound interest. The *South Tyneside* litigation was a situation where the lack of availability of a proprietary remedy meant that compound interest was unavailable. Lord Goff identified this as being a result of the "technical and unrealistic"[49] nature of the equitable approach: favouring a broader approach based on justice and restitution. The traditional equitable approach is considered to be unduly technical on the basis that "[i]t seems strange indeed that, just because the power to trace property has ceased, the court's jurisdiction to award compound interest should also come to an end."[50]

The defence of the equitable approach is set out most clearly by Lord Browne-Wilkinson who devotes a large section of his speech to the dismissal of a broad application of Birks' model of restitution,[51] as applied subsequently by Chambers.[52] His lordship expressed himself to be wary of the ". . . perceived need to strengthen the remedies of a plaintiff claiming in restitution . . ." as involving ". . . a distortion of trust principles."[53] The distortion of trust principles referred to, is said to arise from the elision of property rights and 'rights in "the value transferred" '[54] particularly in the mooted development of the resulting trust as a mechanism to restore property to its former owner.[55] One weakness from which Birks' suffers is the purported imposition of a trust without the trust property needing to be suitably defined.[56]

The second weakness which Lord Browne-Wilkinson identified in Professor Birks' approach is its implication that trusteeship be imposed on a person at a time when they could not know that a trust had arisen. In line with the First Principle of the Equity Approach:

> "[t]his result is incompatible with the basic premise on which all trust law is built, *viz.* that the conscience of the trustee is affected. Unless and until the trustee is aware of the factors which give rise to the supposed trust, there is nothing which can affect his conscience."[57]

---

[47] [1996] 2 All E.R. 961 at 969.
[48] [1991] 2 A.C. 548.
[49] [1996] 2 All E.R. 961 at 978.
[50] *ibid.*
[51] "Restitution and Resulting Trusts" in *Equity and Contemporary Legal Developments* (Goldstein ed., 1992), pp. 335, 364–373.
[52] *Resulting Trusts* (Oxford, 1997).
[53] [1996] 2 All E.R. 961 at 992.
[54] *ibid.*
[55] As considered above, para. 8.033.
[56] See Birks, *Introduction to the Law of Restitution* (Oxford, 1989), p. 361.
[57] [1996] 2 All E.R. 961 at 992.

The result of this approach is that a resulting trust could never be imposed as a restitutionary response to any unjust factor including failure of consideration or mistake. The third objection to Professor Birks' approach is the need:

"to impose on his wider view an arbitrary and admittedly unprincipled modification so as to ensure that a resulting trust does not arise when there has only been a failure to perform a contract, as opposed to total failure of consideration . . ."[58]

8.060   Birks introduces this circumlocution to meet the circumstances where there is an insolvent recipient.[59] Lord Browne-Wilkinson's view of this exclusion is that:

"[t]he fact that it is necessary to exclude artificially one type of case which would logically fall within the wider concept casts doubt on the validity of the concept"[60]

Consequently, in his Lordship's view, this mooted expansion of the doctrine of unjust enrichment ought to be dismissed as likely to produce greater commercial uncertainty.

In conclusion, the view of the majority of the House of Lords was that equity should continue to take priority over the emerging doctrine of restitution by reversal of unjust enrichment. The possibilities offered by an approach based on restitution are dismissed. Lord Browne-Wilkinson explains that in his view the development of a proprietary interest based on restitutionary principles would not be based on sound principle and, while it would be put into effect in the name of unjust enrichment, would be "capable of producing most unjust results".[61]

In considering whether equity is the right mechanism for the resolution of disputes in the context of complex financial transactions, it is important to establish whether or not it will be suitably flexible. The concretisation of equitable principles, considered above, appears to militate against this. The need for a commercially sensible approach is illustrated by Lord Wilberforce in *General Tire and Rubber Co. v. Firestone Tyre and Rubber Co. Ltd*[62]

"In a commercial setting, it would be proper to take account of the manner in which and the time at which persons acting honestly and reasonably would pay."

In the context of the derivatives market, there is similarly some need to take account of the market's typical modes of taking security, allocating risk and achieving termination. In Lord Goff's speech there is an acknowledgement of the concern which the *Hazell* litigation had caused among the commercial community. What is perhaps more problematic is the impact of the *Islington* appeal on that same community. As his lordship held:

---

[58] *ibid.*
[59] Birks, *Introduction to the Law of Restitution* (Oxford, 1989), pp. 356–359, 362.
[60] [1996] 2 All E.R. 961 at 992.
[61] *ibid.*
[62] [1975] 1 W.L.R. 819 at 836; [1975] 2 All E.R. 173 at 188.

". . . I wish to record that it caused grave concern among financial institutions, and especially foreign banks, which had entered into such transactions with local authorities in good faith, with no idea that a rule as technical as the ultra vires doctrine might undermine what they saw as a perfectly legitimate commercial transaction."[63]

8.061 Similarly, Lord Woolf was concerned for the reputation of substantive English commercial law when he held that:

"It is no secret that [the decision in *Hazell*] caused dismay among some of those concerned with the standing abroad of the commercial law of this country. That concern is likely to be increased if the outcome of this litigation is that this appeal has to be allowed by this House because the courts have no jurisdiction to grant compound interest."[64]

What was acknowledged by the House of Lords in *Target Holdings v. Redferns*[65] was that there is a different context between international financial institutions and those who might look to English laws of trusts and restitution for remedies in connection with their own homes. Therefore, it is important that the fundamental principles of trusts law identified in *Islington* are made capable of even application to commercial situations as well as domestic situations. Lord Woolf emphasised the commercial nature of the contract and of the financial contract at issue in the *Islington* appeal, in considering authorities such as *Wallersteiner v. Moir (No. 2)*[66] and in *National Bank of Greece SA v. Pinios Shipping Co. (No. 1), The Maira*.[67] In particular, he approved Hobhouse J.'s award of compound interest on the basis that compound interest would have been payable on an ordinary loan.[68]

The role of equity, on this model, is to supply a remedy where there is an unconscionable lack of recourse at common law. The question is therefore the manner in which such a remedy will be imposed and the circumstances in which it would be appropriate to impose such a remedy. Therefore, based on the above-quoted passage, to achieve the troublesome goal of "full restitution", Lord Woolf considers that it is necessary to award compound interest. The overruling of *Sinclair*[69] means that there is no need to proceed on the basis that the local authority is a fiduciary — rather, the application of general equitable principle would be enough.

In the opinion of Lord Woolf it is particularly instructive to analyse the allocation of risks made by the contracting parties:

"The modern test should be whether the debtor could reasonably foresee that in the ordinary course of things the loss was likely to occur or was on the cards. Who would refuse to impute such knowledge to a debtor? Who would venture to suggest that a defaulting debtor could not reasonably foresee interest as the creditor's loss flowing from the failure to pay?"[70]

---

[63] [1996] 2 All E.R. 961 at 965.
[64] [1996] 2 All E.R. 961 at 1002.
[65] [1996] 1 A.C. 421, [1995] 3 W.L.R. 352.
[66] [1975] Q.B. 373.
[67] [1990] 1 A.C. 637.
[68] It is significant that Lord Woolf seems to be treating the upfront payment as a loan.
[69] In this respect Lord Woolf concurs with Lord Browne-Wilkinson rather than Lord Goff, *infra*.
[70] [1996] 2 All E.R. 961 at 1016; citing, with approval, Dr F.A. Mann "On Interest, Compound Interest and Damages" (1985) 101 L.Q.R. 30.

8.062 On this basis, it is to be considered again why the terms agreed between the parties as to termination and the allocation of risk were not considered by any court to be worthy of examination. It is important that the courts are able to recognise the attempts made by the contracting parties to allocate their risks and provide prudent mechanisms for termination of the contracts. As Atiyah explains the inter-action of the market and the use of contract:

> "In the market, parties were expected to calculate rationally the various risks, whether of past or of future events, which might affect the value of the contract. Provided that there was no fraud, and provided that the bargaining process was itself fair, the result must be deemed to be fair. Unexpected events, unknown factors, whether occurring before or after the contract was made, were not to be allowed to upset the resultant bargains. In principle all such risks were capable of being perceived and evaluated; in practice, not everybody succeeded in doing so. Or doing it very well . . . The whole point of the free market bargaining approach was to give full rein to the greater skill and knowledge of those who calculated risks better . . . He who failed to calculate a risk properly when making a contract would lose by it, and next time would calculate more efficiently."[71]

The commercial common sense approach has an eye on context. In Atiyah's conception, the purpose of the contract is to evaluate the risks between commercial parties. Fully operational markets require that the law recognise the commercial context in which they anticipate the operation of legal remedies. The development of trans-national norms of private international law have the effect of introducing greater commonality of principle. There is a policy requirement for municipal systems of law to prevent the re-location of commercial contracts outside their jurisdictional boundaries because it becomes difficult to enforce policy requirements of each system of rules.

---

[71] Atiyah, *The Rise and Fall of Freedom of Contract* (Oxford 1979), p. 437.

Appendix

Sample Form of Credit Derivative Confirmation

Heading

[Headed paper of Party A]

Date:

To: [Name and Address or Facsimile Number of Party B]

From: [Party A]

Re: Credit Derivative Transaction

Dear

The purpose of this [facsimile] [letter] (this "Confirmation") is to confirm the terms and conditions of the Credit Derivatives Transaction entered into between us on the Trade Date specified below (the "Transaction"). This Confirmation constitutes a "Confirmation" as referred to in the ISDA Master Agreement specified below.

The definitions and provisions contained in the 1999 ISDA Credit Derivatives Definitions (the "Credit Derivatives Definitions"), as published by the International Swaps and Derivatives Association, Inc., are incorporated into this Confirmation. In the event of any inconsistency between the Credit Derivatives Definitions and this Confirmation, this Confirmation will govern.

[This Confirmation supplements, forms a part of, and is subject to, the ISDA Master Agreement dates as of [date], as amended and supplemented from time to

---

THE FOOTNOTES TO THIS CONFIRMATION ARE PROVIDED FOR CLARIFICATION ONLY AND DO NOT CONSTITUTE ADVICE AS TO THE STRUCTURING OR DOCUMENTATION OF A CREDIT DERIVATIVE TRANSACTION.

ISDA has not undertaken to review all applicable laws and regulations of any jurisdiction in which the Credit Derivatives Definitions may be used. Therefore, parties are advised to consider the applications of any relevant jurisdiction's regulatory, tax, accounting, exchange or other requirements that may exist in connection with the entering into and documenting of a privately negotiated credit derivative transaction.

time (the "Agreement"), between you and us. All provisions contained in the Agreement govern this Confiramtion except as expressly modified below.][1]

The terms of the Transaction to which this Confirmation relates are as follows:

1. General Terms:

    Trade Date   [   ]

    Effective Date: [   ]

    Scheduled Termination Date: [   ]

    Floating Rate Payer: [Party A] [Party B] (the "Seller")

    Fixed Rate Payer: [Party A] [Party B] (the "Buyer")

    Calculation Agents:[2]   [   ]

    Calculation Agent City:[3]   [   ]

    Business Day:[4]   [   ]

    Business Day Convention: [Following] [Modified Following] [Preceding] (which shall apply to any date referred to in this Confirmation that falls on a day that is not a Business Day[5]).

    Reference Entity: [   ]

---

[1] Include if applicable. If the parties have not yet executed, but intend to execute, an ISDA Master Agreement include, instead of this paragraph, the following: "This Confirmation evidences a complete and binding agreement between you and us as to the terms of the Transaction to which this Confirmation relates. In addition, you and we agree to use all reasonable efforts promptly to negotiate, execute and deliver an agreement in the form of the [ISDA Master Agreement (Multicurrency-Cross Border)] [ISDA Master Agreement (Local Currency-Single Jurisdiction)] (the "ISDA Form"), with such modifications as you and we will in good faith agree. Upon the execution by you and us of such an agreement, this Confirmation will supplement, form part of, and be subject to that agreement. All provisions contained in or incorporated by reference in that agreement upon its execution will govern this Confirmation except as expressly modified below. Until we execute and deliver that agreement, this Confirmation together with all other documents referring to the ISDA Form (each a "Confirmation") confirming transactions (each a "Transaction") entered into between us (notwithstanding anything to the contrary in a Confirmation), shall supplement, form a part of, and be subject to, an agreement in the form of the ISDA Form as if we had executed an agreement in such form (but without any Schedule except for the election of [English Law] [the laws of the State of New York] as the governing law and [specify currency] as the Termination Currency) on the Trade Date of the first such Transaction between us. In the event of any inconsistency between the provisions of that agreement and this Confirmation, this Confirmation will prevail for the purpose of this Transaction."

[2] If the Calculation Agent is a third party, the parties may wish to consider any documentation necessary to confirm its undertaking to act in that capacity. If a person is not specified, the Credit Derivatives Definitions provide that the Calculation Agent will be the Seller.

[3] If a city is not specified, the Credit Derivatives Definitions provide that the Calculation Agent City will be the city in which the office through which the Calculation Agent is acting for purposes of the Credit Derivative Transaction is located.

[4] The Credit Derivatives Definitions provide a fallback to days on which commercial banks and foreign exchange markets are generally open to settle payments in the jurisdiction of the currency of the Floating Rate Payer Calculation Amount.

[5] Credit Derivatives Definitions provide a fallback to the Modified Following Business Day Convention.

[Reference Obligation(s):][6]   [   ]

                                      [The obligation[s] identified as follows:

                                      Primary Obligor: [   ]
                                      Guarantor: [   ]
                                      Maturity: [   ]
                                      Coupon: [   ]
                                      CUSIP/ISIN: [   ]
                                      Original Issue Amount: [   ]]

Reference Price: [%][7]

2. Fixed Payments:

    [Fixed Rate Payer   [   ]]

    Calculation Amount:[8]

    [Fixed Rate Payer Period End   [   ]]
    Date:[9]

    Fixed Rate Payer Payment   [   ]
    Date[s]:

    [Fixed Rate: [   ]][10]

    [Fixed Rate Day Count   [   ]
    Fraction:[11]

    [Fixed Amount]:   [   ]

3. Floating Payment:

    Floating Rate Payer   [   ]
    Calculation Amount:[12]

---

[6] Specify if required. A Reference Obligation must be specified for Credit Derivative Transactions to which Cash Settlement applies.
[7] If a percentage is not so specified, the Credit Derivatives Definitions provide that the Reference Price will be 100 per cent.
[8] If an amount is not specified, the Credit Derivatives Definitions provide that the Fixed Rate Payer Calculation Amount will be the Floating Rate Payer Calculation Amount.
[9] If a date is not specified, the Credit Derivatives Definitions provide that the Fixed Rate Payer Period End Date will be each date specified in the related Confirmation as a Fixed Rate Payer Payment Date.
[10] The Credit Derivatives Definitions provide that the Fixed Rate means a rate, expressed as a decimal, equal to the per annum rate specified here.
[11] If a Fixed Rate Day Count Fraction is not specified, the Credit Derivatives Definitions provide a fallback to Actual/360 as the Fixed Rate Day Count Fraction.
[12] Specify an amount or, for amortising Transactions, refer to amounts listed in an amortisation schedule.

Conditions to Payment:

Credit Event Notice

Notifying Party: Buyer [or Seller]

[Notice of Intended Physical Settlement][13]

[Notice of Publicly Available Information Applicable][14]

[Public Source(s):[   ]][15]

[Specified Number:[   ]][16]

Credit Events:

The following Credit Event[s] shall apply to this Transaction:

[Bankruptcy]

[[Failure to Pay]

[Grace Period Extension Applicable][17]

[Grace Period:][18]

Payment Requirement: [   ]][19]

[Obligation Default]

[Obligation Acceleration]

[Repudiation/Moratorium]

---

[13] Notice of Intended Physical Settlement is a required Condition to Payment in respect of Credit Derivative Transactions to which Physical Settlement is applicable. It is not applicable in relation to Credit Derivative Transactions to which Cash Settlement is applicable.

[14] If Notice of Publicly Available Information is intended to be a Condition to Payment, the parties should include a reference to it here.

[15] If Notice of Publicly Available Information has been selected by the parties and a Public Source is not specified, the Credit Derivatives Definitions provide that the Public Sources will be Bloomberg Service, Dow Jones Telerate Service, Reuter Monitor Money Rates Services, Dow Jones News Wire, Wall Street Journal, New York Times, Nihon Keizai Shinbun and Financial Times and successor publications (which sources may be referred to collectively in a Confirmation as the "Standard Public Sources").

[16] If Notice of Publicly Available Information has been selected by the parties and a number of Public Sources is not specified, the Credit Derivatives Definitions provide that the Specified Number will be two.

[17] Specify whether the parties intend Grace Period Extension to apply. If Grace Period Extension is not specified here as being applicable, (Grace Period Extension will not apply to the Credit Derivatives Transaction.

[18] If Grace Period Extension is applicable, the parties may also wish to specify the number of days in the Grace Period. Parties should specify whether the Grace Period is to be measured in Business Days or calendar days. If a number of days is not so specified, Grace Period will be the lesser of the applicable grace period with respect to the relevant Obligation and 30 calendar days. If at the later of the Trade Date and the date as of which an Obligation is issued or incurred, no grace with respect to payments or a grace period with respect to payments of less than three Grace Period Business Days is applicable under the terms of that Obligation, a Grace Period of three Grace Period Business Days shall be deemed to apply to that Obligation. Unless Grace Period Extension is specified as applicable to a Credit Derivative Transaction, this deemed Grace Period will expire no later than the Scheduled Termination Date.

[19] Payment Requirement is relevant to the Failure to Pay Credit Event. If a Payment Requirement is not specified, the Credit Derivatives Definitions provide that the Payment Requirement will be US $1,000,000 or its equivalent in the relevant Obligation Currency as of the occurence of the relevant Failure to Pay.

[Restructuring]

[Default Requirement: [   ]][20]

OBLIGATION(S):
Obligation Category   [Payment]
(Select only one):   [Borrowed Money]
                                         [Reference Obligations Only][21]
                                         [Bond]
                                         [Loan]
                                         [Bond or Loan]

Obligation Characteristics   [Pari Passu Ranking]
(Select all that apply):   [Specified Currency: [   ]][22]
                                         [Not Sovereign Lender]
                                         [Not Domestic Currency [Domestic Cur-
                                         rency means: [   ]]][23]
                                         [Not Domestic Law]
                                         [Listed]
                                         [Not Contingent]
                                         [Not Domestic Issuance]

[and:]

[Specify any other obligations of a Reference Entity.]

[Excluded Obligations:][24]   [   ]

4.   Settlement Terms:

     Settlement Method: [Cash Settlement] [Physical Settlement]

     [[Terms Relating to Cash
     Settlement:][25]

---

[20] Default Requirement is relevant to the Obligation Default, Obligation Acceleration, Repudiation/Moratorium and Restructuring Credit Events. If a Default Requirement is not specified, the Credit Derivatives Definitions provide that the Default Requirement will be US $10,000,000 or its equivalent in the relevant Obligation Currency as of the occurrence of the relevant Credit Event.
[21] If Reference Obligations Only is specified as the Obligation Category, no Obligation Characteristics should be specified.
[22] Specify currency. The Credit Derivatives Definitions provide that, if no currency is so specified, Specified Currency means the lawful currencies of any of Canada, Federal Republic of Germany, Japan, Republic of France, Republic of Italy, United Kingdom and the United States of America and the euro (and any successor currency to any such currency). The Credit Derivatives Definitions provide that these currencies may be referred to collectively in a Confirmation as the "Standard Specified Currencies".
[23] If no currency is specified, the Credit Derivatives Definitions provide that Domestic Currency will be the lawful currency and any successor currency of (a) the relevant Reference Entity, if the Reference Entity is a Sovereign, or (b) the jurisdiction in which the relevant Reference Entity is organised, if the Reference Entity is not a Sovereign. In no event shall Domestic Currency include any successor currency if such successor currency is the lawful currency of any of Canada, Federal Republic of Germany, Japan, Republic of France, Republic of Italy, United Kingdom or the United States of America or the euro (or any successor currency to any such currency).
[24] Unless specified here as an Excluded Obligation, the Reference Obligation will be an Obligation.
[25] Include if Cash Settlement applies.

[Valuation Date:][26]

[Single Valuation Date:

[   ] Business Days][27]

[Multiple Valuation Dates:

[   ] Business Days[28]; and
each [   ] Business Days
thereafter[29]
Number   of   Valuation   Dates:
[   ]][30]

[Valuation Time:][31]

[Quotation Method: [Bid] [Offer] [Mid-market]][32]

[Quotation Amount: [   ]
                            [Representative Amount][33]

[Minimum Quotation   ][34]
Amount:

[Dealer(s):   ][35]

[Settlement Currency:][36]

[Cash Settlement Date: [   ] Business Days][37]

[Cash Settlement Amount:][38]

---

[26] Include if the Cash Settlement Amount is not a fixed amount. The Credit Derivatives Definitions provide that if neither Single Valuation Date nor Multiple Valuation Dates is specified here, Single Valuation Date will apply.

[27] If the number of Business Days is not specified, the Credit Derivatives Definitions provide that this will be five Business Days.

[28] If the number of Business Days is not specified, the Credit Derivatives Definitions provide that this will be five Business Days.

[29] If the number of Business Days is not specified, the Credit Derivatives Definitions provide that this will be five Business Days.

[30] If the number of Valuation Dates is not specified, the Credit Derivatives Definitions provide that this will be five Valuation Dates.

[31] If no time is specified, the Credit Derivatives Definitions provide that the Valuation Time will be 11:00 a.m. in the Calculation Agent City.

[32] If no Quotation Method is specified, the Credit Derivatives Definitions provide that Bid shall apply.

[33] Specify either an amount in a currency or Representative Amount. If no Quotation Amount is specified, the Credit Derivatives Definitions provide that the Quotation Amount will be the Floating Rate Payer Calculation Amount.

[34] If no amount is specified, the Credit Derivatives Definitions provide that the Minimum Quotation Amount will be the lower of (i) US $1,000,000 (or its equivalent in the relevant Obligation Currency) and (ii) the Quotation Amount.

[35] Specify the Dealers. If no Dealers are specified here, the Calculation Agent will select the Dealers in consultation with the parties.

[36] If no currency is specified, the Credit Derivatives Definitions provide that the Settlement Currency will be the currency of denomination of the Floating Rate Payer Calculation Amount.

[37] If a number of Business Days is not specified, the Credit Derivatives Definitions specify three Business Days.

[38] If no amount is so specified, the Credit Derivatives Definitions provide that the Cash Settlement Amount will be the greater of (a) Floating Rate Payer Calculation Amount multiplied by the difference the Reference Price and the Final Price and (b) zero.

[Quotations: [Include Accrued Interest]
                                        [Exclude Accrued Interest]][39]

[Valuation Method:[40]   [Market] [Highest][41]
                                        [Average Market] [Highest]
                                        [Average Highest][42]
                                        [Blended Market] [Blended Highest][43]
                                        [Average Blended Market]
                                        [Average Blended Highest]][44]

[Terms Relating to
Physical Settlement:][45]

[Physical Settlement   [   ] Business Days][46]
Period:

[Portfolio: [Include Accrued Interest]
                                        [Exclude Accrued Interest][47]

DELIVERABLE   OBLIGA-
TION(S):

Derivable Obligation Category   [Payment]
(Select only one):   [Borrowed Money]
                                        [Reference Obligations Only][48]
                                        [Bond]
                                        [Loan]
                                        [Bond or Loan]

---

[39] If neither Include Accrued Interest nor Exclude Accrued Interest is specified with respect to Quotations, the Credit Derivatives Definitions provide that the Calculation Agent will determine, after consultation with the parties, based on then current market practice in the market of the Reference Obligations, whether such Quotations shall include or exclude accrued but unpaid interest.

[40] Include if the Cash Settlement Amount is not a fixed amount.

[41] Either of these Valuation Methods may be specified for a Credit Derivative Transaction with only one Reference Obligation and only one Valuation Date. If no Valuation Method is specified in such circumstances, the Credit Derivatives Definitions provide that the Valuation Method shall be Highest.

[42] One of these three Valuation Methods may be specified for a Credit Derivative Transaction with only one Reference Obligation and more than one Valuation Date. If no Valuation Method is specified in such circumstances, the Credit Derivatives Definitions provide that Average Highest shall apply.

[43] One of these Valuation Methods may be specified for a Credit Derivative Transaction with more than one Reference Obligation and only one Valuation Date. If no Valuation Method is specified in such circumstances, the Credit Derivatives Definitions provide that Blended Highest shall apply.

[44] One of these Valuation Methods may be specified for a Credit Derivative Transaction with more than one Reference Obligation and more than one Valuation Date. If no Valuation Method is specified in such circumstances, the Credit Derivatives Definitions provde that Average Blended Highest shall apply.

[45] Include if Physical Settlement applies. Subject to contrary agreement between the parties, the Partial Cash Settlement Terms contained in the Credit Derivatives Definitions apply automatically in the context of events rendering it impossible or illegal for Buyer to Deliver or for the Seller to accept Delivery of any portion of the Portfolio on or prior to the Latest Permissible Physical Settlement Date. This should be distinguished from the Partial Cash Settlement of Loans, Partial Cash Settlement of Assignable Loans and Partial Cash Settlement of Participations provisions, which are elective. If applicable for any reason, the Partial Cash Settlement Terms will apply in the form prescribed in the Credit Derivatives Definitions unless contrary provision is made by the parties in the Confirmation.

[46] If a number of Business Days is not specified, the Credit Derivatives Definitions provide that the Physical Settlement Period will be the longest of the number of Business Days for settlement in accordance with then current market practice of any Deliverable Obligation being Delivered in the Portfolio, as determined by the Calculation Agent, after consultation with the parties.

[47] Specify whether, in respect of Deliverable Obligations with an outstanding principal balance, the Portfolio is to include or exclude accrued but unpaid interest. If neither "include Accrued Interest" nor "Exclude Accrued Interest" is specified here, the Credit Derivatives Definitions provide that the Portfolio shall exclude but unpaid interest.

[48] If Reference Obligations Only is specified as the Deliverable Obligation Category, no Deliverable Obligation Characteristics should be specified.

Deliverable Obligation Characteristics   [Pari Passu Ranking]
(Select all that apply):   [Specified Currency: [   ]]⁴⁹
                                                  [Not Sovereign Lender]
                                                  [Not Domestic Currency
                                                       [Domestic   Currency   means:
                                                  [   ]]]⁵⁰
                                                  [Not Domestic Law]
                                                  [Listed]
                                                  [Not Contingent]
                                                  [Not Domestic Issuance]
                                                  [Assignable Loan]
                                                  [Consent Required Loan]
                                                  [Direct Loan Participation]
                                                  [Indirect Loan Participation Qualifying
                                                       Participation Seller:[   ]]⁵¹
                                                  [Transferable]
                                                  [Maximum Maturity [   ]]⁵²
                                                  [Accelerated or Matured]
                                                  [Not Bearer]

[and:]

[Specify any other obligations of a Reference Entity.]

[Excluded Deliverable   [   ]
Obligations:]⁵³

[Partial Cash Settlement of Loans Applicable]⁵⁴

---

⁴⁹ Specify Currency. The Credit Derivatives Definitions provide that, if no currency is so specified, Specified Currency means the lawful currency of any of Canada, Federal Republic of Germany, Japan, Republic of France, Republic of Italy, United Kingdom or the United States of America or the euro (and any successor currency to any such currency). The Credit Derivatives Definitions provide that these currencies may be referred to collectively in a Confirmation as the "Standard Specified Currencies".

⁵⁰ If no currency is specified, the Credit Derivatives Definitions provide that Domestic Currency will be the lawful currency and any successor currency of (a) the relevant Reference Entity, if the Reference Entity is a Sovereign, or (b) the jurisdiction in which the relevant Reference Entity is organised, if the Reference Entity is not a Sovereign. In no event shall Domestic Currency include any successor currency if such successor currency is the lawful currency of any of Canada, Federal Republic of Germany, Japan, Republic of France, Republic of Italy, United Kingdom or the United States of America or the euro (or any successor currency to any such currency).

⁵¹ If either Direct Loan Participation or Indirect Loan Participation is specified as a Deliverable Characteristics, specify any requirements for the Qualifying Participation Seller here. If requirements are not so specified, the Credit Derivatives Definitions provide that there shall be no Qualifying Participation Seller, with the result that only a Participation pursuant to a Participation agreement between Buyer and Seller will constitute a Direct Loan Participation or an Indirect Loan Participation.

⁵² Specify maximum period to maturity from the Physical Settlement Date.

⁵³ Unless specified as an Excluded Deliverable Obligation, the Reference Obligation will be a Deliverable Obligation.

⁵⁴ Include if the parties intend that the Partial Cash Settlement Terms are to be applicable in relation to Assignable Loans and Consent Required Loans.

[Partial Cash Settlement of Assignable Loans Applicable][55]

[Partial Cash Settlement of Participations Applicable][56]

Escrow: [Applicable] [Not Applicable]

[5. Dispute Resolution Applicable][57]

[6.] Notice and Account Details:

Telephone, Telex and/or
Facsimile Numbers and
Contact Details for Notices:

Buyer: [ ]
Seller: [ ]

Account Details

Account Details of Buyer [ ]

Account Details of Seller: [ ]

[7. Offices[58]

Seller: [ ]

Buyer: [ ]]

---

[55] Include if the parties intend that the Partial Cash Settlement Terms are to be applicable in relation to Assignable Loans.

[56] Include if the parties intend that the Partial Cash Settlement Terms are to be applicable in relation to Direct Loan Participations and Indirect Loan Participations.

[57] Specify whether it is intended that the ISDA Dispute Resolution Guidelines (the "Guidelines") are to be applicable to the Credit Derivative Transaction. If the Guidelines have been published at the Trade Date and Dispute Resolution Applicable is specified here, the Guidelines (as in effect at the Trade Date) will be incorporated by reference into the Credit Derivative Transaction. If the Guidelines have not been published at the Trade Date, specifying Dispute Resolution Applicable here will be of no effect. Upon publication, the Guidelines will not, without further action by the parties, apply to Credit Derivatives Transactions entered into prior to the date of publication of the Guidelines. Until such time as the Guidelines are published, the provisions of Section 10.2 of the Credit Derivatives Definitions shall apply to every Credit Derivative Transaction unless specifically disapplied by the parties.

[58] If necessary, specify the Offices through which the parties are acting for the purposes of the Credit Derivative Transaction.

Closing

Please confirm your agreement to be bound by the terms of the foregoing by executing a copy of this Confirmation and returning it to us [by facsimile].

Yours sincerely,

[PARTY A]

By: _____

    Name:
    Title:

Confirmed on the date
first above written:

[PARTY B]

By: _____

    Name:
    Title:

Index

ACCOUNTING STANDARDS BOARD (ASB), discussion paper, 5.002–5.004
ACCOUNTING TREATMENT, 5.001–5.019
ADD-ONS, 1.062, 1.069
ADDITIONAL TERMINATION EVENTS, 1.049–1.050
AFFECTED PARTIES, 1.039
AMERICAN OPTIONS, 1.011
ANDERSON AND SUNDARESAN (AS) MODEL, 7.017
ANNUAL PAYMENTS, taxation, 6.006–6.008
AS *see* Anderson and Sundaresan model
ASB *see* Accounting Standards Board
ATIYAH, 8.062

BACKGROUND, 1.001–1.018
BANK OF ENGLAND, London Code, 4.031
BANKERS TRUST, 4.026, 4.031–4.032, 4.038, 4.054
BANKING BOOK, capital, 1.065–1.068
BANKRUPTCY
   Credit Events, 1.024–1.026, 1.030–1.031, 3.002–3.004, 3.020, 4.006
   endogenous credit risk models, 7.002–7.003, 7.007–7.013
   Merton model, 7.008–7.010, 7.017
BANKS
   background, 1.002–1.003
   banking book capital, 1.065–1.068
   capital adequacy requirements, 1.061–1.063
   confidentiality, 2.025–2.026
   credit risk transfers, 1.013
   insurance, 2.007
   privileged information, 2.030–2.032
BARCLAYS BANK V. O'BRIEN, 4.039, 4.054–4.055
BASIC STRUCTURES, 1.004–1.005
BASIS RISKS, 1.017
BASLE ACCORD (1988), 1.061–1.062, 1.069
BBA *see* British Bankers Association
BERMUDAN OPTIONS, 1.011
BIRMINGHAM CASE, 8.002
BLACK AND COX MODEL, credit risk, 7.010
BLACK-SCHOLES MODEL, 7.008–7.018
BONDS, 1.053, 5.018
BRITISH BANKERS ASSOCIATION (BBA), 1.015, 5.002–5.003
   see also Statements of Recommended Practice

BROWNE-WILKINSON, LORD, 4.039, 4.054–4.055, 8.003, 8.016, 8.019–8.020, 8.022–8.023, 8.025–8.027, 8.033–8.036, 8.039, 8.046–8.050, 8.057–8.060
BUYERS OF PROTECTION
   concept, 1.004–1.014, 1.017, 2.002–2.003
   Credit Events, 1.024–1.030
   documentation, 1.020–1.022
   other events, 1.026–1.028
   short position, 1.065

CALCULATION AGENT, 1.033, 1.035, 1.040–1.041, 1.048, 1.050
CALCULATIONS
   concept, 4.004, 4.019–4.020
   dispute resolution, 3.014
   fair value, 5.011–5.018
CAPITAL
   adequacy requirements, 1.061–1.070
   banking book, 1.065–1.068
   conclusions, 1.070
   legal issues, 1.061–1.070
   risk, 1.061–1.063
   trading book, 1.065, 1.068
CAPS, 1.003, 1.057, 2.006–2.007
CASE STUDY, sovereign credit derivatives, 3.005–3.009
CASH FLOW, 1.003
CASH SETTLEMENT, 1.005, 1.006–1.007, 1.009–1.011, 1.072
CASH-SETTLED CREDIT DECLINE NOTES, 1.009–1.011
CASH-SETTLED DEFAULT SWAPS, 1.005
CASH-SETTLED TOTAL RETURN SWAPS, 1.006–1.007
CEA *see* Commodity Exchange Act
CFTC *see* Commodity Futures Trading Commission
CHAMBERS, resulting trusts, 8.035–8.036, 8.059
CJA *see* Criminal Justice Act
CLAIMS
   personal restitutionary claims, 8.014–8.015
   seller liabilities, 4.027–4.033, 4.057, 8.004–8.062
CLASSES, insurance, 2.007, 2.012–2.014, 2.017, 4.017–4.018
CLOSE OUT COST, fair value, 5.015
CODE OF MARKET CONDUCT, FSA, 2.030–2.032
COLLIER, RICHARD, 4.011, 6.001–6.015
COMMODITY EXCHANGE ACT (CEA), US, 1.059–1.060